THE 100 GREATEST ADVERTISEMENTS

ADVERTISEMENTS

WHO WROTE THEM AND WHAT THEY DID

By

JULIAN LEWIS WATKINS

DOVER PUBLICATIONS, INC. NEW YORK

Published in Canada by General Publishing Company, Ltd., 30 Lesmill Road, Don Mills, Toronto,
Ontario.
Published in the United Kingdom by Constable
and Company, Ltd., 10 Orange Street, London WC 2.

This Dover edition, first published in 1959, is a revised and enlarged edition of the work originally
published by The Moore Publishing Company in
1949.

Standard Book Number: 486-20540-1
Library of Congress Catalog Card Number: 59-8988

Manufactured in the United States of America
Dover Publications, Inc.
180 Varick Street
New York, N. Y. 10014

Preface to Dover Edition -1959

NEARLY ten years have passed since the first edition of this book (long out of print) came off the presses and literally startled me, and many others, with its instant acceptance, controversy, and success.

This was more than I expected, and more than I deserved. As a matter of fact, the book would never have been attempted, or completed, without the encouragement and assistance of Fred Kendall, long-time editor of the old *Advertising & Selling* which was a sort of bible to us struggling copywriters in the thirties and forties. Fred kept me at it when my spirits sagged — and sag they did, especially when some un-blithe spirit would tell me with great candor (and truth) that nobody but nobody could possibly pick the 100 greatest advertisements.

Of course not. As I wrote in the original *Author's Preface* " . . . the purpose of this book is to provide those who make, buy, sell, teach, or study advertising with a comprehensive reference work which can serve as a new, and I hope, exciting, stimulus to the continuing search for advertising effectiveness."

Lofty aims, and I apologize for my inability to make them loftier. But they seemed to work, ably supported by Raymond Rubicam's wonderful *Foreword.*

And that is why this second edition, with 13 new additions to the original "100 Greatest" came to be.

JULIAN L. WATKINS,
CHICAGO, ILLINOIS.
JANUARY 19, 1959

Author's Preface - 1949

AS I sit here in my office on the twelfth floor of the Statler Building in Boston, Massachusetts, I can see across the rooftops some sixty different advertisements:

Three gasolines, two beverages, a school of dancing, a newspaper, a public utility, and a mayonnaise, are among them.

They look good to me! And in this upset, trembling world too few of us realize that these familiar clarions of commerce are actually the last strong line of free enterprise.

If you switched on your radio this morning or your television last night — you heard and saw them. And in your newspaper or magazine, you face repeatedly some of the finest salesmen in the world.

Jack Cunningham, a distinguished copywriter and executive for Cunningham & Walsh in New York, made a snapshot of an average New York cross-street. He said this about it to a group of advertising men last year:

"I want you to notice the following things — all within forty or fifty feet of the camera: there staring up from the sidewalk, is a handbill announcing that brakes will be relined nearby for $16.90. Next to it is a discarded matchbox telling you to insist on Gillette Blue Blades. Tucked under the man's arm is a newspaper which presents to view the current Macy offerings in furniture. Nearby on the sidewalk is the torn half of the familiar brown Hershey chocolate bar wrapper. The windows on the left are full of advertising. Hanging signs reach out to intercept the vision. A railway express truck goes by with a passing reminder to chew Wrigley's.

"Even the cars parked alongside the curb flaunt their familiar advertising trademarks.

"Here, in a few square yards of city street, are many corporations, big and little, striving and crying for success through their printed voices—advertising."

Well, out of the rumble and thunder of the millions of presses — out of the billions of whispering, shouting, exhorting, cajoling advertising words that have been written over the years — *which ones stand out?*

And what are the stories behind them that will help you appraise their stature and their power?

Now the peculiar thing about advertising is that nowhere do personal opinions differ more widely than in the estimation of advertising copy, and this is especially true among advertising men themselves.

Many a man has challenged me already with this sixty-four-dollar question: "What makes an ad 'great'?"

What it sells? Certainly — in most cases that's what the man who paid for it had in mind, believe me. And as an instrument of sales, advertising has fulfilled its first glowing promise fabulously. Many an advertisement — especially in the mail order field — has produced enough traceable sales to be rated "great" in anybody's book.

But as advertising comes of age, even the die-hards of the rockum and sockum school of hard-selling copy, are beginning to agree that there's much more to it than sending you to "your favorite store." Charles C. Mortimer, Chairman of the Advertising Council, and vice president of General Foods Corporation, measured advertising soberly and intelligently when he said recently that "advertising has acquired new and sometimes frightening responsibilities . . . we have discovered in the last few years that advertising can literally accomplish miracles . . ."

What Mr. Mortimer referred to was advertising's power in the realm of ideas . . . "that in advertising there exists one of the most effective means for inspiring and informing the people that the world has ever known . . ."

Great advertising, like sublime happiness, is a lot of little things. Sometimes these things hang together and sometimes they don't.

Great advertising is not always the most beautiful. In fact, the reverse is often true.

Great advertising, however, does have one or two things in common: an idea, or concept, that can't be buried regardless of presentation, and a sincerity, or belief, that reaches right out from the page and into your heart.

It is not the purpose of this book to dissect and lay bare the many little things that are undoubtedly responsible for the generally accepted success of these one hundred choice examples of our craft. I doubt if anybody on earth could do that. It is the purpose of this book to provide those who make, buy, sell, teach, or study advertising, with a comprehensive reference work which can serve as a new and, I hope, exciting, stimulus to the continuing search for advertising effectiveness.

If advertising is to accept and cash-in on the broader challenge of its responsibility as a growing social and economic force, it can well review, study, and apply, some of the best that has gone before.

The term "great" as I have used it in my title and must use it throughout this book, is both a matter of personal opinion and a matter of record. As to whether my opinion is any better than yours — I don't know. I offer only my fifteen years with N. W. Ayer & Son, Young & Rubicam, J. Walter Thompson Company; and sixteen years as a principal with the H. B. Humphrey Company, Boston. As to the matter of record, I offer more; the one hundred advertisements recorded here have been chosen, primarily, by two kinds of exceptionally well qualified experts — one, the people who read, (or do not read) advertisements — who act, or do not act, upon them . . . and two, *time*.

While compiling my list I wrote to many of the leading advertising men in the country for suggestions, and it is amazing how many of our ablest stand solidly behind Cadillac's "The Penalty of Leadership" — Squibb's "The Priceless Ingredient" — Jordan's "Somewhere West of Laramie" — Book of Etiquette's "Again She Ordered Chicken Salad" — Listerine's "Often a Bridesmaid but Never a Bride" etc!

It is amazing, and significant, because even these few differ so widely in concept and execution that their classification as "great" ads is indeterminable by any rule or method, save by these two: that they are *remembered,* and the ability behind them *respected.*

Persuasion is still the destination of any advertisement, and you can reach it from almost any point on the creative compass if you've got an idea worth traveling in.

Some of the stories behind these selections have never been told before. Some are fascinating examples of far-sightedness. Some are Algeric. Some are immensely American. Some are sheer inspiration. Some are downright funny; with a lot of horse-sense laughing through! Some are intensely human. Some will fill you with the fine old wine of nostalgia.

All are useful as demonstrations of skilled advertising performance. The ability to think, to analyze, and to work like hell for clarity and conviction.

I think, as you go through these pages, you will feel a new pride in the business of advertising, for you will realize again what it has meant to the building and to the preservation of American free enterprise . . . *and how little its surface in that direction has been scratched.*

You will differ perhaps with some of my selections. That is inevitable. My hope is that my list is truly representative of the first hundred years, let's say, of advertising progress.

And if I have helped create in you that solid gold incentive which great performance invariably arouses, then I shall be exceedingly glad.

We have books of great short stories, great plays, great poems, great trials, great paintings, and so forth, but so far as I know, this is the first attempt to marshall the great in advertising, and to present it in compact and convenient reference form.

To Raymond Rubicam, with whom I once had the great privilege of working; to George Cecil and Ken Slifer of N. W. Ayer & Son, where I first saw the light of copy day; to James W. Young, with whom I never worked but always wanted to; to Hayward Anderson, an old and valued friend, and to the Curtis Publishing Company for almost endless photographs from issues long buried in the files — I owe particular thanks for gracious, thoughtful and enormous help.

And, of course, if it hadn't been for Fred Kendall, the astute and friendly editorial director of the Moore Publishing Company, publishers of Advertising Agency, (better known to our generation as Advertising & Selling), the book probably would never have been published at all. Fred liked the idea from the start and encouraged me to do it — supplying both valued data from his files and genuine enthusiasm from his heart. In fact, the book's title is his. He admits that I may know a good ad when I see one but that he knows a title that will sell books!

My files are filled with wonderful letters from other men and women about whom you will hear later, and who, in turn, have filled my heart with a very special quality and quantity of gratitude. This is really *their* book; I've simply put it together.

BOSTON, MASSACHUSETTS
OCTOBER, 1949

☆

Foreword

by

RAYMOND RUBICAM

AS Julian Watkins intimates in his dedication of this book, anyone who attempts to name *"The 100 Greatest Advertisements"* is not settling the matter, but is merely starting something. Because I think Mr. Watkins is starting a good thing, I am glad that he asked me to write the Foreword to his book.

When I began as a copywriter, a book like this would have been worth more money to me than I owned. A week's salary would have been a bargain price. Possession of such a collection of ads, and insight into how they were produced and what they accomplished, would have paid dividends on the spot — and would have continued to pay them for years afterwards while I was a developing copywriter,

and for many more years during which I hired, taught, trained and tried to inspire other copywriters.

Writers and artists do not learn best from textbooks, but by doing and by absorbing through their pores, from the work of others, the particular qualities which appeal to them and stimulate their own potentialities. It is harder for teachers of advertising in schools and colleges to know and obtain the great advertisements, or even the successful ones, than it is for teachers of literature to know and obtain the great or successful books. We in the advertising business have not been adequately cooperative in providing teaching material, particularly information which will help teachers and students distinguish between the superlatively effective, the fairly effective, and the ineffective, in copy.

There are many successful ads, few great ones. A great ad by virtue of the very adjective applied to it, must be not merely successful, but phenomenally so. Yet phenomenal results alone — whether in number of readers, or inquiries, or even sales, do not make people feel that an ad is great unless its message is made memorable by originality, wit, insight, conviction or some other notable quality of mind or spirit. And even those qualities do not make it great if its claims are dishonest, if it impairs the good will of the customer toward the advertiser either before or after the sale, or if it impairs the good will of the public toward advertising. The best identification of a great ad is that its public is not only strongly sold by it, but that both the public and the advertising world remember it for a long time as an admirable piece of work.

A single agency or advertising department cannot as a rule do much better than the schools in putting before the beginner enough ads that can be called great. The agency or department may produce much excellent work, but seldom does that work span the wide variety of tasks that advertising can perform, or the widely varied styles and methods by which similar goods and services can be and have been sold.

Of course, there is always on display in current media the daily and weekly grist of all the advertising mills, but current advertising style can be as monotonous as current automobile style, and pre-occupation with it merely sets up the need for a strong antidote, lest the pressure of standardization ruin the youngster for life.

Advertising is no exception to the rule that superlative work has an unequalled thrill for the craftsman. The great ads will contribute mysteriously but potently to any beginner who has a spark that can be struck. And, let me add, Mr. Watkins' Combination Panorama and Close-up of the Ads that Folks Remember can be just as enlightening and even more profitable to the Boss himself.

To the hundred (or more)
great ads I must have missed!

Contents

Page

THE 100 GREATEST
ADVERTISEMENTS

MEN WANTED for Hazardous Journey. Small wages, bitter cold, long months of complete darkness, constant danger, safe return doubtful. Honor and recognition in case of success — Ernest Shackleton.

WANTED: *Volunteers For The South Pole*

THIS advertisement, written by Ernest Shackleton, the famed polar explorer, appeared in London newspapers in 1900. In speaking of it later, he said: "It seemed as though all the men in Great Britain were determined to accompany me, the response was so overwhelming."

Of course, the lure of adventure had a great deal to do with the success of this simply written copy. So did the power of deadly frankness.

EASTMAN KODAK — *"You Press The Button — We do The Rest"*

OVER the years the Eastman Kodak Company has published many advertisements that would unquestionably rate as "great", but probably none greater than this. *"You Press the Button — We Do the Rest"* is one of the greatest of advertising ideas.

It was literally edited-out of a long piece of copy by George Eastman himself. In a day when glass plate cameras enjoyed but limited and difficult use, Mr. Eastman's Kodak Camera, emulsion film, and advertising sense opened a market as rich as any in the world.

The advertisement shown here appeared in 1890 and was among the first to shake loose the home-picture-making instinct of the nation. Lovers of short copy will find here strong backing for their arguments, and ah yes, that's a testimonial (and a good one) in italic type.

The famous Eastman *"Brownie"* Kodak, *"Kodak As you Go"* and other variations of the button-pressing idea were much later developments. And who of us old enough to remember the first war to end wars, will ever forget the Kodak advertisement that appeared in full-page rotogravure in 1917: the illustration was of course a photograph, showing an Army officer sitting in front of a field tent gazing raptly at a sheaf of snapshots fresh from a letter. There was but one line of copy, and only one line was needed. It read: *"Pictures from Home."*

The late L. B. Jones, famous advertising manager of the Eastman Kodak Company, wrote it, and it is one of the shortest and most effective pieces of human-interest copy ever written. Mr. Jones didn't write it that way at first. In fact, he wrote it quite the other way, for it was three hundred words long to begin with! Three hundred words of very fine copy no doubt under the headline *"Pictures from Home."* "The longer I looked at it," Mr. Jones told me years later, "the more I realized that the *picture* told the story, so I began cutting, and finally cut the text out altogether!"

"Come let's to bed", says Sleepy Head.
"Tarry awhile", says Slow;
He got a whiff of Campbell's Soup
And didn't want to go!

It takes a bright and sparkling flavor
to attract children!

Flavor—flavor—what has the flavor?... That's a game every child's appetite loves to play... Remember how inquisitive your sense of taste was, back in those childhood days?... Poking into all kinds of things to eat — giving the "tongue test" to everything (not always confined to foods)... finding some things that really "hit the spot". Every youngster has decided preferences in food.

You like Campbell's Tomato Soup. Of course, you do... for it is a distinctive flavor universally acclaimed.

And your children have a taste that is keener than yours — fresh — appreciative. See how instantly and eagerly the youngsters go for this soup, with its enchanting bright red color and its taste that sets the tongue a-tingling!

At least once every day the children should get the invigorating benefits of wholesome soup, for its nourishing food and its aid to digestion... And they *always* greet Campbell's Tomato Soup with delight... especially if it's prepared with milk as Cream of Tomato.

21 kinds to choose from . . .

Asparagus	Mulligatawny
Bean	Mushroom (Cream of)
Beef	Mutton
Bouillon	Noodle with chicken
Celery	Ox Tail
Chicken	Pea
Chicken-Gumbo	Pepper Pot
Clam Chowder	Printanier
Consommé	Tomato
Julienne	Vegetable
Mock Turtle	Vegetable-Beef

LOOK FOR THE RED-AND-WHITE LABEL

Campbell's Tomato Soup

Double rich! Double strength!

Campbell's Soups are made as in your own home kitchen, except that they are double strength. So when you add an equal quantity of water, you obtain twice as much full-flavored soup at no extra cost.

CAMPBELL'S SOUP — *"The Campbell Kids"*

ALTHOUGH the Campbell's Soup advertisement shown here appeared in *The Saturday Evening Post,* April 6, 1935 the famous Campbell Kids appeared on car cards as long ago as 1899. Certainly no book of great advertisements would be complete without an example of this truly outstanding series beloved by young and old alike for more than half a century — already.

There seems to be no exact record, (which is unfortunately true of so many great advertisements) as to who wrote the original jingles. Miss Grace Drayton was the first illustrator and her style has been faithfully followed by different successors.

Nobody knows how much soup the Campbell Kids have sold, but you might take a look at the huge kitchens down in Camden, New Jersey and at the first advertising page following reading matter in countless years of *The Post.* The red and white Campbell label is a familiar landmark in American advertising history, and the Campbell Kids have been a lively, human, endearing part of your growing up, and mine.

figures, will have a good effect in many whether worn by some character or over a piece of furniture. At the same reat care should be taken to avoid the a and vulgar error of combining too gay colors. Indeed, the two great of the want of artistic effect in tableaux, monly arranged, are, first, too much nd, second, too much color. In almost tableau where more than three figures one, at least, should be in shadow, l by something light behind. The fol-diagram will show how the shadow may ed:

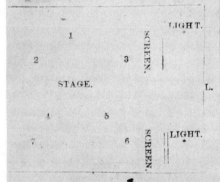

ose the figures 1, 2, 3, 4, 5, 6, 7 to repre-performers. The two lights indicated lluminate the back of the stage, form-ght background. Figure 1 will then be e of both lights; figure 2 will be par-aded by figure 5; figure 3 will be par-aded by the rear screen; figures 4 and e in full light; figure 6 in the deep from both screens; and figure 7 dimly ated by the rear light only. Here we different degree of light for almost haracter and the effect will be found a g one. Foot-lights should hardly ever l in arranging tableaux, as they give s exactly the opposite of picturesque. hts should be brilliant, placed high up, in number. A good effect may some-e got by cross-lights; but generally t to have them all on one side of the

d lights are capable of being used with ppy results, and it is by no means a diffi-tter to produce them, either by colored ch as are used at the theaters, or by lobes with colored liquids and placing front of the lamps, like those we see indows of the chemists's shops.

VERS TO PUZZLES OF DEC. 14TH.

TRANSPOSITIONS.

I.

grin—vinegar; 2, train me—raiment; r—her Tom; 4, ray comes—sycamore;

THE "IVORY" is a Laundry Soap, with all the fine qualities of a choice Toilet Soap, and is 99 44-100 per cent. pure.

Ladies will find this Soap especially adapted for washing laces, infants' clothing, silk hose, cleaning gloves and all articles of fine texture and delicate color, and for the varied uses about the house that daily arise, requiring the use of soap that is above the ordinary in quality.

For the Bath, Toilet, or Nursery it is preferred to most of the Soaps sold for toilet use, being purer and much more pleasant and effective and possessing all the desirable properties of the finest unadultered White Castile Soap. The Ivory Soap will "float."

The cakes are so shaped that they may be used entire for general purposes or divided with a stout thread (as illustrated) into two perfectly formed cakes, of convenient size for toilet use.

The price, compared to the quality and the size of the cakes, makes it the cheapest Soap for everybody for every want. TRY IT.

SOLD EVERYWHERE.

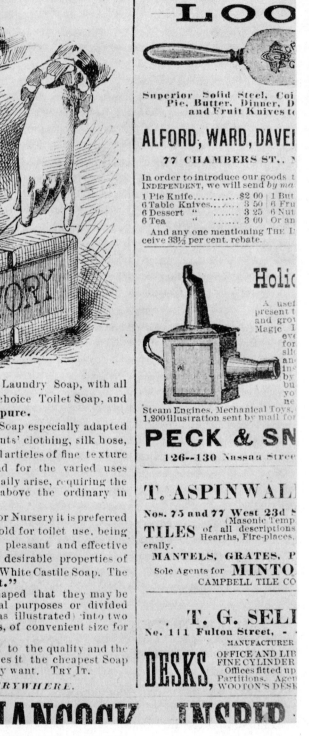

IVORY SOAP — $99^{44}/_{100}\%$ *Pure* — *(1882)*

BACK in December, 1882 this advertisement for Ivory Soap appeared in many newspapers throughout the land. Nobody remembers the exact schedule or the writer's name, but it was unquestionably among the first of the famous 99 44/100 percent pure series. Copywriters please note the substantial reason-why "sell" all the way through this compact "reader" copy. Pretty solid stuff. Few ads in that long-gone day were any better. Few soaps either; and that was a combination hard to beat. In my book, it rates as among the great ads of all time because it is truly representative of an imaginative and resourceful advertising policy that has led Procter & Gamble from small beginnings to a very distinguished place in the sun. They had a good idea, and they stuck to it, varying only its interpretation as the years went by.

PHOEBE SNOW — *"The Road of Anthracite"*

I HAVE a special interest in a girl named Phoebe Snow. I saw her first on a Clinton Street trolley back in my hometown, Elmira, New York. I fell in love with her at first sight and my devotion has remained constant through the years.

Phoebe was selling the Lackawanna Railroad then — and she still is. She used to say things like this to me as I rode to work —

> Like aeroplanes
> My favorite trains
> O'ertop the lofty mountain chains
> There's cool delight
> At such a height
> Upon the Road of Anthracite.

Yes, Phoebe was a car card then — probably the first great railroad selling symbol in print. She has been selling the Delaware, Lackawanna & Western since 1900, and she has done so well at it that the railroad now calls itself *The Route of Phoebe Snow* and an entire modern passenger train is named in her honor.

Phoebe Snow was the pin-up rage of her day, created by Earnest Elmo Calkins and first painted by Harry Stacy Benton — not Penrhyn Stanlaws, as has so often been reported. The model was a Mrs. Murray, one of the very first models to be used in advertising, long before Powers and Conover established their picturesque services.

Phoebe Snow was created to sell the idea of cleanliness in traveling on a railroad which used sootless anthracite coal exclusively as locomotive fuel. Phoebe always wore a spotless white dress — was always cool-looking, comfortable, corsaged with violets. She became so popular as a symbol of cleanliness, and lodged so surely in the hearts and minds of Lackawanna travelers and shippers, that they've printed her name on all rolling stock. Booklets with her verses and story have been distributed by the hundreds of thousands.

But I am indebted to Mr. Calkins (via Fred Kendall) for the real story behind the story of Phoebe Snow. Mr. Calkins wrote it only three years ago and I quote —

"Forty-five years ago, Wendell P. Colton, then, advertising manager of the D. L. & W., now head of his own advertising agency, prepared and ran a series of street car cards based on the nursery rhyme, *The House That Jack Built,* the heroine of which was a girl in white, *All in Lawn."* When that came to a logical end, he turned to us for an idea to continue the advertising. Taking our cue from the previous set, we gave the girl a name and produced an endless set of jingles.

"The form of the verses was suggested by an onomatopoetic rhyme in *The Humorous Speaker,* one of the elocution books so numerous when I was a boy — "Riding on the Rail." Its jigging meter was supposed to imitate the song of the rushing train. Rhyming advertisements were popular then. Kenneth Fraser's "Spotless Town" and Charles Snyder's "See that Hump" lilted from every street car card and boarding; constant repetition gave them currency.

"Mrs. Murray was posed before the camera in and out of cars, talking with the crew, eating in the diner, having her berth made up, as that was easier than painting in such inconvenient environments, and those photographs were the basis of the colored paintings made by Benton. The resulting pictures had little of the glamour of today's pin-up girls. The American ideal was something quite different in those double pre-war days. Phoebe was demure and circumspect, innocent as her white gown, as safe traveling alone on the Road of Anthracite as her spotless attire. Sex appeal existed, but it wasn't named, and 'pin-up' was as unknown as 'roomette'. As your story intimates, Phoebe Snow had her day, became a proverb, a symbol, and a simile in her time, and had her tribute of burlesque, parody, cartooning and allusion that were evidence of the world's familiarity.

"An amusing story could be made of the manner in which the higher criticism was applied to the apotheosis of Phoebe Snow. One of the Lackawanna's officers explained learnedly (after the fact) that Phoebe was the only woman's name that had the right psychological appeal, that this perfect name was not hit upon until after experiments with other names, that Mary was tried and failed to click, that when Phoebe was adopted the public responded one hundred percent. All of which was vastly entertaining to the man who created Phoebe, named her without giving a thought to the laws of mental science, mnenomics, or the subtle influence of association of ideas. And he realized that thus are legends made.

"It is evidence of advertising's flexibility that Phoebe Snow, her very reason for existence wiped out by wars and coal strikes, her personality dated by post-war ideas of feminine charm, is being transformed into a new symbol, that of women's advent in to the emphatically masculine industry of railroading, with hostesses on streamlined trains to add the hospitable touch that neither Pullman porter, nor conductor can supply. And it is a curious coincidence that Best Foods, which is the residuary legatee of one of the earliest flake breakfast foods, Force, is inquiring into the history of Sunny Jim, another character at whose birth I was at least the midwife.

"The last jingle I perpetrated in the Lackawanna series was:

> Miss Phoebe's trip
> Without a slip
> Is almost o'er.
> Her trunk and grip
> Are right and tight
> Without a slight.
> "Good bye, old Road of Anthracite!"

— Earnest Elmo Calkins

I have a very *special* interest in Phoebe Snow, not alone because of her classification as a great ad, but more because she led me into advertising. I was so entranced by her rhymed selling that I did a little rhymed selling of my own . . . in the form of an application for a job! I sent out sixteen letters, got five favorable replies, one by telegram. Those *were* the good old days, weren't they?

SMITH BROTHERS COUGH DROPS

PROBABLY the world's most famous brothers are *"Trade"* and *"Mark"* Smith! Since 1852 when the first advertisement for a "Cough Candy" appeared in Poughkeepsie newspapers over the signature of William Smith, these deftly bearded gentlemen have been selling cough drops as cough drops were never sold before — or since.

Ten years or so ago, practically an entire 40-page edition of the *Poughkeepsie-New Yorker* was devoted to the 100th Birthday Celebration of this famous industry which had produced enough cough drops up to that time to ease the roughened throats of all the people in the world!

Five generations of Smith Brothers have carried on this fantastically successful business which contains all the ingredients of the American dream . . . log cabin beginnings, first product made over kitchen stove, sold from door to door, and then the slow ascent to great wealth and world influ-

ence. Just pull out the stops and bear down on the keys!

And if you could ask either *"Trade"* or *"Mark"* or any of their fortunate descendants what one thing — beyond the product — was the big booster along the upward road, the voice that answered would undoubtedly say: "Continuous advertising, small space, plenty of insertions, simple copy . . ."

Maybe you won't call the pictures of *"Trade"* and *"Mark"* that I've reproduced here either "great" or "famous" advertisements. You're right — technically; but I imagine more people know these gentlemen and what they make, than know the reasons why the product's good for them . . .

Even today's Smith Brothers advertising says, *"Don't Let Those Beards Fool You!"* And then it goes on with *"Modern Science Recognizes The Effectiveness of This Trusted Formula . . ."* Trying to modernize *"Trade"* and *"Mark"* are they? Is *nothing* sacred?

[11]

This is the butcher of Spotless Town,
His tools are bright as his renown.
To leave them stained were indiscreet,
For folks would then abstain from meat,
And so he brightens his trade you know
By polishing with

SAPOLIO

This is the maid of fair renown
Who scrubs the floors of Spotless Town.
To find a speck when she is through
Would take a pair of specs or two,
And her employment isn't slow.
For she employs

SAPOLIO

This is the Mayor of Spotless Town,
The brightest man for miles around.
The shining light of wisdom can
Reflect from such a polished man,
And so he says to high and low:
"The brightest use

SAPOLIO

SAPOLIO — "Spotless Town"

DOWN from Cornell, where he drew and wrote for the college papers while earning an engineering degree, came J. K. Fraser. "No one wanted an advertising man like me. Had to eat so made a deal with the mate and cook of a ship who had opened up a restaurant on 23rd Street. Every week I put a poster in the window inviting people to come in and eat. In payment, whenever I felt hungry I went in myself and ate on the house. I got the posters back. With these samples I landed a job with Ward & Gow who controlled street car advertising space. Mr. Ward also managed Sapolio advertising. One day I told Mr. Ward that I would like to try my hand at some Sapolio car cards. When I showed him the Spotless Town series he said: 'Fine! I am going to keep that series in the cars so long people will get sick and tired of seeing it, and when it makes you famous don't forget to give me some of the credit.' I wrote the jingles and drew the pictures. I was 24."

Spotless Town deserves a place in any collection of great ads, and Mr. Ward in any charting of far-sightedness. For Spotless Town (while selling Sapolio by the ton) was parodied in many papers and one syndicated political series ran all over the country. At one time four theatrical road companies booked shows called Spotless Town . . . and one community changed its name permanently thereto. Out of the Spotless Town success, rose J. K. Fraser to head the old Blackman Company (now Compton Advertising), to retire a wealthy, healthy and respected man, to take up golf and "I can still put them out beyond the 200-yards marker." And this person doesn't doubt it. JK could always call his shots. Love that man!

VICTOR TALKING MACHINE COMPANY — *"His Master's Voice"*

THIS is *our* dog — yours and mine! We grew up with this beloved fox terrier listening to his master's voice. It symbolized so perfectly, so warmly that first grand instrument of home entertainment, the Vic. It gave to the struggling Victor Talking Machine Company in the early days of this cyclonic century, an expression of performance that instantly went to the hearts of young and old alike. Many great ads have appeared over the Victor and later the RCA-Victor name, but none more valuable certainly than the dog everybody knows.

The idea was the inspiration of Francis Barraud, an English painter. One day his dog Nipper — for that was the terrier's name — sat hunched before a talking machine listening quizzically to the voices coming from the horn. Nipper's pose caught the eye of his master . . . and one of the greatest trade-marks in the world was born. Barraud gave it the title which has never changed *"His Master's Voice"* and sold the English rights to the picture to the Gramophone Company, London. In 1901, the Victor Talking Machine Company acquired the American rights to the painting and adopted it as its trade-mark, and has featured it for more than half a century in advertising and retail display.

The moral of all this — if one is needed — is that good ideas are everywhere. But you have to know one when you see it.

FISK RUBBER COMPANY — *"Time To Retire"*

HERE is a young man who has never had time to practice what he preaches. He is anything but retired — in fact, he has been inordinately busy since 3 o'clock one morning in the year 1907 . . .

Burr Giffin, an agency art director, (according to James L. Collings in the March 29, 1947 issue of *Editor & Publisher*) who frequently did work for the Fisk Tire Company was stirring at that early hour because he had an idea and the urge to do something about it.

He sat down on his bed and made a rapid sketch of a small boy with his right arm encircling a tire and his left hand holding a candle. Then he gave his work a title *"Time to Retire."*

The next morning he showed the sketch to his boss who thought it good enough to present to Fisk. Fisk in turn liked it so much that a poster ad was immediately whipped into shape. Thus, one of the most human, most famous trade marks in America started its long and illustrious advertising career.

An interesting sidelight is that Edward Egleston, an artist whose son was rumored to be the first model, made the first painting in oil in 1916. Through the years, however, that original painting was spoiled by too many retouchings.

In 1939 when the U. S. Rubber Company acquired Fisk they found among the drawings and paintings an oil of the Fisk boy of apparently indifferent quality.

The new management sent the painting to the Metropolitan Museum of Art to be restored — a process that revealed many layers of retouching which probably represented the over-the-years opinions of various engravers and lithographers as to where lights and shadows should fall and how color could be improved.

After the final restoration it was found that each change had been far from an improvement because the original was a completely charming picture.

The Fisk boy has had many millions of advertising dollars invested in him. He is kept up to date by employing different models each year in essentially the same pose. Recently he was animated and given lines, but essentially the original idea remains intact.

UNEEDA BISCUIT

HERE is the young man who took crackers out of the cracker barrel, put them into neat, sanitary packages, and sold, what is still after sixty years of competition, the most famous "biscuit" in the world! Actually, of course, the story is far more significant than that. A. W. Green, Chairman of the Board of the National Biscuit Company just before and after the turn of the century, was the prime mover in an idea that was probably the forerunner of the packaged food business in this country. For this was the day of bulk selling. Crackers — and almost every other item in the grocery stores of that day — were sold from barrels or boxes. You bought your groceries and you took your chances; sometimes you got them clean and fresh, and sometimes you got them stale, fly-specked and smelling of kerosene.

Mr. Green recommended to his Board a *home* PACKAGE of crackers—a package containing a quantity that would be quickly consumed by the average family, that would be packed in a container free from contamination and protected from moisture, dust, germs and odors. Mr. Green also recommended a mass price of 5¢ (this was 1899, remember) and some novel method of advertising and merchandising this absolutely revolutionary scheme.

The Board was unenthusiastic. Its mind was still in the cracker barrel. With rare foresight, it pessimistically predicted failure. But fortunately it wasn't boss. And also, fortunately, the National Biscuit Company had appointed N. W. Ayer & Son as its advertising agency.

Serving the National Biscuit account was one of Ayer's strongest men: H. N. McKinney. Mr. McKinney was just as foresighted in his field as Mr. Green in his, and the result of that combination was the name UNEEDA and a coordinated plan for reaching the public through newspapers, magazines, street car cards, posters and painted signs.

The campaign was an over-night sensation and new bakeries were built in different parts of the country to supply the fantastic demand, but neither National Biscuit nor N. W. Ayer probably realized the extent to which they were remolding our daily lives. Today's brightly illuminated markets with their neatly arranged rows of packaged foods, each with its own trade mark, had its origin in this first bold step taken but fifty years ago.

The famous boy in boots, sou'wester and slicker, with a package of Uneeda Biscuits in his arm, was the work of Joseph J. Geisinger, an associate of Mr. McKinney's at N. W. Ayer & Son. It was Mr. Geisinger's job to illustrate the original Uneeda campaign — to give it novelty and freshness and human appeal. He did. He did it so well that the slickered lad (Mr. Geisinger's nephew, Gordon Stille, by the way) is still one of the best-known advertisements in the world.

"AH RECKON AS HOW HE'S DE BES' KNOWN MAN IN DE WORL'"

Painted by Rowland M. Smith for Cream of Wheat Co.

CREAM OF WHEAT -- *"Ah Reckon As How He's De Bes' Known Man In De Worl' "*

A GOOD idea somehow never dies and nobody can quite analyze what accounts for its longevity. You'd think perhaps that the Cream of Wheat Chef had long ago lost his identity in the constant boil of change, yet a recent survey showed that this famous Negro is still one of the first three or four best-known trade-marks in the country.

The Cream of Wheat trademark originated with Colonel Mapes, one of the founders of the Company and its general manager of many years. One day in the early 1900's he was lunching in Kohlsaat's Restaurant, Chicago, and was served by a handsome colored waiter. He was so impressed by the waiter's friendly smile that he secured his picture and release for its use. Since that time the waiter's face has appeared on all Cream of Wheat packages and in all Cream of Wheat publicity.

G. Barnard Clifford, Treasurer and Sales Manager of the Cream of Wheat Company, adds this interesting footnote to the story: "Up until a few years ago hardly a year passed that we were not approached by various gentlemen claiming to be the original chef. However, Colonel Mapes had a secret way of identifying the original man and we have never found him. Perhaps he is gone to his reward these many years . . ."

Well — as the advertisement across the way says: *"Ah Reckon As How He's de bes' Known Man In de' Worl' "*.

Advertisement reproduced through the courtesy of The Cream of Wheat Corporation. Reg. U. S. Pat. Off.

The
PENALTY OF LEADERSHIP

IN every field of human endeavor, he that is first must perpetually live in the white light of publicity. ¶Whether the leadership be vested in a man or in a manufactured product, emulation and envy are ever at work. ¶In art, in literature, in music, in industry, the reward and the punishment are always the same. ¶The reward is widespread recognition; the punishment, fierce denial and detraction. ¶When a man's work becomes a standard for the whole world, it also becomes a target for the shafts of the envious few. ¶If his work be merely mediocre, he will be left severely alone—if he achieve a masterpiece, it will set a million tongues a-wagging. ¶Jealousy does not protrude its forked tongue at the artist who produces a commonplace painting. ¶Whatsoever you write, or paint, or play, or sing, or build, no one will strive to surpass, or to slander you, unless your work be stamped with the seal of genius. ¶Long, long after a great work or a good work has been done, those who are disappointed or envious continue to cry out that it can not be done. ¶Spiteful little voices in the domain of art were raised against our own Whistler as a mountebank, long after the big world had acclaimed him its greatest artistic genius. ¶Multitudes flocked to Bayreuth to worship at the musical shrine of Wagner, while the little group of those whom he had dethroned and displaced argued angrily that he was no musician at all. ¶The little world continued to protest that Fulton could never build a steamboat, while the big world flocked to the river banks to see his boat steam by. ¶The leader is assailed because he is a leader, and the effort to equal him is merely added proof of that leadership. ¶Failing to equal or to excel, the follower seeks to depreciate and to destroy—but only confirms once more the superiority of that which he strives to supplant. ¶There is nothing new in this. ¶It is as old as the world and as old as the human passions—envy, fear, greed, ambition, and the desire to surpass. ¶And it all avails nothing. ¶If the leader truly leads, he remains—the leader. ¶Master-poet, master-painter, master-workman, each in his turn is assailed, and each holds his laurels through the ages. ¶That which is good or great makes itself known, no matter how loud the clamor of denial. ¶That which deserves to live—lives.

CADILLAC -- *"The Penalty Of Leadership"*

THE list of famous advertisements selected for this book is not entirely my own. When the work began, I wrote to perhaps fifty leading advertising men explaining my belief in the need and usefulness of a volume like this and asked them to name some of the advertisements which, over the years, had made a profound impression upon them. *"The Penalty of Leadership"* appeared on every list!

Much has been written about this perhaps greatest of all advertisements, the conditions which prompted it, etc., but the significant fact to me is this: the advertisement, contrary to popular belief, appeared but once: January 2, 1915 in *The Saturday Evening Post,* yet after more than thirty years, hardly a week goes by that either Cadillac or its agency, MacManus, John & Adams, Detroit, do not get requests for one or more copies. Millions have been distributed.

"That which deserves to live — lives."
Its author: Theodore F. MacManus.

"Well, Bob, it's five minutes past two. What's the story going to be?"
"Oh, I'll tell her we had a blowout."
"That would never get past MY wife. She knows I use Kelly-Springfield."

KELLY-SPRINGFIELD — *The Fellowes Series*

EARNEST Elmo Calkins and other advertising men whose opinions on advertising are always respected, have called the Kelly-Springfield Tire advertising of the era 1918 to 1931, the most outstanding tire campaign ever run in national magazines. The sample on the opposite page is typical of this series. Henry Hurd, then advertising manager of Kelly-Springfield and Laurence Fellowes, a free lance artist, did them.

"At that time," writes Mr. Hurd, "we were the Tiffany of the tire industry. We felt that for an ambitious million dollar advertising budget, we needed something more than merely a punning (Lotta Miles) trade character such as we had been using in our outdoor display, and I was casting about for an idea when Laurence Fellowes walked in with a suggestion for a house organ cover. In those days Fellowes did fineline drawings without the wash which he later adopted; when it came to drawing smart cars and smart types of people he was in a class by himself. The drawing he brought in to me that day gave me the idea for the Kelly magazine series which for so many years I wrote and he illustrated. Sometimes I would send him the copy and he would do a drawing to fit the text; sometimes I would run dry and write copy to whatever picture he felt like producing..."

CAMEL CIGARETTES — *First Big Time Cigarette Campaign*

ONE of the heartening things about doing this book has been the interested, all-out cooperation received from advertisers and agencies — none more heartening than that from my advertising alma mater, N. W. Ayer & Son. And none more enlightening than this story about the first big league advertiser of cigarettes, R. J. Reynolds Company. Here is the story of Camels as related to Ayer Vice President, Clarence L. Jordan by William M. Armistead, long dean of Ayer executives, who got and handled the Reynolds account for many years:

The Cigarette Industry — like so many industries in the early days of the 20th Century — began its development with sectional brands.

In the South-Atlantic States Piedmonts were a big seller — and down in New Orleans, Home Runs and Picayunes were popular. Fatimas were demanded in the East and Middle-Atlantic — and out in San Francisco they were selling a brand almost exclusively which had a "mouthpiece."

R. J. Reynolds, who had just completed overcoming sectional brands in a pipe tobacco — making Prince Albert a national seller — made up his mind to attempt the same thing in a cigarette.

After a long time in studying the various sectional brands, Mr. Reynolds decided he had perfected the proper blend for a national cigarette. He bought the name "CAMEL" from a small independent company in Philadelphia for $2,500.00.

Mr. Reynolds then said to Mr. Armistead, who handled the advertising account for N. W. Ayer & Son, that they were ready to proceed and offered him an appropriation of $250,000 to introduce the Camel brand.

This initial appropriation was refused, with the following statement: "While it is true that all of those around the Reynolds Tobacco Company who have tried the new cigarette think it is a great blend, some of them may have expressed that belief because they thought it would please you, Mr. Reynolds. If you spend a quarter million dollars on that cigarette — and the public does not like it — you will kill the brand, as well as lose a quarter million dollars. Public approval is the only way to test the product. If this cigarette will not sell without advertising — it certainly will not sell with advertising."

We then went on to recommend that one carton of Camel Cigarettes be distributed to each of 125 of the best retail stores in Cleveland, with the understanding that the carton be left on top of the counter — and figures furnished on repeat orders by stores.

The cigarette immediately began to repeat.

Then, the same system was tried out in other sections of the country where various sectional brands were being sold. Again and again, the product started to repeat without any advertising.

Based on this method of testing in all sections of the country, it became clear that this new blend could overcome sectional prejudices.

Then — and not until then — was advertising recommended to introduce the brand on a full-scale basis.

This introduction was done by Sales Divisions, of which there were 87 in the United States. Each Division Manager was instructed to notify the Home Office as soon as he had perfected a complete distribution in his area.

The advertising campaign started off with teaser copy in newspapers, approximately forty inches in size.

The first advertisement was a very simple teaser display — using the words *"The Camels Are Coming."*

The second advertisement featured the wording *"Tomorrow There Will Be More Camels in This Town Than in Asia and Africa Combined."*

The third advertisement stated *"Camels Are Here,"* and proceeded to describe the brand.

From that point on, consistent newspaper space was used on a campaign which was built around the theme that Camel Cigarettes did not offer any premiums — such as were popular with most cigarettes at the time — because the cost of the tobaccos used in the Camel blend was too great to permit anything except the quality product itself.

That was the introductory period and — as could be expected — it stung competition into quick action.

Camels started moving rapidly in nearly all sections, except for New York City. That city had been left for the last. Sales there were controlled largely by the Metropolitan Tobacco Company, who had advised the R. J. Reynolds Tobacco Company that if they would keep their salesmen out of New York City they would give them distribution in about 17,000 stores that were tops, in one week — just as soon as they were convinced the product would sell.

Reynolds agreed, and the last division opened was New York, through the Metropolitan Tobacco Company, using exactly the same technique — with advertising spreading to magazines and billboards, in addition to newspapers, but still using the same hard-selling theme.

Camels grew from 4th place to 1st place in five years, securing about 40% of the entire cigarette business.

Naturally, competition switched its tactics from sectional sellers to national blends that could compete on a national basis with the success of Camels — and the big cigarette battle, which is still going on, got under way with millions of dollars of advertising being spent each year on each of the leading national brands.

An amusing incident developed one of the greatest slogans in this cigarette battle.

A sign painter was painting a billboard one day and a man walked up and asked him if he could give him a cigarette. The painter said "yes" and offered him a Camel. The stranger thanked him with enthusiasm, and said *"I'd Walk A Mile For A Camel."*

The sign painter was smart enough to report the incident as a suggestion for a billboard and from this incident grew one of the best and most familiar slogans in advertising.

DR. ELIOT'S FIVE-FOOT SHELF — *"This Is Marie Antoinette Riding To Her Death"*

THIS ad belongs in my book for two reasons: first, it worked! And second, it is probably the first important copy ever written by one of America's truly distinguished copy men: Bruce Barton.

I wrote Mr. Barton for the story and I could give you no more interesting information about this significant demonstration of his ability than this quote from his letter:

"Tom Beck, who had been sales manager for Procter & Gamble, was hired by Robert Collier to take charge of sales of Collier's Weekly and the Collier books including the famous Five-Foot Shelf of Books selected by Dr. Eliot. Beck came from a business that depended wholly on advertising into a business that never had had any advertising, a business in which the salesman did not want advertising because every salesman worked his own way and sometimes his way was open to considerable ethical debate. Each salesman pretended to be the general manager out on a special trip to consult subscribers; or an executor of the estate of the publisher who was seeking to dispose of a few fine sets at bargain prices in order to close up the estate, etc.

"Beck believed that books could be advertised and sold ethically and he hired a great national advertising agency to prepare advertisements for the Five-Foot Shelf of Books to be run in Collier's Weekly. A number of these advertisements were double spreads. Their theme was the joy and satisfaction of owning and reading great books.

"Part of my duties as Beck's assistant was to supervise the advertising, and I complained to the agency that, while the advertisements were very fine advertisements, they did not produce any coupons and without coupons which the salesmen could follow up we had no chance to recoup our advertising expense from added sales.

"One day the superintendent of the press room called me up and said the magazine was about to go to press and that there was one vacant quarter-page which we of the sales department might have for a book advertisement if I could get the copy through immediately. I took a volume from one of our pulled sets (sets on which the subscriber had failed to keep up his payments), opened it almost at random, tore out the picture of Marie Antoinette, had a cut made, and wrote under the picture: *This is Marie Antoinette riding to her death. Have you ever read her tragic story?*

"Marie pulled eight times as many coupons in that quarter-page* as we had ever received from a double-spread! She was such a good puller that she continued to run in the magazine for years after I left Collier's.

"While I had written one or two pieces of copy previously, she was my first major operation.

"I don't know how you could get a photostat of her except from the files of Collier's. She must have appeared first somewhere between 1910 and 1913."

---

*Sorry we haven't the quarter-page Mr. Barton mentions. The half-page shown, however, is but the enlarged use of the original quarter-page copy. It required a major research operation to get this, and I am indebted to the good people in Collier's Boston and New York offices for digging it out of ancient files.

There isn't a girl who can't have the irresistible, appealing loveliness of perfect daintiness

Within the Curve of a Woman's Arm
A frank discussion of a subject too often avoided

A woman's arm! Poets have sung of its grace; artists have painted its beauty.

It should be the daintiest, sweetest thing in the world. And yet, unfortunately, it isn't, always.

There's an old offender in this quest for perfect daintiness—an offender of which we ourselves may be ever so unconscious, but which is just as truly present.

Shall we discuss it frankly?

Many a woman who says, "No, I am never annoyed by perspiration," does not know the facts—does not realize how much sweeter and daintier she would be if she were *entirely* free from it.

Of course, we aren't to blame because nature has so made us that the perspiration glands under the arms are more active than anywhere else. Nor are we to blame because the perspiration which occurs under the arm does not evaporate as readily as from other parts of the body. The curve of the arm and the constant wearing of clothing have made normal evaporation there impossible.

Would you be absolutely sure of your daintiness?

It is the chemicals of the body, not uncleanliness, that cause odor. And even though there is no active perspiration—no apparent moisture—there may be under the arms an odor unnoticed by ourselves, but distinctly noticeable to

others. For it is a physiological fact that persons troubled with perspiration odor seldom can detect it themselves.

Fastidious women who want to be absolutely sure of their daintiness have found that they could not trust to their own consciousness; they have felt the need of a toilet water which would insure them against any of this kind of underarm unpleasantness, either moisture or odor.

To meet this need, a physician formulated Odorono—a perfectly harmless and delightful toilet water. With particular women Odorono has become a toilet necessity which they use regularly two or three times a week.

So simple, so easy, so sure

No matter how much the perspiration glands may be excited by exertion, nervousness, or weather conditions, Odorono will keep your underarms always sweet and naturally dry. You then can dismiss all anxiety as to your freshness, your perfect daintiness.

The right time to use Odorono is at night before retiring. Pat it on the underarms with a bit of absorbent cotton, only two or three times a

week. Then a little talcum dusted on and you can forget all about that worst of all embarrassments—perspiration odor or moisture. Daily baths do not lessen the effect of Odorono at all.

Does excessive perspiration ruin your prettiest dresses?

Are you one of the many women who are troubled with excessive perspiration, which ruins all your prettiest blouses and dresses? To endure this condition is so unnecessary! Why, you need *never* spoil a dress with perspiration! For this severer trouble Odorono is just as effective as it is for the more subtle form of perspiration annoyance. Try it tonight and notice how exquisitely fresh and sweet you will feel.

If you are troubled in any unusual way or have had any difficulty in finding relief, let us help you solve your problem. We shall be so glad to do so. Address Ruth Miller, The Odorono Co., 719 Blair Avenue, Cincinnati, Ohio.

At all toilet counters in the United States and Canada, 60c and $1.00. Trial size, 30c. By mail postpaid if your dealer hasn't it.

Dr. Lewis B. Allyn, head of the famous Westfield Laboratories, Westfield, Massachusetts, says:

"*Experimental and practical tests show that Odorono is harmless, economical and effective when employed as directed, and will injure neither the skin nor the health.*"

Address mail orders or requests as follows:
For Canada to The Arthur Sales Co., 61 Adelaide St., East, Toronto, Ont. For France to The Agencie Américaine, 38 Avenue de l'Opéra, Paris. For Switzerland to The Agencie Américaine, 17 Boulevard Helvetique, Geneve. For England to The American Drug Supply Co., 6 Northumberland Ave., London, W. C. 2. For Mexico to H. E. Gerber & Cia, 2a Gante, 19, Mexico City. For U. S. A. to The Odorono Co., 719 Blair Avenue, Cincinnati, Ohio.

ODORONO — *"Within The Curve Of A Woman's Arm"*

TIMES may change, says the JWT News, but a good basic advertising appeal does not. A J. Walter Thompson advertisement for a deodorant, which appeared about 40 years ago, used the same type of illustration — a woman in a man's arms, her one arm upraised, and the same *"You may offend without knowing it"* appeal as is being used in today's modern "Fresh" (JWT-NY) advertising.

James Young, who wrote the 1919 deodorant advertisement says that it was so startling at that time that some 200 *Ladies' Home Journal* readers cancelled their subscriptions and "publishers begged us to stop the copy." Times *have* changed, but not basic advertising appeals. (Mr. Young adds a P.S.: "Several women who learned that I had written this advertisement said they would never speak to me again — that it was 'disgusting' and 'an insult to women.' But the deodorant's sales increased 112% that year.")

You will learn more about James W. Young in this book but nothing more important than his copy philosophy, as expressed to me in a letter from Rancho Canada, Pena Blanca, New Mexico, written in September 1948, and I quote: "I learned to write copy as a seller of books by mail — to Methodist ministers! Hence I have always believed in two things: first, that people read ads; second, that they will respond to them if you use them to make a complete sales canvass. These convictions, in turn, have never made me afraid of 'long copy.'

"When I write an ad I first try to get in mind a very sharp conception of the kind of person I am going to talk to. Then I try to formulate, very clearly, the proposition I am going to make him or her — why he should buy something, think something, or do something.

"Then I try to think out where this person's interests or problems and the proposition come together, and from this try to work out the headline and main illustration which, as one unit, will take hold of them. I usually think out many headlines before I get the one which satisfies me. And also usually labor equally to get the one right illustration for the headline. Where possible, as in the Webb Young advertising, I test headlines for their relative effectiveness, knowing from these tests that some headlines can be twice as effective as others.

"As I write the body of the ad I keep thinking about the reader, asking myself: Have I made this clear? — What doubt will he have here? — Have I made this interesting? — and so on.

"Some ads come easier than others, of course, but usually the actual writing process is not difficult for me. I do not begin it, as a rule, until I have clearly seen the completed ad in my own mind — headline, main illustration, format, and general course of the copy story. When that has come about, then I sit down and put it on paper, and the first draft usually stands, with few revisions."

Brown's Job

Brown is gone, and many men in the trade are wondering who is going to get Brown's job.

There has been considerable speculation about this. Brown's job was reputed to be a good job. Brown's former employers, wise, gray-eyed men, have had to sit still and repress amazement, as they listened to bright, ambitious young men and dignified old ones seriously apply for Brown's job.

Brown had a big chair and a wide, flat-topped desk covered with a sheet of glass. Under the glass was a map of the United States. Brown had a salary of thirty thousand dollars a year. And twice a year Brown made a "trip to the coast" and called on every one of the firm's distributors.

He never tried to sell anything. Brown wasn't exactly in the sales department. He visited with the distributors, called on a few dealers, once in a while made a little talk to a bunch of salesmen. Back at the office he answered most of the important complaints, although Brown's job wasn't to handle complaints.

Brown wasn't in the credit department either, but vital questions of credit usually got to Brown, somehow or other, and Brown would smoke and talk and tell a joke, and untwist his telephone cord and tell the credit manager what to do.

Whenever Mr. Wythe, the impulsive little president, working like a beaver, would pick up a bunch of papers and peer into a particularly troublesome and messy subject, he had a way of saying, "What does Brown say? What does Brown say? What the hell does Brown say? —Well, why don't you do it, then?"

And **that** was disposed.

Or when there was a difficulty that required quick action and lots of it, together with tact and lots of that, Mr. Wythe would say, "Brown, you handle that."

And then one day, the directors met unofficially and decided to fire the superintendent of No. 2 Mill. Brown didn't hear of this until the day after the letter had gone. "What do you think of it, Brown?" asked Mr. Wythe. Brown said, "That's all right. The letter won't be delivered until tomorrow morning, and I'll get him on the wire and have him start East tonight. Then I'll have his stenographer send the letter back here and I'll destroy it before he sees it."

The others agreed, "That's the thing to do."

Brown knew the business he was in. He knew the men he worked with. He had a whole lot of sense, which he apparently used without consciously summoning his judgment to his assistance. He seemed to think good sense.

Brown is gone, and men are now applying for Brown's job. Others are asking who is going to get Brown's job—bright, ambitious young men, dignified older men.

Men who are not the son of Brown's mother, nor the husband of Brown's wife, nor the product of Brown's childhood—men who never suffered Brown's sorrows nor felt his joys, men who never loved the things that Brown loved nor feared the things he feared—are asking for Brown's job.

Don't they know that Brown's chair and his desk, with the map under the glass top, and his pay envelope, are not Brown's job? Don't they know that they might as well apply to the Methodist Church for John Wesley's job?

Brown's former employers know it. Brown's job is where Brown is.

B B D & O — *"Brown's Job"*

BROWN'S job, by the late F. R. Feland, former treasurer of BBDO, is one of those pieces of advertising copy that is legend up and down the industry. It floors me every time I read it — and it must a good many others, too, because requests still come into BBDO for copies or permission to reprint.

Mr. Feland wrote the text in 1920 for the BBDO house organ "The Wedge" or perhaps it was called "Batten's Wedge" then (one of the oldest house organs in the country, incidentally),

and it was used later as a full page advertisement in the *New York Times.* In both uses, it created tremendous interest, receiving much editorial praise as an outstanding piece of agency propaganda. "Just why," Mr. Feland once commented, "is a little hard to understand, inasmuch as, beyond our signature, it makes no reference to agency operation."

Mr. Feland was indeed modest.

And, incidentally, where else in the world will you find a *treasurer* who thought like that!

LITTLE brother, would you be
    Very tall and strong like me?
Then you will, if you are wise,
    Take your daily exercise.

Even though you cannot talk,
    And have not begun to walk
You are big enough to own
    A Kiddie-Kar, and ride alone.

Don't you think that it is pleasant
    To have a birthday and a present?
Now that you are one year old
    You must be a warrior bold.

I'm sure you will enjoy it more
    Than simply creeping on the floor.
There is very little to it,
    Let me show you how to do it.

Never fear that you will fall,
    See, it does not tip at all.
Sit upon this comfy seat
    And push it onward with your feet.

Then as soon as you can learn
    To travel swiftly and to turn,
You shall come outdoors and see
    What fun it is to race with me.

Gaily, gaily we shall ride
    On our journeys, side by side.
And come in these frosty nights
    With O! such awful appetites!

Be sure this mark
is on the seat.

KIDDIE-KAR is the one universal vehicle for children of all ages, from babyhood up to seven or eight years. Your child should have one on the first birthday, or the first Christmas, after passing one year old. It is a great help in learning to walk. And for the older children, both girls and boys it affords healthful exercise, outdoors and in. It is the only practical indoor vehicle and is used the year round.

It is perfectly safe—close to the ground, and almost impossible to tip over—nothing to pinch fingers—no sharp corners—no paint to come off—no adjustments to get out of order.

You will find Kiddie-Kar wherever juvenile vehicles are sold.

Note the list of sizes and prices at the lower left-hand corner of this page.

Don't wait until Christmas. Your dealer may be sold out.

REAL KIDDIE-KARS ARE MADE ONLY BY WHITE

Made in five sizes

No. 1—for 1-2 years, $1.25
No. 2—for 2-3 years, 2.00
No. 3—for 3-4 years, 2.50
No. 4—for 4-5 years, 3.00
No. 5—for over 5 years, 3.50

Higher west of the Mississippi

MADE IN AMERICA FOR AMERICAN GIRLS AND BOYS

The only genuine KIDDIE-KAR is made by the H. C. White Company of North Bennington, Vt. The name KIDDIE-KAR is a registered trade mark; it is always on the seat. The KIDDIE-KAR is protected by four patents.

KIDDIE KAR — *"The Dick Walsh Series"*

ADVERTISING in 1919 was refreshed with this handsome, effective campaign for Kiddie-Kars. "The verses, of course," says Richard J. Walsh, who wrote them, "are frank imitations of Stevenson." Well, it takes a darn good man to imitate Stevenson, and when Dick Walsh gave up the writing of advertising copy for the publishing business, advertising lost one of its most gifted men.

The Kiddie Kar verses became so popular that they were published in the form of a book for children by Lippincott. Sarah Stilwell Weber did the wonderful illustrations. Richard J. Walsh is now president of The John Day Company.

The University of the Night

THE young Lincoln, poring over borrowed school-books far into the night—seeking in the dim light of his log fire the transforming light of knowledge—eager to grow—eager to do—here is a picture that has touched the hearts of men in every country on the earth—here is an example which, for three score years, has inspired the man who strives against the odds of circumstance to make his place in the world.

To-night, in cities and towns and villages, on isolated farms and on the seven seas—thousands of men will drop their daily labors to fight, beneath the lamp, the battle that Lincoln fought—to wring from the hours of the night the education of which circumstance deprived them in the days when they might have gone to school.

Up from the mines, down from the masts of ships, from behind counters and plows, from chauffeurs seats and engine cabs, from factories and offices—from all the places where men work they will go home and take up their books because they yearn to grow, because they seek higher training, greater skill, more responsibility, lives more profitable and work more satisfying.

Some of them are men who work in one field whereas their talents and desires are in another. Some, happy enough in their field of work, are halted in their progress because they do not understand the higher principles of their business or profession. Some of them left school in boyhood because poverty made it necessary; some left because they did not realize then as they do now the value of an education. And some have need of special training which they could not have anticipated, or which they could not have obtained in public schools.

Fifty years ago these men, some of them married, all of them with a living to earn by day, would have had no place to turn for the courses of study and for the personal guidance that they need.

Thirty-two years ago there was founded a school to help them—a school created for their needs and circumstances—a school that *goes to them* no matter where they are—a school whose courses are prepared by the foremost authorities, whose textbooks are written for study in the home, whose instructors guide their students by personal correspondence.

Created in response to a need, the International Correspondence Schools have developed their scope and usefulness with the growth of that need. Beginning with a single course in coal mining, these schools have become to-day an institution with courses in 304 subjects, covering almost every technical field and practically every department of business.

In the thirty-two years of their history the International Correspondence Schools have furnished instruction to more than two and a half million men. Many of them now occupy positions of leadership in their fields. Most of them have been helped to greater earning power, to higher skill or craftsmanship, to the added responsibility, character and good citizenship that come with increased knowledge.

For the most part, these Scranton Schools have served men who could have been served by no other type of educational medium. They have served a larger number, and in a greater number of fields, than any other educational institution.

INTERNATIONAL CORRESPONDENCE SCHOOLS
Scranton, Pennsylvania

Offices in leading cities of the United States and Canada, and throughout the world

I. C. S. — *"The University Of The Night"*

PERHAPS the most famous university in the world is *The University of the Night* in Scranton, Pennsylvania, known colloquially as I. C. S. Its campus lights shine every night in thousands of homes and its graduates flourish in every industry in the land. I. C. S. has depended almost entirely upon advertising to get its story to the most important group of people in the world: men and women who want to study and get ahead. Thus, I. C. S. has published many an advertisement. but none more important than this highly effective example of institutional advertising, written by Raymond Rubicam and headlined by George Cecil, of N. W. Ayer & Son, as great a copy team as ever was.

The University of the Night is obviously not one of those I. C. S. ads to which you can attribute concrete sales of courses, but it will be hard for any student of advertising to believe that it did not fertilize many a mind for a later ad that advertised a course. Also, in my book, it is an excellent example of advertising that does its selling with dignity and poise, and, for the good of advertising, can we have too much of that?

Ray Rubicam tells me, incidentally, that this was the last ad he wrote before leaving N. W. Ayer to form his own agency with John Orr Young. He stayed at the office late one night to do it, sending it off without a headline to George Cecil who was waiting in Scranton. George Cecil, who has written hundreds of I. C. S. ads over the years, gave it that powerful and appealing title.

The GREATEST MOTHER in the WORLD

Stretching forth her hands to all in need; to Jew or Gentile, black or white; knowing no favorite, yet favoring all.

Ready and eager to comfort at a time when comfort is most needed. Helping the little home that's crushed beneath an iron hand by showing mercy in a healthy, human way; rebuilding it, in fact, with stone on stone; replenishing empty bins and empty cupboards; bringing warmth to hearts and hearths too long neglected.

Seeing all things with a mother's sixth sense that's blind to jealousy and meanness; seeing men in their true light, as naughty children — snatching, biting, bitter—but with a hidden side that's quickest touched by mercy.

Reaching out her hands across the sea to No Man's land; to cheer with warmer comforts thousands who must stand and wait in stenched and crawling holes and water-soaked entrenchments where cold and wet bite deeper, so they write, than Boche steel or lead.

She's warming thousands, feeding thousands, healing thousands from her store; the Greatest Mother in the World—the RED CROSS.

Every Dollar of a Red Cross War Fund goes to War Relief

AMERICAN RED CROSS, WORLD WAR I — *"The Greatest Mother In The World"*

I ASKED several prominent advertising men of my generation what they remembered as the most famous ad of the first World War. Without exception it was Courtland N. Smith's *"The Greatest Mother in the World"* created for the American Red Cross.

Court Smith has been a partner in the advertising agency, Alley & Richards, for many years, and has written some excellent copy since the wave of World Wars began, but none perhaps of such memorable distinction as the *"Greatest Mother"* piece. As a poster, the idea became so popular that Great Britain asked for and obtained permission to use it for Red Cross drives over there. It was the only instance where an American ad was accorded such an honor. Court tells this story as to how it all came about:

"I was asked (along with other agency men) by the War Advertising Committee to contribute an idea for a Red Cross advertisement. I recall that the late L. B. Jones, Advertising Manager of Eastman Kodak Co. was one of that committee; I believe the chairman.

"Riding back from Sag Harbor where I'd been calling on a client, I hit upon the idea, *'The Greatest Mother in the World.'* It seemed to me to typify something of the service rendered by that great organization.

"I made my own rough sketch and called in a finish artist (the late A. E. Foringer). He caught the spirit of the thing — allegorical figure typifying motherhood — holding a wounded stretcher case in her arms — and that was that.

"I remember that when I submitted it to the Committee, Jones put up a battle that I call it, *'The Tenderest Mother in the World.'* You now know who won out!"

THE STRANGER AT THE GATE

In the feudal days of old, when cities were armed camps, when the stranger was an enemy, until he proved himself a friend, the merchant who came from one city to another was challenged at the gate.

Today, by thousands, to every city in the land, come the salesmen of manufacturers in distant places. There are no walls of stone to bar their entrance; no city gates where sentries challenge. But there are other gates within the city; there are other walls than walls of stone.

What salesman does not know the little gate that leads the way—or bars it—to the inner office of the buyer? What salesman does not know that important moment when his card goes in —and he waits the word? And if his product is unknown—how often he is halted at the gate!

Then the gates of the homes—the millions of homes—in cities and towns and villages, and on the farms, where dwell the people. Of these there are so many that the manufacturer cannot send his salesmen to them; yet the success or failure of his product hangs upon its reception at these gates. And here again, the unknown product is challenged, while the gates swing wide for the known.

In the old days there were certain illustrious persons upon whom was conferred a key to the city, symbolizing the good-will of the inhabitants and betokening that all places were open to them. Today, in the world of industry, there are those who hold a similar key. They are the ones who know the power of advertising.

N. W. AYER & SON
ADVERTISING HEADQUARTERS

NEW YORK   BOSTON   PHILADELPHIA   CLEVELAND   CHICAGO

THE AYER HOUSE ADS — *"The Stranger At The Gate"*

N. W. AYER & SON was probably the first advertising agency to advertise both advertising and itself in national as well as trade publications. Its first advertisements appeared as early as 1870 and for many years, beginning in 1919, the N. W. Ayer "house" ads ran regularly in The *Saturday Evening Post*. Many Ayer writers contributed to the different campaigns. As I remember it, W. M. Gerdine and Amos Stote were two of the earlier men whose work appeared over the Ayer signature. Certainly none became more famous, however, than Raymond Rubicam who followed them, and who wrote such memorable pieces as *The Stranger at the Gate, The Maverick* and *The Apple that Never Was Picked.*

Back in the early 20s, a large segment of

industry was still unsold on the usefulness and value of advertising. The Ayer series of Rubicam's time undertook to help make advertisers out of non-advertisers and was a highly important contributor to that agency's distinguished and sustained success, and to advertising as a whole. What Rubicam did so well was to illustrate the advertising point he was making by leading off with some simple, highly pointed, easily recognized and engaging parallel in some field outside of advertising.

Not only did Rubicam's series arouse the enthusiasm and improve the morale of the Ayer sales force and staff, but it began to draw a heavy mail — including invitations from prominent national advertisers to call on them.

SQUIBB — *"The Priceless Ingredient"*

IN 1921, Squibb had never advertised to the public, but wanted to advertise certain "household" drug products which are on most bathroom shelves. Squibb did a large business with the medical profession and felt that the profession would scrutinize very critically any advertising to the public that it might do. So the problem given to Raymond Rubicam, then a writer at N. W. Ayer & Son, was to produce a series of advertisements which would sell Squibb to the public and not offend the publicity sensitive medical profession.

Squibb had done a masterly job of convincing young Rubicam of its high professional standards and the importance of its contributions to the science of medicine. So much so that Rubicam admits to this day that his efforts to produce something off the beaten track "are still painful in my mind." He became obsessed with the problem and covered dozens of yellow sheets with headlines, both in the office and at home. One night at two in the morning, he seemed as far away from the solution as ever. Wearily gathering up his yellow sheets before going to bed, he took one more look through the mass of headlines he had written. "Suddenly," he writes, "two separate word combinations popped out at me from two different headlines. One was *The Priceless Ingredient* and the other *Honor and Integrity*. Instantly, the two came together in my mind and I knew I had the headline and the slant that solved the problem: *The Priceless Ingredient of Every Product is the Honor and Integrity of its Maker*. The next day I wrote a full piece of copy around this, and Jim Mathes and I submitted it personally to the late Mr. Theodore Weicker, who was then vice president, and later president, of Squibb.

"The first text did not contain the parable about Hakeem, the Wise Man, which finally was used to lead-off the text, with Hakeem pronouncing *The Priceless Ingredient* sentence just as I first wrote it."

The parable was introduced by Mr. Weicker.

Both Raymond Rubicam and Theodore Weicker have been widely credited with the origination of *The Priceless Ingredient* idea, but the foregoing is the actual story of what happened.

The phrase, *The Priceless Ingredient of Every Product is the Honor and Integrity of its Maker*, became a permanent part of Squibb advertising and appears on practically everything bearing the Squibb name. During the more than quarter century of its use, the Squibb advertising appropriation has grown to many times its 1921 size.

STEINWAY

The Instrument of the Immortals

There has been but one supreme piano in the history of music. In the days of Liszt and Wagner, of Rubinstein and Berlioz, the preeminence of the Steinway was as unquestioned as it is today. It stood then, as it stands now, the chosen instrument of the masters— the inevitable preference wherever great music is understood and esteemed.

STEINWAY & SONS, Steinway Hall, 107-109 E. 14th Street, New York

Subway Express Stations at the Door

STEINWAY — *"The Instrument Of The Immortals"*

WHEREAS, The Priceless Ingredient idea came only after protracted and painful work, the Steinway phrase *The Instrument of the Immortals* came "in a flash." No one can tell the story better than its author, Raymond Rubicam: "Just after I had been hired as a copywriter by N. W. Ayer & Son late in 1919 I was assigned to a writing paper account and was busy trying to cook up some ads for it when a 'copy order' was laid on my desk instructing me to prepare three full page ads for Steinway, to be used in what was then known as 'The Quality Group' of magazines. I was also instructed to follow, in the words of the copy order, the same 'policy' as that of three previous ads. Because I was having trouble making thoughts flow on the writing paper account, I decided to look at the file about Steinway piano and then to look up the past ads. From the file I learned that the piano had been used by practically all the greatest pianists and most of the great composers since Wagner. But when I found the ads in the proof book I discovered that they consisted of photographs of lovely ladies sitting at pianos in lovely drawing rooms, and that the text (without headlines) told nothing of the great Steinway story. Without effort, the phrase formed in my mind, *The Instrument of the Immortals.* I wrote it on a piece of yellow paper and it looked so good that I was afraid to accept my own estimation of it. I decided to put it away in a desk drawer, go back to work on the writing paper account, and then take another appraising look at it in a few days.

"When I looked at it again it still seemed good. So I went downstairs to the Art Department and got hold of Arthur Sullivan, who was then Ayer's Art Director. He told me that somewhere in a big vault Steinway had a collection of oil paintings of the great masters who had played their piano, and that there was, in fact, a book of these paintings called *The Steinway Collection.* But Sullivan told me that for some reason unknown to him Ayer was forbidden to use the paintings in advertising, even though a book of reproductions of them was given to purchasers of pianos. This was a blow, but Sullivan and I decided on a ruse to save *The Instrument of the Immortals.* Lejaren à Hiller was then making the photographs for Steinway advertising. Knowing Hiller's ability in dramatic photography Sullivan and I decided to have him dress up a model to look like 'an immortal' of the Franz Liszt type, and to pose him with a strong beam of light from above illuminating him and his piano. We were not going to say whom we were portraying, but we were going to be certain that everybody knew we were picturing an immortal of music. I was going to write brief but strong text that would build the Steinway case around the fact that the instrument had been played by the overwhelming majority of the great masters since its beginning. When the ad was finished I showed it to Jerry Lauck, the account executive, and by that time I was so enthusiastic about *The Instrument of the Immortals'* idea that I urged him to persuade Steinway to use the phrase not just for one ad but for a whole series,

and to get them to let us use real portraits of real 'immortals'. Lauck shared my enthusiasm for the idea, but said that Steinway did not believe in 'slogans'. I remember saying 'all right, don't call it a slogan, call it an advertising phrase — but do your best to get them to agree to use it regularly'. I contended that as dignified as Steinway might be there was nothing in that phrase that would injure their dignity. Lauck got the initial advertisement OK'd easily enough, but could not get Steinway to agree to continue using it.

"The thing that converted it into a permanent campaign phrase was the spontaneous response to the ad. A few days after the ad ran in the magazines the treasurer of Steinway, who strangely enough was in charge of the advertising, sent for Lauck and told him that for the first time in 25 years of advertising they had actually received a considerable number of voluntary and wholly favorable comments on an ad. The treasurer's response to this was to tell Lauck that he and his associates had changed their minds and that the company would run the phrase *The Instrument of the Immortals* as the central idea in a series of advertisements. They also gave us permission to have portraits made of the greatest living 'immortals' of the piano. We did not want to use immediately the paintings in the Steinway Collection because all the immortals in that collection were dead, and we wanted to establish the point that the living ones — Paderewski, Rachmaninoff and Hofmann — played the Steinway, before we called on the past. At a later date the client also released the Steinway collection for our use.

"At the time *The Instrument of the Immortals* was originated, Steinway spent some $25,000 or $30,000 a year for advertising and had been an advertiser on about this scale for more than a quarter of a century. In the next several years, the Steinway appropriation grew steadily until, at one time it reached, I believe, $500,000. *Although the total production of pianos was decreasing during this period the sale of Steinway pianos increased steadily.* This was not all due, of course, to the 'Instrument of the Immortals' idea. One of the productive things we did to supplement it was to advertise, for the first time, that Steinway pianos could be bought on installment terms. It was somewhat amazing to discover how many people had a hankering for a Steinway but assumed that Steinways were not sold on easy terms, although in fact they were. Another thing we did was to persuade Steinway to reopen the famous old concert hall connected with their then offices in lower New York, and to invite their prospective customers to hear without charge, some of the good concert pianists in recital on a Steinway. These were not my ideas, but Lauck's, or Steinway's, or both.

"We also undertook an aggressive full-page rotogravure campaign in New York City which cost much more than Steinway had ever spent nationally. It took considerable Steinway courage to approve the cost of this, but the reward was substantial success."

Down *from* Canada
came tales of a wonderful beverage

How Canada's famous old ginger ale was brought to this country and adopted by New York's most exclusive clubs, restaurants and hotels. Now sold in this city.

FOR years and years, visitors to Canada have come back with tales of a wonderful ginger ale. They described its exquisite flavor—they told of drinking it in the Houses of Parliament in Ottawa, in the residence of the Governor-General, and in the Royal Canadian Yacht Club.

Friends would listen and smack their lips and ask if there wasn't some way to purchase it in this country. And the answer was always "No."

Then in 1921 the Canadian owners were induced to open a selling agency in this country and "Canada Dry," for the first time, was officially brought to the United States.

A carload was sold the very first week, without a line of printed advertising, and in two short years "Canada Dry" became the accepted ginger ale for smart functions in the most exclusive clubs, hotels and restaurants in New York.

As a matter of fact, the demand grew so rapidly that a separate plant was soon made necessary in this country—one of the most impressive tributes to quality in the history of American business. The reason for the remarkable success of "Canada Dry" is simply that it is

A real ginger ale

This is an important point to remember The dark, brownish color of the ordinary ginger ale is no indication of the quality. That strong, burning, biting taste of the ordinary ginger ale is due largely to the excessive use of capsicum, or red pepper, which is often substituted for the genuine Jamaica ginger.

Because it is *real* ginger ale, and is made from real Jamaica ginger and other absolutely pure ingredients, "Canada Dry" blends delightfully with other beverages—it will not bite the tongue or burn the lips—it has none of that flat, syrupy flavor—it leaves no "brassy" after-taste or recurring "*back kick*," as some people call it—it is friendly to the stomach!

"Canada Dry" has been served for years in the leading hospitals in Canada because of its purity and quality. It is one of the very, very few ginger ales that physicians recommend with absolute confidence.

A truly wonderful flavor!

The minute you break the golden seal of the beautiful bottle and pour a bit of "Canada Dry" slowly down the side of the thin-edged glass, as the connoisseur would pour a glass of fine old wine, you will know that here, at last, is *real* ginger ale.

Hold it to the light. See how clear it is! How it gleams and sparkles! The life and vitality of it! The pale, "dry" champagne color.

And then—*taste it!* Here is a revelation in ginger ale quality—a delicate, alluring "dry" flavor that intrigues your taste—a flavor unlike that of any other ginger ale you have ever tasted!

For "Canada Dry" is made from a formula known to only three men! This formula took fifteen years to perfect—it is handed down from father to son—it is one of the most carefully guarded commercial secrets in the world!

Truly it has been said that until you try "Canada Dry" you have no idea how good ginger ale ought to be. It is so different from the ordinary ginger ale that it might almost be called by another name.

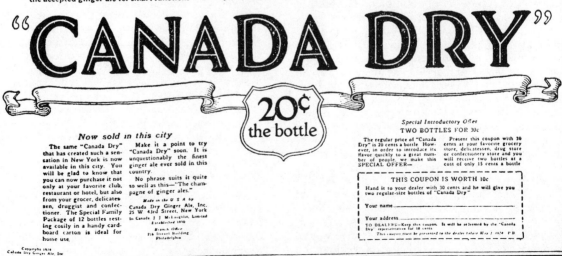

"CANADA DRY"

20¢ the bottle

Now sold in this city

The same "Canada Dry" that has created such a sensation in New York is now available in this city. You will be glad to know that you can now purchase it not only at your favorite club, restaurant or hotel, but also from your grocer, delicatessen, druggist and confectioner. The Special Family Package of 12 bottles resting cosily in a handy cardboard carton is ideal for home use.

Make it a point to try "Canada Dry" soon. It is unquestionably the finest ginger ale ever sold in this country.

No phrase suits it quite so well as this—"The champagne of ginger ales."

Made in the U S A by
Canada Dry Ginger Ale, Inc.
25 W 43rd Street, New York
In Canada J J McLaughlin, Limited
Established 1890

Branch Office
216 Locust Building
Philadelphia

Copyright 1924
Canada Dry Ginger Ale, Inc

CANADA DRY — *"Down From Canada Came Tales Of A Wonderful Beverage"*

GEORGE CECIL, of N. W. Ayer & Son, who wrote the first Canada Dry advertising ever to appear in the United States is one of my favorite people. A favorite because the man is a superb advertising writer, a keen wit, and above all — a sensitive human being.

George has written many great ads and his share of the greatest. *"Down from Canada"* is as fine a piece of emotionalized reason-why selling as ever was put into print. I commend it to copymen old and young. Read it — every word of it — and you'll pick up a pencil with new determination.

The Canada Dry series was written by George following a gang-up — that is, a group meeting of top writing brass at which the creative problems of launching Canada Dry were discussed. George came up two days later with the winning series of which the ad across the page was the first. There

were many more, and it would be hard to pick a "best".

The results story behind this campaign is just as inspiring as the copy." The morning after the first advertisement appeared, three New York jobbers telephoned orders totaling 500 cases. In thirty days the plant was working overtime. In ninety days, it was 300% oversold. During almost all of 1923 orders were five to ten times the capacity of the New York plant. A new plant was built at Hudson, N. Y. At the time the plans were drawn, it was thought that this plant would be large enough for all future needs. But it was necessary to order still another unit, for orders booked during the first month of 1924 were twice those received during *all of* 1923.

"There is no doubt that 'Canada Dry' is one of the greatest retail successes of all time."

WOODBURY SOAP — *"The Skin You Love To Touch"*

ACCORDING to the records of the Andrew Jergens Company, the famous phrase *"The Skin You Love to Touch"* was originally the title of a Woodbury booklet about the skin and how to care for it. Although records are missing, somebody must have seen the value of that phrase because it became an advertisement and was first published in quarter-page space in the *Ladies Home Journal* for May, 1911. Again, there is no record as to what happened as a result of this relatively minor use of Woodbury's famous booklet title, but it must have caught on because

it next crops up as a full color page in the September 1915 issue of the *Journal*.

Certainly, Woodbury's *"The Skin You Love to Touch"* is one of advertising's most famous advertisements, and though ads, like hats, change in appearance, certain fundamentals behind them do not. The current advertising (see illustration) for Woodbury's Facial Soap in no way resembles the advertising thirty years ago — but the fundamentals behind both are in perfect likeness — and the phrase *"The Skin You Love to Touch"* goes on.

Somewhere West of Laramie

SOMEWHERE west of Laramie there's a broncho-busting, steer-roping girl who knows what I'm talking about. She can tell what a sassy pony, that's a cross between greased lightning and the place where it hits, can do with eleven hundred pounds of steel and action when he's going high, wide and handsome.

The truth is—the Playboy was built for her.

Built for the lass whose face is brown with the sun when the day is done of revel and romp and race.

She loves the cross of the wild and the tame.

There's a savor of links about that car—of laughter and lilt and light—a hint of old loves—and saddle and quirt. It's a brawny thing—yet a graceful thing for the sweep o' the Avenue.

Step into the Playboy when the hour grows dull with things gone dead and stale.

Then start for the land of real living with the spirit of the lass who rides, lean and rangy, into the red horizon of a Wyoming twilight.

EDWARD S. (NED) JORDAN* — *"Somewhere West Of Laramie"*

OH . . . James . . . fetch me my harp AND sweep off that top step of the golden stairs. I'm going to tell the story of the IMMORTAL Playboy before they take my bones somewhere west of Laramie and bury them out on the lone prairee-e-e — out where Henry Ewald wants to erect a monument to the man who wrote better copy than that one.

Just to get you in the mood: "I am the rose of Sharon and the lily of the valley . . . As the lily among the thorns, so is my love among the daughters. . ."

Oh . . . excuse me, I must have been thinking of the fundamentals of all advertising . . . all FICTION . . . all of life, which include LOVE, MONEY, ADVENTURE and SPIRIT (or religion).

■ Those who are already dry behind the ears will remember 1918, when 2,000,000 girls were waiting for 2,000,000 boys to come back from "over there." They called them "doughboys." I knew the name would be anathema to the lads just as soon as they gladly put on their "civvies." So I stole the name Playboy from Synge, the Irish playwright, whose play, "The Playboy of the Western World," had been brought to Broadway by Lady Gregory. You see I'd been selling Ramblers and Jefferys for ten years, according to the engineers' ideas of promotion — offset crank shafts, straight line drives, and ejector manifolds. Then Kettering perfected the Delco starting and lighting system. Now any woman could crank a car without breaking her arm. A brand new market had been created. So . . . we got together $300,000 and started for town. Those were the days when we were happily "tiptoeing on eggs" — we just had complete faith in the IDEA.

Walking the floor one dreary Saturday afternoon, waiting for good old "slew foot Barger," our Toledo dealer, to come in with a check for two cars to drive back home. He appeared and we met our meager payroll. Dancing that night at the Mayfield Country Club with Eleanor Borton, age 17, a fine outdoor girl, who could play any position on any guy's team. "Mr. Jordan, why don't you build a car for the girl who loves to swim and paddle and shoot and for the boy who loves the roar of the cutout?" "Thanks, nice girl, for a million dollar idea."

■ Next day . . . New York, in Harry Harrington's Packard Custom Body shop . . . A swanky roadster designed for Flo Ziegfeld as a gift to his wife, Billie Burke. Sketch the job in outline on an envelope. Get to Buffalo where it could be bumped out of aluminum on inexpensive wooden dies. Ship it to Cleveland . . . hide it in the warehouse. Keep your mouth shut.

Plaster it with everything that women want in a car . . . to hell with the old mechanical chatter. Make it look like a woman likes to look to the man who likes to look at her.

Call all the dealers in. Sell 'em from soup to nuts on the regular production line . . . Then *WHAM* comes the Playboy up the boulevard. A regular riot started.

"Hey, Ned, when can we get 'em?" . . . "Never. We can't sell an expensive car. We just built one for the fun of it. You guys can't sell an expensive car. You can't think of anything but price." "The hell we can't . . . I can sell a hundred of those babies at $3,000."

"Okay, brave boys, write down your prices . . . drop them in a hat. We'll build one for each of our 85 distributors. The price will be the lowest figure any dealer puts in the hat and he'll get the first Playboy." Baker, our Detroit distributor, put in the figure $2,175. WELL . . . that gave us $500 net profit in every job and every time we made 2,000 jobs . . . WE MADE ONE MILLION DOLLARS.

Call that BLUE SKY?

Next I wrote ONE advertisement for *The Saturday Evening Post*. It went like this:

"We might as well tell it . . . the secret will soon be out . . . it's a wonderful companion for a wonderful girl and a wonderful boy. How did we happen to think of it? WHY . . . a girl who loves to swim and paddle and shoot described it to a boy who loves the roar of the cutout. So we built one just for the love of doing it . . . and stepped on it . . . AND . . . the chickens ran and the dogs barked. It's a shame to call the Playboy a roadster . . . so full is this brawny thing of the vigor of boyhood and morning."

Then followed a deluge of letters from women all over America. The best was from a girl in West Park, O., who wrote:

Dr. Mr. Jordan: I do not want a position with your company. I just want to meet the man who wrote that advertisement. I am 23 years of age, a brunette, weight 120 pounds, and my wings are spread. All you've got to do is say the word and I'll fly to you."

Now, I might safely answer the question which has been asked a thousand times . . . "Did you?" My answer was "N-O-O," because there were only 24 hours between sunset and sunset . . . NOW . . . I MIGHT . . .

P.S. The Jordan made 1900% for the original stockholders. We started liquidation in 1928 when our statement showed 3½ in assets to 1 of liabilities and the boom was on, but we could see the depression looming over the horizon, and knew that the volume manufacturers were going to build 5,800,000 cars, which, with all the trading, would bankrupt thousands of dealers — WHICH IT DID. THANK THE LORD we quit just in time. Our families have since been enjoying the trust funds which the Playboy earned.

— Reprinted in part with permission from the January 28, 1952 issue of *Advertising Age*.

*Edward S. (Ned) Jordan, 76, died December 29, 1958 and obituaries in many leading magazines and newspapers featured this great Jordan ad, which has so surely left an imperishable imprint on the advertising of our time.

Why men crack . . .

An authority of international standing recently wrote:
"You have overeaten and plugged your organs with moderate
stimulants, the worst of which are not only alcohol and tobacco,
but caffein and sugar." . . . He was talking to men who crack
physically, in the race for success.

YOU know them. Strong men, vigorous
men, robust men—men who have never
had a sick day in their lives. They drive.
They drive themselves to the limit. They
lash themselves *over* the limit with stimulants. They crack. Often, they crash.

You have seen them afterward. Pitiful
shells. The zest gone, the fire gone. Burnt-out
furnaces of energy.

"He was such a healthy-looking man—"

He was. His health was his undoing. His
constitution absorbed punishment. Otherwise he might have been warned in time.

"*For every action there is an equal and contrary reaction.*" You learned the law in
physics. It applies to bodies.

For every ounce of energy gained by
stimulation, by whipping the nerves to
action, an ounce of reserve strength is
drained. If the reserve is great, its loss may
not be felt immediately. But repeated with-
drawals exhaust any reserve. Physical
bankruptcy. Then the crash.

The last ten years have been overwrought.
Men have disregarded much that they know
about hygiene—about health. "Keeping up
with the times." Inflated currency, stimu-
lated production, feverish living, goaded
nerves. It is time to check up.

It is time to get back to normal, to close
the drafts, to bank some of the fires. It is
time to remember some of the simple lessons
of health you learned in school.

Avoid stimulants. What is good for the
boy is good for the man. Life is worth living
normally. The world looks good in the morning to the man whose head does not have to
be "cleared."

Borrowed Energy Must be Repaid!

Two million American families avoid
caffein by drinking Postum. And two million
American families are better off for it. They
have deprived themselves of nothing.

The need they feel for a good, hot drink is
amply satisfied by Postum. They like its
taste. They like its wholesomeness. They

prefer the energy—*real energy*
of body-building grain in place
of artificial energy *borrowed
from the body's own reserve* by
drug stimulation.

Postum is made of whole
wheat and bran roasted. A little
sweetening. Nothing more.

It is not an imitation of
coffee or anything else. It is an
excellent drink in its own right.
It has a full, rich flavor inher-
ited directly from nourishing
wheat and system-toning bran.
Instead of retarding or upset-
ting digestion, it is an actual
help, making the meal more
appetizing and warming the
stomach without counteracting
these good effects by drugging.

There isn't a wakeful hour, a taut nerve,
or a headache in it. You can drink it every
meal of the day, relish it, crave it, knowing
that it is a help, not a hindrance, to health
and efficiency.

A Sporting Proposition

You have a good many years yet to live,
we hope. A good many years to do with as
you please. We are going to ask you, in
the interest of your health, usefulness and
happiness during these remaining years, to
try Postum for thirty days.

To make it a sporting proposition, we will
give you the first week's supply of Postum.
Enough for a cup with every meal for a week.
But we want you to carry on from that point
for thirty days. You can't expect to free yourself from the accumulated effect of a habit of
years in two or three days, or even a week.

There is a woman in Battle Creek,
Michigan, famous for her Postum. She has
traveled all over the country, preparing it.
She has personally served it to over half a
million people, at expositions, food fairs, and
at Postum headquarters in Battle Creek,
where she has 25,000 visitors yearly.

Her name is Carrie Blanchard. Men who
have tasted Carrie Blanchard's Postum

have the habit of remembering its goodness.

We have asked her to tell men about
Postum made in the Carrie Blanchard way.
She wants to start you on your thirty-day
test with her own directions—in addition to
the week's supply.

You men who have not cracked—it might
be well to accept Carrie Blanchard's offer.

Carrie Blanchard's Offer

"Men have always been partial to my Postum. Anybody can make it as well as I can—
but there are a few simple things to remember.

"I have written these things down, and will
be mighty glad to send my directions to anyone who will write. I also want to send
enough Instant Postum, or Postum Cereal
(the kind you boil), to get you well started
on your thirty-day test.

"If you will send in your name and address,
I'll see that you get the kind you want,
right away."

TEAR THIS OUT—MAIL IT NOW

YOUR GROCER SELLS POSTUM IN TWO FORMS. Instant Postum, made in the cup by adding boiling water is the easiest drink in the world to prepare. Postum Cereal (the kind you boil) is also easy to make, but should be boiled 20 minutes. Either form costs less than most other hot drinks.

POSTUM — "*Why Men Crack*"

FOR a long time this advertisement hung in Young & Rubicam's third floor reception room, and was proudly, if inaccurately, referred to as "our first ad."

Y & R had been in business a trifle more than a year when it appeared in one of the May issues of the *Post,* (1924). I was a cub with Ayer at the time, but I remember how eagerly every one in the old shop read it and felt pretty happy about it, too. For its authors were both graduates of "Advertising Headquarters".

The idea and headline are Rubicam's and the text is by Lew Greene, retired Vice President and Group Head, J. Walter Thompson Company, New York.

I consider this excellent example of sincere, persuasive writing "great" for a number of reasons. First, the general conception back of the campaign, of which WHY MEN CRACK was but the first

expression; second, the long, narrative-type copy, never-before used, I believe, in the cereal field, copy long enough to tell a full and convincing story; third, the absence of the conventional shouting slug so much used at that time; fourth, the coupon and its "Carrie Blanchard" offer; and fifth, it was, in a sense, the first ad with what became a very definite Young & Rubicam style, or stamp, or whatever you want to call the things that so graphically identify the work of the different agencies. And when you consider where Y & R ranks in the agency parade, that's a pretty important stamp.

WHY MEN CRACK and its immediate successors set the advertising world talking in 1924, and sent Postum sales from an old low to a new high within twelve months. The Postum campaign was so successful, in fact, that Postum awarded Y & R with the best "Oscar" of them all: more, and more, General Foods business!

★

WRITTEN AFTER HOURS

It is after hours and most of the people have gone home.

There is a chess game in the office of the production manager and a light still burns in the cashier's cage.

From the outer room comes the untutored click of a typewriter—an office boy is taking the Y. M. C. A. course in advertising.

Across the areaway a man bends over his desk, writing. A green visor shades his eyes.

From his twenty-eighth story window as he glances up from time to time he can look down on the jewelry of lights.

It is after hours, but he works on.

He will whip his copy into finished form before he leaves.

One of the layout men has put his drawing board aside and is going out to the elevators.

Under his arm he carries a tissue pad. A new idea is stirring in his mind. It will be roughed out in pencil before morning comes.

Six months from now you will feel it tugging at your purse strings.

It is after hours and most of the people have gone home.

But out in Bronxville and Great Neck, in London and Paris, in Chicago and San Francisco—in hotel rooms, on Pullman cars, on speeding planes and ocean liners this company's people are thinking about other people's businesses, working for men who are all unaware such work is going on.

A few hurried notes scrawled on the back of an old envelope tonight may be the key to next year's most productive advertising campaign.

Between the acts at the theatre an idea may come that will make sales history.

At home beneath the reading lamp a man may solve a merchandising problem.

Once a famous trademark came back from a camping trip.

These are phases of our service that perhaps not even our own clients have ever thought of before.

There is no mention of it in our Terms and Conditions. But all our clients have been the gainer for it and will be many times again.

Why such devotion on the part of men who have already given us their day?

Of no one here is asked more than he can do.

The client does not require it.

Again, why?

Anyone who deals regularly with men will tell you this is the kind of work that money alone cannot buy.

It is work done purely of free will and its real pay is pride in work well done.

Those who understand the creative mind will know just what we mean by that.

They know that the good workman, in advertising as elsewhere, asks no question save, how well can this be done?

Most of our men turned to this organization because they felt that with us they could approach their work in just that spirit.

All of us here hold that good advertising is advertising which is seen, is read and is believed— advertising which makes friends, builds good

will—advertising which returns to the advertiser his investment with a profit.

To contrive with words and pictures advertising which can do these things is a challenge to men of fine talent and quick imagination who like to write and like to draw.

It is not an easy thing to do, and if we have been unusually successful at it, that is because we love the job and have given it our best.

The men who write advertisements for the clients of this firm would succeed in any branch of journalism.

Some of them have been on university faculties. One has edited a newspaper. Others are contributors to the magazines.

They know how to appeal to the public in the printed word.

They know how to sell.

The men who lay out and design our advertising are men at the top of their profession.

They are men who, were they not advertising men. would be well known illustrators and artists.

They know how to catch the public's eye by picture and design.

They know how to sell.

The men in charge of merchandising and contact responsibilities are seasoned business men.

One of them headed a great selling organization for many years.

They know how to fit the wings of advertising to the fuselage of business.

They know how to sell.

Research department? Expert media men? Direct advertising department? Merchandising department? Export facilities?—We have them all.

We have them all developed to a degree not equaled by any other organization that we know. And these departments are all essential in the rounding out of the service this house has made its own.

But quite the finest thing we have to give to those who come to us for counsel is the high enthusiasm of our men and a devotion to their work which is measured neither by the dollar nor the clock.

This, too, was written after hours.

ERWIN, WASEY & COMPANY, INC., *Advertising*

420 Lexington Avenue, New York • 230 N. Michigan Avenue, Chicago

ERWIN, WASEY & COMPANY — *"Written After Hours"*

WRITTEN AFTER HOURS by the late O. B. Winters of Erwin, Wasey & Company, is one of the finest pieces of advertising agency promotion ever written. The phrase "after hours" has been adapted to many uses since this famous ad first appeared more than twenty years ago. The agency has long since lost track of the thousands of requests for reprints.

The copy itself tells the story as to where the idea came from and why it was written. In my book, O. B. Winters stands erect as one of the finest of inspirational writers.

A later piece titled THE OLD MAN and

published as a full page newspaper ad by Erwin, Wasey in 1939 when the world was sorely infected by the dangerous ideologies of Hitler and Mussolini, is a simple, stirring, rallying presentation of the American way, that was quoted, reprinted and distributed nobody knows how many times.

Students of effective advertising should make these two pieces of copy required reading at least twice a year. When you can put words together with such striking simplicity, sincerity and conviction, you can work where you want to at the price you want to get — and love it — and be loved.

TECLA PEARLS — *"A $10,000 Mistake"*

I NEVER saw the man who wrote this advertisement but almost from the first day I stepped inside an advertising agency as a wide-eyed, impressionable youngster, my betters spoke his name reverently: Frank Irving Fletcher.

Stories about Fletcher, his work, his writing habits, his austerity, his fabulous fees, are legion. I know that he is a passionate disciple of brevity, that he works entirely as a free lance, has few friends among advertising men, is caustic, blunt and somewhat contradictory — but always able. He does most of his writing at night.

The advertisement A $10,000 MISTAKE is a classic example of Frank Irving Fletcher at his best.

THE GLORY OF THE UPWARD PATH

As told in the letters of men who are travelling it

TWO paths begin at the bottom of the hill of life.

One of them winds about the base, thru years of routine and drudgery. Now and then it rises over a knoll representing a little higher plane of living made possible by hard earned progress; but its route is slow and difficult and bordered with monotony.

The other mounts slowly at first, but rapidly afterwards, into positions where every problem is new and stirring, and where the rewards are comfort, and travel and freedom from all fear.

Let us glance for a moment at the letters men write who are treading this fortunate path. Such letters come to the Alexander Hamilton Institute in every mail; they are the most thrilling feature of the Institute's business day.

Exultant letters they are, full of hope and happiness; the bulletins of progress on the upward path.

My income has increased 750 per cent

HERE is one from an official in the largest enterprise of its kind in the world. "In the past eight years my income has increased 750%. The Course has been the foundation in my business training."

Another from an officer in a successful manufacturing company: "Last Friday was a happy day for me; I was elected a member of the Board of Directors of this company. The day when I enrolled with the Alexander Hamilton Institute was the turning point in my career"

Whole volumes could be filled with letters of this sort. A few of them have been printed in the Institute's book entitled "Forging Ahead In Business." Thousands of others are open records in the Institute's offices.

In the past ten years the Alexander Hamilton Institute has enrolled thousands of men in its Modern Business Course and Service; and to-day the monthly rate of enrolment is more than three times as great as ever before.

They are men who are moving up

THESE were men, not boys, when they enrolled. Their average age was thirty-three years. They had already made their start in business; they were successful in one department—in selling, or accounting, in production, or banking, or insurance, or factory or office management.

The Alexander Hamilton Institute rounded out their knowledge by giving them the fundamentals of all departments of business. Few men in business ever gain that all-round knowledge; so few that the demand for them is always in excess of the supply.

They are the men who reach the heights of executive responsibility and reward which lie at the end of the upward path.

You are paying whether you profit or not

IT may sound strange to say that you are paying for business training whether you take it or not. Nevertheless it is true.

You are paying in years of moderate progress when the progress might be rapid and sure; paying in opportunities that pass you by because you have not the training or self-confidence to reach out and grasp them; paying in years of routine service when you might enjoy the stimulus and the glory of the upward path.

Send for "Forging Ahead in Business"

THOUSANDS of men have taken the first definite step up, by sending for the 116 page book which the Alexander Hamilton Institute publishes entitled "Forging Ahead In Business." It contains worth while business information, and letters from men in positions exactly similar to yours. It will be sent without obligation; there is a copy for every man of serious purpose. Send for your copy to-day.

ALEXANDER HAMILTON INSTITUTE — *"The Glory Of The Upward Path"*

REMEMBER the advertisements for the Alexander Hamilton Institute? Bruce Barton wrote them in his human, inspiring style, and they remain to this day, among the finest examples of the narrative technique in advertising.

But to me advertisements like this are notable for still another reason: sincerity. Bruce Barton's partner of Alexander Hamilton Institute days, Roy Durstine, says it very well in his famous (and still about the most readable book on advertising ever written) MAKING ADVERTISEMENTS AND MAKING THEM PAY* —

"People often point out the great variation between the advertisements of two successful advertisers.

'Which one is good advertising?' they ask. 'This one violates every standard of taste and yet there is something about it that gives it as much power as that beautiful advertisement.'

"Sincerity is the reason. Two advertisements may be as different as a subway guard and an Episcopal bishop and yet each one will make its appeal. Advertisements are like people. If a man is sincere you can forgive him almost anything. One salesman comes to see you with a manner that is so abrupt or so shy that your first impulse is to tell

him to go out again into the rain which drove him into your office. And yet if he is sincere, if he honestly believes in what he is selling, and you give him half a chance, he will probably leave as good an impression with you as the man whose manners carry a high polish.

"It's equally true that a lack of sincerity can ruin the best materials ever used in the construction of an advertisement. Take a drawing made by an artist whose technique is faultless but who has the idea that he is going slumming whenever he dips into commercial art, combine it with a few vapid words by a writer whose chief interest in the advertisement is to finish it before lunch, have these words put into type and the two elements arranged by a designer whose life is spoiled because he didn't think of making Type Charts before Ben Sherbow did, and what do you have? A pleasing advertisement, perhaps, representing several hundreds of dollars in its manufacture and several thousands in its progress to the public eye through magazine space, but without a flicker of spirit and life and what has been latterly called jazz.

"There ought to be something about an advertisement as contagious as the measles. Without sincerity an advertisement is no more contagious than a sprained ankle."

*MAKING ADVERTISEMENTS and Making Them Pay, by
Roy S. Durstine, Charles Scribner's Sons, New York, 1921.

Listen—

You Biggest City in the World!

Always in a hurry—aren't you? You are so crowded for time that you can never spare more than half an hour to watch a man crawl up the face of a skyscraper, or to study how a chauffeur puts on a new tire, or to learn from a window demonstrator about an automatic necktie.

Give me one minute and I'll show you how to enjoy shaving every morning for the rest of your life. Isn't that a more instructive use of a minute than to watch them frying flapjacks in a Childs' window?

The reason that you find shaving so painful is because you rub half dissolved, caustic soap into the pores, raising a lot of tiny blood blisters which the razor slices off. The trouble isn't that your beard is tough or your skin tender — your soap is bad and your method is wrong.

Get a tube of Mennen Shaving Cream—which perfectly softens the toughest beard without rubbing in with fingers. Squeeze half-an-inch of cream onto a brush that is full of cold water. Whip up a lather on the point of your chin and spread gradually over the face, adding water constantly. Use three times as much water as any ordinary lather will carry. Work this Mennen lather in for three minutes with the brush only. Keep your fingers out of it.

Then enjoy the most glorious shave of your shaving career. Note afterwards that your face doesn't feel as if someone had rubbed salt into it but on the contrary is smooth and free from smart.

Come on—New York—be a sport!

Give Mennen's a trial and be not only the biggest but the happiest city.

Jim Henry
MENNEN SALESMAN

Jim Henry says—"What I like about New York is that it reminds me of every other country town."

MENNEN'S SHAVING CREAM

Trade Mark

GERHARD MENNEN CHEMICAL CO
NEWARK, N.J. U.S.A.

MENNEN'S SHAVING CREAM — *"Listen — You Biggest City In The World!"*

ADVERTISING men face the problem continually of saying something usually considered commonplace in a fresh and interesting way — so people will read what they say and do what they ask them to. Wilbur Corman and Jim Adams found the answer in the famous Jim Henry series for Mennen's Shaving Cream of which *LISTEN — You Biggest City in the World* is an outstanding example.

The copy flatters its cosmopolite readers, and the first person technique is highly effective. There wasn't a lot of first person stuff in those days (circa 1919) and it is hard to believe that the Jim Henry series wasn't the inspiration for the raft of it which followed — and it's good writing, when ably done, as it was here, for it helped enormously in putting Mennen's Shaving Cream on the list of best sellers, and keeping it there.

The Diary
of a Lonesome Girl

Dear Diary: **May 12**

Another day gone—another day just like a hundred days before. Oh, if only something new would happen!

I hate to think of getting up and dragging myself through another day—facing the same four walls of my little world—never going anywhere—never having any good times.

Nobody seems to care what happens to me . . . sometimes I wonder if I care myself.

I know I shouldn't talk like that, but tonight I just can't help it. For it's moonlight, Diary, and I can hear them singing over at Mary Robinson's party. It doesn't seem right that they should be so happy when I'm so miserable.

Oh, yes, Mary asked me to come, but I think she knew I wouldn't accept. I just couldn't wear that old blue crepe again . . . I just couldn't!

Oh, Diary—please help me find a way to get pretty clothes like other girls . . . before Tom forgets.

May 13

Mary came over today to tell me about the party. It must have been wonderful, Diary, and it made me more miserable than ever just to hear about it.

Mary started right in by saying she had danced four times with Tom and then began describing all the new dresses.

But I can't tell you what she said, Diary. All the time she was talking I kept repeating to myself—"She danced four times with Tom" . . . "She danced four times with Tom."

Please don't let her take him away from me, Diary—please don't let her take him away.

June 8

More trouble, Diary. Little Fred is sick and Mother told me today that we'd have to use the money we've been saving for my new dress to help pay the doctor's bill.

Poor Mother! She tries so hard to make both ends meet on Dad's salary and mine, but every time we get a little money saved up, something happens.

I tried to be brave and tell her it didn't really matter. But when I got up to my room I felt so blue that I cried myself to sleep.

If Mother and I could only sew better and make clothes that have real style—then things would be different. Isn't there some way I can learn, Diary?

June 23

I feel better today, Diary, happier than I've felt in months. Remember Myrtle Wright who used to live in our block before she was married?

She and her husband were passing through on their vacation and she dropped in to see me.

She looked even younger than before she was married and she was dressed so beautifully that I just couldn't help but feel a little envious.

She seemed surprised that I wasn't married, and when she asked me why, I poured out the whole story—about clothes . . . about money . . . about Mary . . . about Tom.

"Don't worry, dear," she said. "I've been through it all myself and I know how you feel. Just you listen to me and everything will turn out all right."

Then she told me that she *makes* all her smart lovely clothes—even her coats—and at such savings. That a year ago she couldn't sew any better than I do. But that she had found a school that had taught her right in her own home to make dresses in the smartest, newest styles.

She gave me the address and I wrote tonight. Oh, if it's only true, Diary! Think what it will mean to me!

June 26

More good news, Diary. You know Mrs. Devereaux, who has that dressmaking shop on Broad Street? She's the best dressmaker in town. I asked her yesterday

Among the readers of "McCall's Quarterlies" there are thousands of girls like this. Yes, and just around the corner there are thousands of men like Tom. There's a real and timely message here for every woman and girl who wants to know the happiness of having pretty clothes.

if she had studied in Paris. "No—not in Paris, my dear, but right here in my own home. Everything I know about dressmaking and designing I learned from the Woman's Institute."

Do you hear that, Diary? Why, that's the very school I wrote to the other night.

June 27

Early today the postman brought me a good thick letter from the Woman's Institute. I fairly snatched it from his hand. Guess he thought it was a love letter.

I've read it over three times! It made me so happy I felt like singing all day long.

Think of it, Diary! While I've been so unhappy, thousands of other girls have been learning right at home to make just the kind of smart, becoming clothes they've always wanted at, oh, such wonderful savings.

If *they* can learn, why can't I? I *know* I can and I'm *going to!*

October 15

I know I've neglected you for almost four months, Diary, but I've been so busy since I enrolled with the Woman's Institute that I haven't had time to do anything but be happy.

Here it is only the middle of October and already I have more pretty fall clothes than I ever had in my life. And altogether they cost me no more than one really good dress would have cost me ready-made. Oh, there's a world of difference in the cost of things when you have to pay only for materials!

My friends are all wondering at the change in me, but we know what did it, Diary, don't we?

And you should see Mother in her new dress! You'd hardly know her, and Dad says he's beginning to fall in love with her all over again. You don't know how happy that makes her feel. She's just as much interested in the Woman's Institute as I am.

November 20

More good news! Mother and I have started making clothes for other people. I thought it would be hard, but it isn't. Seems as if everybody in the neighborhood wants clothes like ours.

Just last week we made two dresses for Mrs. Harris and one for Mrs. Patterson. And they really were stylish, if I do say it myself. Mrs. Harris paid $23.50 and Mrs. Patterson paid $15, and they were too delighted for words when they saw how they turned out.

We've earned nearly $80 in the last four weeks and I have three more dresses promised for next week.

And just think . . . I'm going to have a big party in December. I mailed the invitations tonight. And listen, Diary . . . I sent one to Tom!

December 10

Well, the party's over and it was a wonderful success. You should have heard the girls when they saw my new dress. Even Mary Robinson said it was the prettiest dress there.

Tom wanted me to give him every dance, but I told him the hostess couldn't do that. But I did save the last dance for him, and as he drew me close I don't believe I have ever been so happy in all my life.

And he isn't engaged to Mary Robinson, Diary—he's coming to see me Wednesday night.

January 4

The most wonderful, wonderful thing has happened, Diary! Tom has asked me to marry him! It's to be in the spring—just as soon as I can get my trousseau ready. It's going to be the dearest trousseau any girl ever had, too, every stitch of it worked by my own hands.

And to think that just a few months ago I was so miserable and discouraged that I didn't know which way to turn!

The Woman's Institute has certainly made a wonderful change in my life and I'll never forget what it has done for me. I hate to think where I'd be today if Myrtle hadn't told me about it just when she did.

THE WOMAN'S INSTITUTE — *"The Diary Of A Lonesome Girl"*

"PEOPLE won't read long copy" . . . these words are exasperatingly familiar to advertising men who have disproved them time and again — but never more amazingly than in a series for the Woman's Institute, written by George Cecil of N. W. Ayer & Son. *"The Diary of a Lonesome Girl"* is a fine example.

"People" not only read this human, sincere exposition of a lonely girl's despair and her ultimately rewarding experience with the Institute coupon, but they bought courses on dress making as never before.

The Diary of a "Lonesome Girl" pulled so well that it was followed by an advertisement of sim-ilar technique headed "The Letters of a Young Bride."

When Lynn Sumner, the advertising manager, was reading the copy and helping to polish it, he looked up with a smile and said, "George, if you write any more advertisements like this I don't want to be seen with you after six o'clock."

Long copy — or short — you'll find many examples of each in this book . . . just make it interesting, cut it out of the whole cloth of everyday experience, and they'll read it.

Anthony Adverse was a long job of more than a thousand pages. *Good-bye Mr. Chips* was a short job of little more than a hundred pages. Both were best sellers.

LIFT UP YOUR EYES !

How long ago did Orville Wright circle the drill field at Fort Myer while a few score of astonished witnesses stared open-mouthed at the sight of this first man to fly with wings for more than an hour? . . .

How long ago did the intrepid Bleriot hop in his flimsy, scorched monoplane from France to land precariously on the cliffs of Dover? . . .

How long ago did Graham-White circle the Statue of Liberty, struggling dexterously with his hands to maintain equilibrium? . . .

It seems only yesterday!

Yet in the few brief years since then man has learned a new technic in existence. He has explored the earth's atmosphere, his noble machine climbing on after human faculties had failed. . . . He has skimmed lightly over the impenetrable ice barriers of the polar regions. . . . He has taken in his flight not only the gray, fog-blanketed waters of the North Atlantic, but the empty blue seas of the South Atlantic — the Mediterranean—the Pacific—the Indian Ocean—the

Gulf of Mexico. . . . He has soared confidently over the sands of Sahara and the Great Arabian Desert, where only the camel had dared venture before. . . . He has skimmed the terrible dark jungles of the Amazon, and scaled high above the silent places of Alaska. . . . He has flown in squadrons from the Cape of Good Hope to London. . . . In squadrons he has circled South America. . . . *In squadrons he has circumnavigated the globe!*

And in the ordinary routine of transportation service he travels on fixed schedules over airways that streak the skies of Europe and North America. Mail. Passengers. Express. The world is rapidly assigning special duties to this safe vehicle that cuts time in two.

Is there any epoch in all history that has been so sudden in growth from birth to universal achievement? . . . so dramatic in its nature and accomplishments? . . . so rich in promises for the future?

Perhaps the most significant thing in

the great accomplishment of young Colonel Lindbergh is that in him the world sees *the first outstanding example of a generation that is born air-conscious!* Just as the past generation was born to steam, accepting railway transportation as an accomplished fact—and just as the present generation has accepted the automobile as a customary vehicle—so does the rising generation lift up its eyes to the skies! It may be hard still for many of us to accept the fact, but it is certain that the aeroplane will give as great an impetus to advancing civilization as did the automobile.

In this firm belief the Ford Motor Company is devoting its activities and resources to solving the problems that still face commercial aviation. In factory equipment, in laboratory experiment, in actual flights, the Ford Motor Company is establishing a foundation for one of the greatest industries the world has yet known. Within the last two years pilots have flown over ·the established Ford air routes, carrying freight, on regular daily schedules, a distance of more than 700,000 miles.

FORD AIR TRANSPORT — *"Lift Up Your Eyes"*

HERE is the *first* advertisement of the *first* advertising campaign ever to sell air transportation to the general public. It was published by the Ford Motor Company during 1928, and was written by William Ashley Anderson then of N. W. Ayer & Son.

There were seventeen advertisements in the original series. They appeared in leading magazines headed by *The Post* and were widely and favorably commended. "We cannot tell the number who have found inspiration in them. We cannot measure the good they have accomplished. We know only that they are helping effectively to win new

and different appreciation of the meaning of winged vehicles." This from the Foreword of Ford's booklet commemorating the series.

And from the March 1928 *Aero Digest* . . . "His (Ford's) advertising has done more to popularize flying among the reading public than all the stunts that ever have been stunted, at risk of neck and limb . . ."

William Ashley Anderson, an old friend and neighbor of my Philadelphia days, is also a well-known contributor of excellent adventure fiction to *The Saturday Evening Post* and other leading magazines.

Again She Orders —
"A Chicken Salad, Please"

FOR him she is wearing her new frock. For him she is trying to look her prettiest. If only she can impress him—make him like her—just a little.

Across the table he smiles at her, proud of her prettiness, glad to notice that others admire. And she smiles back, a bit timidly, a bit self-consciously.

What wonderful poise he has! What complete self-possession! If only *she* could be so thoroughly at ease.

She pats the folds of her new frock nervously, hoping that he will not notice how embarrassed she is, how uncomfortable. He doesn't—until the waiter comes to their table and stands, with pencil poised, to take the order.

"A chicken salad, please." She hears herself give the order as in a daze. She hears him repeat the order to the waiter, in a rather surprised tone. Why *had* she ordered that again! This was the third time she had ordered chicken salad while dining with him.

He would think she didn't know how to order a dinner. Well, did she? No. She didn't know how to pronounce those French words on the menu. And she didn't know how to use the table appointment as gracefully as she would have liked; found that she couldn't create conversation—and was actually tongue-tied; was conscious of little crudities which she just knew he must be noticing. She wasn't sure of herself, she didn't *know*. And she discovered, as we all do, that there is only one way to have complete poise and ease of manner, and that is to know definitely what to do and say on every occasion.

Are You Conscious of Your Crudities?

It is not, perhaps, so serious a fault to be unable to order a correct dinner. But it is just such little things as these that betray us—that reveal our crudities to others.

Are you sure of yourself? Do you know precisely what to do and say wherever you happen to be? Or are you always hesitant and ill at ease, never quite sure that you haven't blundered?

Every day in our contact with men and women we meet little unexpected problems of conduct. Unless we are prepared to meet them, it is inevitable that we suffer embarrassment and keen humiliation.

Etiquette is the armor that protects us from these embarrassments. It makes us aware instantly of the little crudities that are robbing us of our poise and ease. It tells us how to smooth away these crudities and achieve a manner of confidence and self-possession. It eliminates doubt and uncertainty, tells us exactly what we want to know.

There is an old proverb which says "Good manners make good mixers." We all know how true this is. No one likes to associate with a person who is self-conscious and embarrassed; whose crudities are obvious to all.

Do You Make Friends Easily?

By telling you exactly what is expected of you on all occasions, by giving you a wonderful new ease and dignity of manner, the Book of Etiquette will help make you more popular—a "better mixer." This famous two-volume set of books is the recognized social authority—is a silent social secretary in half a million homes.

Let us pretend that you have received an invitation. Would you know exactly how to acknowledge it? Would you know what sort of gift to send, what to write on the card that accompanies it? Perhaps it is an invitation to a formal wedding. Would you know what to wear? Would you know what to say to the host and hostess upon arrival?

If a Dinner Follows the Wedding—

Would you know exactly how to proceed to the dining room, when to seat yourself, how to create conversation, how to conduct yourself with ease and dignity?

Would you use a fork for your fruit salad, or a spoon? Would you cut your roll with a knife, or break it with your fingers? Would you take olives with a fork? How would you take celery—asparagus—radishes? Unless you are absolutely sure of yourself, you will be embarrassed. And embarrassment *cannot* be concealed.

Book of Etiquette Gives Lifelong Advice

Hundreds of thousands of men and women know and use the Book of Etiquette and find it increasingly helpful. Every time an occasion of importance arises—every time expert help, advice and suggestion is required—they find what they seek in the Book of Etiquette. It solves all problems, answers all questions, tells you exactly what to do, say, write and wear on every occasion.

If you want always to be sure of yourself, to have ease and poise, to avoid embarrassment and humiliation, send for the Book of Etiquette at once. Take advantage of the special bargain offer explained in the panel. Let the Book of Etiquette give you complete self-possession; let it banish the crudities that are perhaps making you self-conscious and uncomfortable when you should be thoroughly at ease.

Mail this coupon *now* while you are thinking of it. The Book of Etiquette will be sent to you in a plain carton with no identifying marks. Be among those who will take advantage of the special offer. Nelson Doubleday, Inc., Dept. 3911, Garden City, New York.

A Social Secretary for Life!

The Famous Book of Etiquette
Nearly 500,000 Sold for $3.50

NOW ONLY $1.98

We have on our shelves at the present time several thousand sets of the Book of Etiquette in the regular $3.50 edition. To clear the shelves quickly and make room for new editions now being printed, Nelson Doubleday, Inc., makes this unusual offer: To the next few thousand people who order the Book of Etiquette, the special bargain price of $1.98 will be extended. In other words, if you act without delay you can secure the complete, two-volume set of the Book of Etiquette at practically *half* the usual cost.

Use the special coupon. It will bring the Book of Etiquette to you promptly, at the special bargain price.

BOOK OF ETIQUETTE

Nelson Doubleday, Inc., Dept. 3911
Garden City, New York

I accept your special bargain offer. You may send me the famous two-volume Book of Etiquette, in a plain carton, for which I will give the postman only $1.98 (plus delivery charges) on arrival—instead of the regular price of $3.50. I am to have the privilege of returning the books within 5 days and having my money refunded if I am not delighted with them.

Name..

Address...

☐ Check this square if you want these books with the beautiful full-leather binding at $2.98 with same return privilege.

(Orders from outside the U. S. are payable $2.44 cash with order. Leather binding, outside U. S., $3.44 cash with order.)

THE BOOK OF ETIQUETTE — *"Again She Ordered Chicken Salad"*

HERE is an ad that will bring back fond memories of the days of Addison Sims of Seattle (by the late Wilbur Ruthrauff, co-founder of Ruthrauff & Ryan), and many other book-selling masterpieces of fabulous sales-history. In a February, 1935 issue of *Time* Magazine's by-gone house organ *Letters,* this excellent story about Lillian Eichler's phenomenal *Book of Etiquette* ads, appeared:

"The girl who repeatedly ordered chicken salad (to the dismay of her tony escort); who never could decide whether or not to invite him into the house late at night; and who practically wrecked her marriage in advance by seizing the arm of a stray usher instead of her father's as they started the wedding march — disappeared from the advertising scene about 1925, but not until she had sold 2,000,000 copies of Publisher Nelson Doubleday's *Book of Etiquette.*

"The miserable lady was the creation of a smart young copywriter named Lillian Eichler. In 1919 Miss Eichler went to work for the Manhattan advertising agency of Ruthrauff & Ryan. About the same time Publisher Doubleday engaged the agency to advertise Eleanor Holt's *Encyclopedia of Etiquette,* of which he had about 1,000 copies on hand. Lillian Eichler, then 18, was assigned to the job. She produced a piece of copy showing an agitated guest spilling a cup of coffee on the table-cloth. Caption: 'Has this ever happened to you?' As a result of the advertisement the 1,000 copies were almost immediately sold; and at the end of the five-day trial offer most of the 1,000 returned to roost on Publisher Doubleday's shelves. Reason: the book had been written before 1900, and its text and pictures were ludicrously archaic.

"However, Doubleday reflected that if Miss Eichler could write such effective copy, she could rewrite the book. In a few months she finished the new *Book of Etiquette.* Equally famed was her slogan: *'What's Wrong In This Picture?'* The advertisements ran for 26 months in national magazines best adapted to mail-order business. Supplemented by direct mail solicitation, the campaign cost $1,500,000, sold 2,000,000 copies at $1.98.

In 1925 Miss Eichler rewrote the book and as recently as a year ago brought it up-to-date again under the title of *The Standard Book of Etiquette.* It is still selling nearly as briskly in bookstores as it once sold by mail.

In the ensuing years, Miss Eichler has found time somehow to marry Dr. Tobias M. Watson, have two children and write fifteen books!

Do You Make These Mistakes in English?

Sherwin Cody's remarkable invention has enabled more than 100,000 people to correct their mistakes in English. Only 15 minutes a day required to improve your speech and writing.

MANY persons use such expressions as "Leave them lay there" and "Mary was invited as well as myself." Still others say "between you and I" instead of "between you and me." It is astonishing how often "who" is used for "whom" and how frequently we hear such glaring mispronunciations as "for MID able," "ave NOO," and "KEW pon." Few know whether to spell certain words with one or two "c's" or "m's" or "r's" or with "ie" or "ei," and when to use commas in order to make their meaning absolutely clear. Most persons use only common words—colorless, flat, ordinary. Their speech and their letters are lifeless, monotonous, humdrum.

Why Most People Make Mistakes

What is the reason so many of us are deficient in the use of English and find our careers stunted in consequence? Why is it some cannot spell correctly and others cannot punctuate? Why do so many find themselves at a loss for words to express their meaning adequately? The reason for the deficiency is clear. Sherwin Cody discovered it in scientific tests which he gave thousands of times. *Most persons do not write or speak good English simply because they never formed the habit of doing so.*

What Cody Did at Gary

The formation of any habit comes only from constant practice. Shakespeare, you may be sure, never studied rules. No one who writes and speaks correctly thinks of *rules* when he is doing so.

Here is our mother-tongue, a language that has built up our civilization, and without which we should all still be muttering savages! Yet our schools, by wrong methods, have made it a study to be avoided —the hardest of tasks instead of the most fascinating of games! For years it has been a crying disgrace.

In that point lies the real difference between Sherwin Cody and the schools! Here is an illustration: Some years ago Mr. Cody was invited by the author of the famous Gary System of Education to teach English to all upper-grade pupils in Gary, Indiana. By means of unique practice exercises *Mr. Cody secured more improvement in these pupils in five weeks than previously had been obtained by similar pupils in two years under old methods.* There was no guesswork about these results. They wer proved by scientific comparisons. Amazing as this improvement was, more interesting still was the fact that the children were "wild" about the study. It was like playing a game!

The basic principle of Mr. Cody's new method is habit-forming. Anyone can learn to write and speak correctly by constantly using the correct forms. But how is one to know in each case what is correct? Mr. Cody solves this problem in a simple, unique, sensible way.

100% Self-Correcting Device

Suppose he himself were standing forever at your elbow. Every time you mispronounced or misspelled a word, every time you violated correct grammatical usage, every time you used the wrong word to express what you meant, suppose you could hear him whisper: "That is wrong, it should be thus and so." In a short time you would habitually use the correct form and the right words in speaking and writing.

If you continued to make the same mistakes over and over again, each time patiently he would tell you what was right. He would, as it were, be an everlasting mentor beside you—a mentor who would not laugh at you, but who would, on the contrary, support and help you. The 100% Self-Correcting Device does exactly this thing. It is Mr. Cody's silent voice behind you, ready to speak out whenever you commit an error. It finds your mistakes and concentrates on them. You do not need to study anything you already know. There are no rules to memorize.

Only 15 Minutes a Day

Nor is there very much to learn. In Mr. Cody's years of experimenting he brought to light some highly astonishing facts about English.

SHERWIN CODY

For instance, statistics show that a list of sixty-nine words (with their repetitions) *make up more than half of all our speech and letter-writing.* Obviously, if one could learn to spell, use, and pronounce these words correctly, one would go far toward eliminating incorrect spelling and pronunciation.

Similarly, Mr. Cody proved that there were no more than one dozen fundamental principles of punctuation. If we mastered these principles, there would be no bugbear of punctuation to handicap us in our writing.

Finally he discovered that twenty-five typical errors in grammar constitute nine-tenths of our everyday mistakes. When one has learned to avoid these twenty-five pitfalls, how readily one can obtain the facility of speech which denotes the person of breeding and education!

When the study of English is made so simple, it becomes clear that progress can be made in a very short time. *No more than fifteen minutes a day is required.* Fifteen minutes, not of study, but of fascinating practice! Mr. Cody's students do their work in any spare moment they can snatch. They do it riding to work or at home. They take fifteen minutes from the time usually spent in profitless reading or amusement. The results really are phenomenal.

Sherwin Cody has placed an excellent command of the English language within the grasp of everyone. Those who take advantage of his method gain something so priceless that it cannot be measured in terms of money. They gain a mark of breeding that cannot be erased as long as they live. They gain a facility in speech that marks them as educated people in whatever society they find themselves. They gain the self-confidence and self-respect which this ability inspires. As for material reward, certainly the importance of good English in the race for success cannot be overestimated. Surely, no one can advance far without it.

FREE — Book on English

It is impossible in this brief review, to give more than a suggestion of the range of subjects covered by Mr. Cody's new method and of what his practice exercises consist. But those who are interested can find a detailed description in a fascinating little book called "How You Can Master Good English in 15 Minutes a Day." This is published by the Sherwin Cody School of English in Rochester. It can be had by anyone, free upon request. There is no obligation involved in writing for it. The book is more than a prospectus. Unquestionably, it tells one of the most interesting stories about education in English ever written.

If you are interested in learning more in detail of what Sherwin Cody can do for you, send for the book "How You Cán Master Good English in 15 Minutes a Day."

Merely mail the coupon, a letter or postal card for it now. No agent will call. SHERWIN CODY SCHOOL OF ENGLISH, 8811 B. & O. Building, Rochester 4, N. Y.

SHERWIN CODY — *"Do You Make These Mistakes In English?"*

I TRACKED down Max Sackheim, author of this famous Sherwin Cody ad, by way of Victor O. Schwab, President of Schwab & Beatty, and Mr. Harry Scherman, President of The Book-of-the-Month Club, both of whom had been credited with writing it.

"Yes," wrote Mr. Sackheim, "I did the Sherwin Cody ad when I was with Ruthrauff & Ryan sometime before 1919.

"As with many other successful ads, this one was written to sell the writer himself. Having had no formal education, I was concerned about the mistakes in English I might have been making in my own writing. I was, there-fore, a good prospect — and I wrote what I thought would sell me.

"Strangely enough, the original copy contained several errors in English. Mr. Cody corrected most of them, and Walter Patterson and Charles Lennon who conducted the School in Rochester, N. Y., (and still do) corrected some others. From time to time thereafter readers of the advertisement challenged the construction of some of the sentences and the usage of some of the words — and further grammatical changes were made.

"In any event, the advertisement still seems to pay — perhaps because no one (no-one? no-body?) is sure he doesn't make some mistakes in English. Between you and I, I ain't sure but what I can't hardly help making some myself."

Mr. Sackheim's frank, amusing reply to my letter for data tells only part of the story about this great piece of copy. Some years ago Mr. Victor Schwab wrote a story about this advertisement titled *"An Advertisement that is Never Changed."*

At the time Mr. Schwab's article was published this particular Sherwin Cody advertisement had been used for fifteen years without change except for slipping a new and better testimonial into the copy occasionally. And here it is 1959 and Mr. Sackheim's advertisement is about the only thing that isn't changing in this changing world!

No exact figures are, of course, available, but it is safe to say that inquiries run into millions, with *dollars* not far behind.

"Can he really play?" a girl whispered.
"Heavens no!" Arthur exclaimed. "He
never played a note in his life."

They Laughed When I Sat Down
At the Piano
But When I Started to Play!—

ARTHUR had just played "The Rosary." The room rang with applause. I decided that this would be a dramatic moment for me to make my debut. To the amazement of all my friends, I strode confidently over to the piano and sat down.

"Jack is up to his old tricks," somebody chuckled. The crowd laughed. They were all certain that I couldn't play a single note.

"Can he really play?" I heard a girl whisper to Arthur.

"Heavens, no!" Arthur exclaimed· "He never played a note in all his life. . . But just you watch him. This is going to be good."

I decided to make the most of the situation. With mock dignity I drew out a silk handkerchief and lightly dusted off the piano keys. Then I rose and gave the revolving piano stool a quarter of a turn, just as I had seen an imitator of Paderewski do in a vaudeville sketch.

"What do you think of his execution?" called a voice from the rear.

"We're in favor of it!" came back the answer, and the crowd rocked with laughter.

Then I Started to Play

Instantly a tense silence fell on the guests. The laughter died on their lips as if by magic. I played through the first few bars of Beethoven's immortal Moonlight Sonata. I heard gasps of amazement. My friends sat breathless — spellbound!

I played on and as I played I forgot the people around me. I forgot the hour, the place, the breathless listeners. The little world I lived in seemed to fade — seemed to grow dim—unreal. Only the music was real. Only the music and visions it brought me. Visions as beautiful and as changing as the wind blown clouds and drifting moonlight that long ago inspired the master composer. It seemed as if the master

musician himself were speaking to me—speaking through the medium of music—not in words but in chords. Not in sentences but in exquisite melodies!

A Complete Triumph!

As the last notes of the Moonlight Sonata died away, the room resounded with a sudden roar of applause. I found myself surrounded by excited faces. How my friends carried on! Men shook my hand—wildly congratulated me—pounded me on the back in their enthusiasm! Everybody was exclaiming with delight—plying me with rapid questions. . . "Jack! Why didn't you tell us you could play like that?". . . "Where *did* you learn?"—"How long have you studied?"—"Who *was* your teacher?"

"I have never even *seen* my teacher," I replied. "And just a short while ago I couldn't play a note.'.

"Quit your kidding," laughed Arthur, himself an accomplished pianist. "You've been studying for years. I can tell."

"I have been studying only a short while," I insisted. "I decided to keep it a secret so that I could surprise all you folks."

Then I told them the whole story.

"Have you ever heard of the U. S. School of Music?" I asked.

A few of my friends nodded. "That's a correspondence school, isn't it?" they exclaimed.

"Exactly," I replied. "They have a new simplified method that can teach you to play any instrument by mail in just a few months."

How I Learned to Play Without a Teacher

And then I explained how for years I had longed to play the piano.

"A few months ago," I continued, "I saw an interesting ad for the U. S. School of Music—a new method of learning to play which only cost a few cents a day! The ad told how a woman had mastered the piano in her spare time at home—and *without a teacher!* Best of all, the wonderful new method she used, required no laborious scales— no heartless exercises — no tiresome practising. It sounded so convincing that I filled out the coupon requesting the Free Demonstration Lesson.

"The free book arrived promptly and I started in that very night to study the Demonstration Lesson. I was amazed to see how easy it was to play this new way. Then I sent for the course.

"When the course arrived I found it was just as the ad said — as easy as A.B.C.! And, as

the lessons continued they got easier and easier. Before I knew it I was playing all the pieces I liked best. Nothing stopped me. I could play ballads or classical numbers or jazz, all with equal ease! And I never did have any special talent for music!"

*   *   *   *

Play Any Instrument

You too, can now *teach yourself* to be an accomplished musician—right at home—in half the usual time. You can't go wrong with this simple new method which has already shown 350,000 people how to play their favorite instruments. Forget that old-fashioned idea that you need special "talent." Just read the list of instruments in the panel, decide which one you want to play and the U. S. School will do the rest. And bear in mind no matter which instrument you choose, the cost in each case will be the same—just a few cents a day. No matter whether you are a mere beginner or already a good performer, you will be interested in learning about this new and wonderful method.

Send for Our Free Booklet and Demonstration Lesson

Thousands of successful students never dreamed they possessed musical ability until it was revealed to them by a remarkable "Musical Ability Test" which we send entirely without cost with our interesting free booklet.

If you are in earnest about wanting to play your favorite instrument—if you really want to gain happiness and increase your popularity—send at once for the free booklet and Demonstration Lesson. No cost — no obligation. Right now we are making a Special offer for a limited number of new students. Sign and send the convenient coupon now — before it's too late to gain the benefits of this offer. Instruments supplied when needed, cash or credit. **U. S. School of Music, 1031 Brunswick Bldg., New York City.**

Pick Your Instrument

Piano	'Cello
Organ	Harmony and
Violin	Composition
Drums and	Sight Singing
Traps	Ukulele
Banjo	Guitar
Tenor	Hawaiian
Banjo	Steel Guitar
Mandolin	Harp
Clarinet	Cornet
Flute	Piccolo
Saxophone	Trombone
Voice and Speech Culture	
Automatic Finger Control	
Piano Accordion	

U. S. SCHOOL OF MUSIC — *"They Laughed When I Sat Down At The Piano"*

I LAUGH as I sit down to write about John Caples and his many famous advertisements. I laugh because unlike John's hero at the piano, I can't come through. Only Caples could do justice to the Caples formula.* But certainly, in my book, this able writer of outstanding copy, deserves a very strong salute.

The remarkably successful piano ad (and others) was written by Mr. Caples in 1925 when he was a mere copy cub in the house of Ruthrauff & Ryan. The late Ev Grady was his boss and the story of this promising neophyte and his development has been ably told by James D. Woolf in *Advertising & Selling*, under the title *"Triumph of Walter Mitty."*

Mr. Caples is now a Vice President of BBD&O.

*List of Caples' books on copy
  TESTED ADVERTISING METHODS
  ADVERTISING IDEAS
  ADVERTISING FOR IMMEDIATE SALES
  MAKING ADS PAY

Often a bridesmaid but never a bride

EDNA'S case was really a pathetic one. Like every woman, her primary ambition was to marry. Most of the girls of her set were married—or about to be. Yet not one possessed more grace or charm or loveliness than she.

And as her birthdays crept gradually toward that tragic thirty-mark, marriage seemed farther from her life than ever.

She was often a bridesmaid but never a bride.

*   *   *   *

That's the insidious thing about halitosis (unpleasant breath). You, yourself, rarely know when you have it. And even your closest friends won't tell you.

Sometimes, of course, halitosis comes from some deep-seated organic disorder that requires professional advice. But usually—and fortunately—halitosis is only a local condition that yields to the regular use of Listerine as a mouth wash and gargle. It is an interesting thing that this well-known antiseptic that has been in use for years for surgical dressings, possesses these unusual properties as a breath deodorant.

It halts food fermentation in the mouth and leaves the breath sweet, fresh and clean. *Not* by substituting some other odor but by really removing the old one. The Listerine odor itself quickly disappears. So the systematic use of Listerine puts you on the safe and polite side.

Your druggist will supply you with Listerine. He sells lots of it. It has dozens of different uses as a safe antiseptic and has been trusted as such for a half a century. Read the interesting little booklet that comes with every bottle.
—*Lambert Pharmacal Company, Saint Louis, U. S. A.*

For HALITOSIS use LISTERINE

THE ONE HUNDRED GREATEST ADVERTISEMENTS

LISTERINE — "Often A Bridesmaid, But Never A Bride"

PROBABLY one of the best-known headlines in all advertising is *"Often a Bridesmaid, but Never a Bride,"* written by the late Milton Feasley of Lambert & Feasley for Listerine. But not so well known is the story behind the genesis of the halitosis idea itself of which *"Often a Bridesmaid, but Never a Bride"* is but a single expression. Here it goes, given to me by Gordon Seagrove of Lambert & Feasley, who was in at the beginning and who is still writing the bulk of the Listerine (halitosis) copy to this day —

"Gerard and Marion Lambert, returning from World War I, got interested in the Lambert Pharmacal Company, in which both were owners. Up to this time Listerine had been more or less of an ethical product with a fairly commanding position in the professional field.

"The brothers Lambert called Milt and me to St. Louis to discuss what we could do to put Listerine into the commercial field. No one had any particularly trenchant thoughts, so Dr. Deacon, chief chemist of the company, was called in to tell us something about the product and its uses. As he read along in a singsong voice, he mentioned halitosis. Everybody said: 'What's that?'— I think it was Milt or Gerard who said, 'Maybe that's the peg we can hang our hat on.'

"There was considerable discussion as to whether we could handle a delicate subject like that in the newspapers and magazines and get away with it.

"The agency that had the account at that time gave the idea a very cold reception, but both Marion and Gerard Lambert were extremely hot about it and Feasley and I went to work. The rest is more or less history. The ads were amplified and repeated over and over again for a number of years, being placed with Lambert & Feasley which started out in New York about 1923.

"Milt died in 1926 and I came down in the fall of that very same year.

"And if you want any explanation of my grey hairs, I've been the sole creator of all Listerine advertising for twenty-two years. If I look something like a rabbit, it's because I've been sniffing at myself and everybody else for these twenty-two years!"

"We could be just as crowded at Macy's, and not get wet!"

BRISK, exhilarating football weather is upon us once more and as thousands converge joyously on bowl and stadium. There may be some who shiver in their shoes, and wish they dared admit that they prefer steam heat to the great open spaces. We have a few suggestions for both the rugged and the frostbitten. As specialists in companionable crowds (which have made us what we are today — the World's Largest Store) we enjoy them, and delight in divining what they will want and need, and forthwith selling it to them, at low cash prices geared to make 94 cents act like a buck. That's why we are so well prepared at this moment to suggest that whether your corpuscles boldly respond to the challenge of rain, snow, and frost, or whether they'd, rather just hang around where it's warm, we can make all Autumn expeditions pleasanter by fitting you out with appropriate woolies. So be your age, even though it's a mere thirty (it's smart to be thirty) and come to Macy's for warm socks, boots, underwear, sweaters, blankets, furs, coats, and ear muffs, before you set forth to exhilarate. We'll conserve your cash, as well as your body heat. As just another great popular American sport dependent on enthusiastic crowds, we are all in favor of football, but believe weather is something someone should do something about—and we've done it! For men, women, and small fry. So come to Macy's before you go to the game, and rub elbows with the smart and thrifty. Our low cash prices attract appreciative crowds. And crowds keep our prices low—a far from vicious circle in these taxing days when *everyone* feels the urge to save.

It's smart to be thrifty 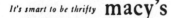 **macy's**

R. H. MACY — *"We Could Be Just As Crowded At Macy's And Not Get Wet!"*

I DON'T know who discovered who: whether Margaret Fishback discovered Macy's or vice versa — but is was certainly one of the most important discoveries ever made in that spastic, price-tagged world of department store advertising. As evidence, I offer the ad at the left.

I wish there was room to show you dozens more, for among them you would find that to a Fishback facts are never dull, even when they're negative!

Margaret's copy for Macy's is fabulous. To her the most commonplace merchandise had an interesting, human angle, usually expressed with a light and entertaining touch. *"You don't need sulphur and molasses — you just need a new spring hat"* is another headline that only someone who wasn't smart enough to be thrifty, could ignore.

My advice to all copywriters is to get a file of Macy advertisements of the Fishback era and read them like the Bible. If you ever write another dull piece of copy after that prepare to go to the copywriters' hell — and in a hack.

CHESTERFIELD CIGARETTES — *"Blow Some My Way"*

PERHAPS the most important four words of copy ever written were these *"Blow Some My Way"* which appeared on a poster for Chesterfield Cigarettes in 1926. Daringly, they introduced, for the first time, *a woman in cigarette advertising,* and great was the furor thereof. But no greater certainly than the vast market to which they paved the way.

Newell-Emmett was the agency and I can't quite pry out of them which writer was responsible (if any one writer was) for this revolutionary idea and the succinct text. I like to think it was Jack Cunningham, who is to Cunningham & Walsh copy what words are to a dictionary.

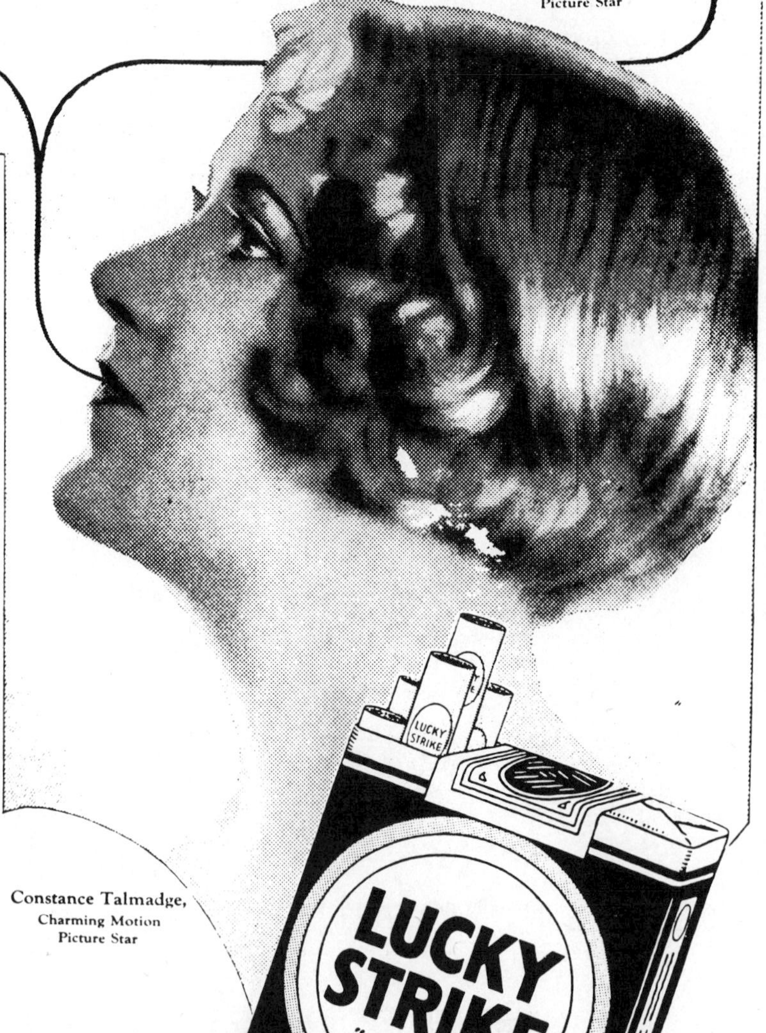

LUCKY STRIKE — *"Reach For A Lucky Instead Of A Sweet"*

IN the November 19, 1948 issue of *Printers' Ink,* Vincent Riggio, President of The American Tobacco Company, relates the alerting story of one of the most famous of all sales-building cigarette campaigns —

"Some years ago, I was riding up town with George W. Hill, and we had gone about five miles through New York City without Mr. Hill having spoken one word. He was thinking deeply about something, and knowing Mr. Hill, I did not interrupt his trend of thought.

"This went on for a while, and we were obliged to stop for a traffic light. The car was standing there for a few minutes, and Mr. Hill grabbed me and said, 'I've got it.' Then, 'Look,' he said, pointing to a stout woman who was standing on the sidewalk waiting to cross the street. This woman had a big piece of candy in her hand and was eating it. A taxicab had pulled up between the sidewalk and our car, the occupant of which was a slender, nice looking woman smoking a cigarette. I noticed the contrast immediately. Mr. Hill said again, 'I've got it . . . *"Reach for a Lucky Instead of a Sweet."* '

"During the rest of the journey we discussed the possible use of this idea. Mr. Hill's enthusiasm was really remarkable. He could talk of nothing else . . . Well, it took a great deal of work to develop this idea so that it could be properly presented to the public . . . I don't have to tell you what this idea did for Lucky Strikes, despite the protests that it raised from the confectionery industry. In 1925 the profits of the American Tobacco Co. were $21,000,000. Principally through this idea, *'Reach for a Lucky Instead of a Sweet,'* these profits had increased by 1931 to $46,000,000. (In 1947 operating profits were $62,254,645.) Many in marketing today believe that campaign created more women smokers than any other single promotional effort."

Who else wants a *whiter* wash
—with no hard work?

HOW would you like to see your wash come out of a simple soaking—whiter than hours of scrubbing could make it!

Millions of women do it every week. They've given up washboards for good. They've freed themselves *forever* from the hard work and reddened hands of washday.

Now they just soak—rinse—and hang out to dry! In half the time, without a bit of hard rubbing, the wash is on the line—*whiter than ever!*

Dirt floats off—stains go

The secret is simply Rinso—a mild, granulated soap that gives rich, lasting suds even in the hardest water.

Just soak the clothes in the creamy Rinso suds—and the dirt and stains float off. Rinse—and the wash is spotless.

Even the most soiled parts need only a gentle rub between the fingers to make them snowy. Thus clothes last longer, for there's no hard rubbing against a board.

Safe for clothes, easy on hands

No laundry soap is easier on clothes or on hands than Rinso. Contains no acids, harsh chemicals or bleaches—nothing to injure white clothes or fast colors.

Rinso is all you need on washday. No bar soaps, chips or powders. Get Rinso for small cost from your grocer. Follow easy directions on package.

Use in washing machines

Rinso is wonderful in washers. Recommended by 23 leading washing machine makers for safety, and for a whiter, cleaner wash.

Guaranteed by the makers of Lux
Lever Bros. Co.

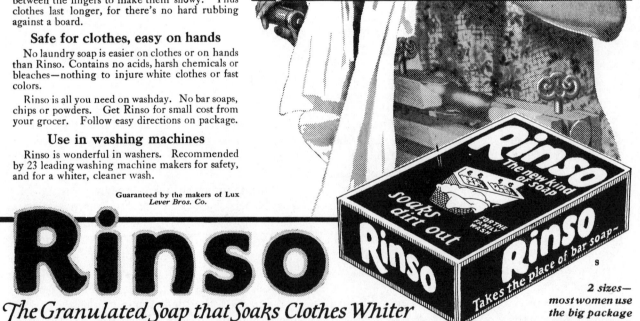

Mrs. G. N. Tapp, a Hub woman, says:

Rinso
The Granulated Soap that Soaks Clothes Whiter

Rinso
The new kind of soap
soaks dirt out
FOR THE FAMILY WASH
Rinso
Takes the place of bar soap—

s

2 sizes—
most women use
the big package

RINSO — *"Who Else Wants A Whiter Wash—With No Hard Work?"*

Several agencies were commissioned in 1926 to study Rinso's advertising needs. Among them was Ruthrauff & Ryan, who interested Lever because of their successful experience in mail-order advertising. R & R were appointed after submitting a local-testimonial newspaper campaign which told housewives how to get whiter clothes with less elbow grease — a result which all women wanted from laundry soaps, according to R & R's field research.

Lever continued to use testimonials in Rinso's advertising for nearly a decade, in newspapers, magazines, and finally in radio. The keynote of Rinso's advertising since 1926 has always been "whiter clothes." Since the original local-testimonial campaign, Rinso sales have multiplied well over 10 times. For many years Rinso has been the leading laundry soap of the country.

THUS, in Western Union style, reads the bolts-and-nuts story behind the phenomenal success of RINSO. The ad at the left is one of the originals in this famous series.

But behind that story is still another, and I learned it one day while playing golf with Grafton Perkins* up on one of the finest courses in this part of the world.

It seems that the whole business revolves around a trifling meeting on the street. Lever decided to appoint a new agency for Rinso. Perkins was given a modest appropriation to pay certain pre-selected New York agencies for getting up recommendations, copy, etc. The appropriation was expended and Perkins was hurrying toward Grand Central on the way back to Cambridge when he ran into an old friend, C. J. McCarthy, who said he was working for Ruthrauff & Ryan. Over a fast drink, Perkins mentioned his mission but said that he had no more money. Sorry, pal, but you weren't on the list anyway.

Cal McCarthy allowed as how he didn't give a hoot about the money — all he wanted was a chance to submit something. That was okay with Grafton B. Perkins.

Now here's the part of the story I like! I hope it happened just the way I'm telling it. Anyway, came the day when the official presentations were all in (including the orphan from Ruthrauff & Ryan) and set up in the office of the President of Lever Brothers Company without identifying marks as to who did what. The President walked slowly around the room studying and reading each memorandum and each piece of copy.

Finally, he came back to Ruthrauff & Ryan's submission and said: "That's it."

---

*Grafton B. Perkins, former Vice President, in Charge of Advertising, Lever Brothers Company; now deceased.

(Lillian Eichler of *Book of Etiquette* fame wrote the Rinso copy for about 10 years.)

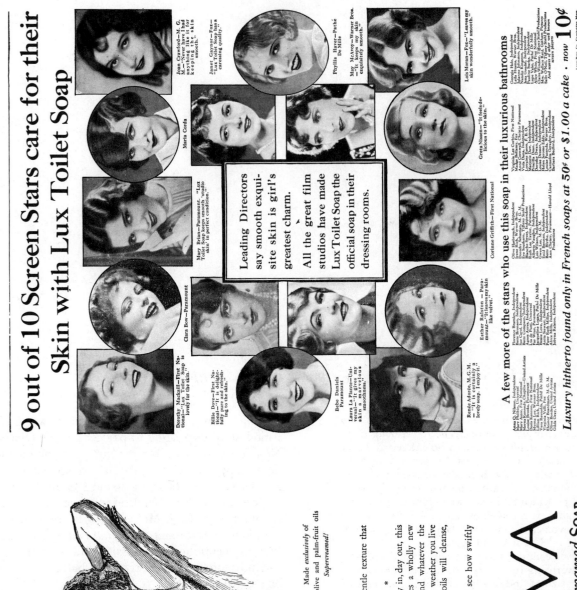

LUX TOILET SOAP —

"9 Out Of 10 Screen Stars Use Lux Toilet Soap For Their Priceless Smooth Skins"

J. Walter Thompson Company groomed Lux Toilet Soap and Lux Flakes for the marketplace. The campaign which introduced this new Lever product in 1925 and 1926, as it slowly gained national distribution, emphasized its superiority even to high-priced imported soaps. In late 1927, however, there appeared the *"9 out of 10 Screen Stars"* campaign which has continued basically unchanged for twenty years. Sales have grown meanwhile until they are over 5 times what they were when the "Hollywood" campaign started. For a decade Lux Toilet Soap has been the biggest seller in its field.

THAT'S the story, friends — or part of it anyway (the part that usually comes up from the auditor's office). Sure, it's got the facts, and the ad at the left is a perfect example of the lusty beginnings of this super soap seller, but there's another story behind the launching of this famous campaign, and it's got everything, including cloak-and-dagger stuff that would be a credit to the FBI.

While advertising for Lux Toilet Soap (under the original name of Lux Toilet Form) was being tested in Taunton and Framingham, Massachusetts, Lever Brothers simultaneously tested a green soap called OLVA in three up-state New York cities. 24-sheet posters with at least 10 colors were used and changed every month (in only 3 cities, mind you), with occasional rotogravure spreads on Sundays to liven things up. A leading competitor or two went nuts at such goings on, first wondering how Lever could afford to package and sell OLVA for a dime when it looked like a quarter job to say the least. Second, the competition shook with Scotch ague at the way Lever spent launching money for the extra elaborate advertising, and the additional extravagant sampling, couponing and store promotion. Dozens of competitive sleuths were thrown into the area to check every move Lever made. Retaliatory ads of 100 lines each were run under such headlines as "BEWARE!" and "WARNING!"

So while competition was running itself ragged spying Lever's OLVA moves, Lever Brothers cashing in on their feint, quietly put LUX Toilet Soap into most of the stores in most of the cities throughout the nation!

The whole ruse was so successful, I am told, that even after OLVA efforts in the three cities were reduced considerably, competition was so fascinated at the prospect of what might happen to the new green soap and profligate backers, that they refused to get excited at the growing distribution given white Lux.

All that happened was that Lever abruptly stopped all promotion on OLVA and whammed Lux across as telegraphed in the brief communique several paragraphs above!

In New York
TELL IT TO SWEENEY!
⟨*The Stuyvesants will understand*⟩

SWEENEY lives in an apartment in Brooklyn, on upper Manhattan, in the Bronx, or has a house on Staten Island or in Nutley, N. J.

It is Sweeney who swells the Municipal Marriage License Bureau each spring and fall. He marries comparatively early and raises a family—usually a good sized one.

Sweeney's children grow fast. They need baby carriages, foods, medicines, shoes, clothing, books, pianos, bathing suits, Christmas trees, tonsilotomy, tuition, trousseaux, phonograph records—in fact, everything.

Sweeney's sons filled both rear and front ranks in the late war; some of them stood ahead of the ranks. They drive trucks, belong to trade unions, work in offices, sell goods and run businesses.

Sweeney's daughters go to school, some of them to college; some of them work in factories, pound typewriters, sell retail merchandise, design Paris frocks. Eventually 75% of them marry.

*   *   *

SWEENEY and Mrs. Sweeney are ambitious and expectant of Life. They believe in God, the United States and life insurance. They respect education, and want the kids to have plenty of it. They look forward to grapefruit for breakfast, their own homes, a little car, money in the bank and a better future for the Sweeney juniors. Today some of the Sweeneys are buying Pierce Arrows and Long Island estates; more of them will, tomorrow. The Sweeneys know what they want—and get it. They *want the best*, and whenever possible—get it.

*   *   *

SWEENEY'S name in New York may be Smith, or Cohen, or Muller, or Nelson, or La Voie—or Sweeney.

There are a million families of Sweeneys in and around New York, with incomes from $6,000 *down*.

You men who aspire to sell large bills of goods to New York, remember the Sweeneys. They comprise 75% of any large city's population. Address your advertising, your sales messages, to them, because they are your best customers. They keep right on living and dying, earning and spending money, buying and using merchandise. They are not hard to sell, and they *are* good folks to do business with. And remember, when you talk to Sweeney, the people of bluer blood and more money who read The News will understand; whereas if you talk to Stuyvesants, the Sweeneys won't listen. You can't lose by saying it so Sweeney understands.

TELL It to Sweeney—in The News, bought by more than *two-fifths* of all the people in New York City who buy an English language morning newspaper.

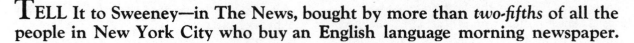

NEW YORK DAILY NEWS — *"Tell It To Sweeney"*

EXAMINE this one a good long time. It is one of a series that made a guy named Sweeney the best-known citizen of New York, and Sweeney's newspaper the greatest conveyor of display advertising in America.

The first *"Tell it to Sweeney"* advertisement was born of necessity and written in the heat of battle. Promotion-minded Leo E. McGivena, first manager of publicity for the *New York News,* was helping it fight for acceptance as a mass market advertising medium. That was in the early 1920s. Selling to the masses was a new idea. *The News* itself was a new kind of newspaper. It was the first tabloid-size newspaper in America. It had a novel way of condensing the day's news. Its use of photos was new. The Public liked it so well that *The News* became the first mass circulation newspaper and the largest daily in the United States while still only four years old. But advertisers were conservative and habit-bound. They could not see that the masses buy more every day than the classes. And they would not be shown. They regarded *The News* as an upstart, often refusing to discuss advertising at all with News salesmen. The resistance of advertisers filled McGivena with righteous indignation. There must be *some* way, he reasoned, to open their minds to the idea that it would be good business to advertise to the masses of people who read *The News.* After a year and a half of effort to express the value, importance, influence and buying capacity of the growing circulation of *The News* he decided to *personalize* the circulation, to

take a single family of the whole mass, and let it represent the whole. Suggested caption *"Tell it to Smith."* And then the recollection of the Marine's famous byword *"Tell it to Sweeney."*

The first *"Tell it to Sweeney"* copy appeared August, 1922. An extended series on the "Sweeney" theme in advertisements and in promotional folders began in January, 1923 and continued at intervals until 1937. *"Tell it to Sweeney"* proved to be the turning point in *The News* campaign to persuade advertisers break with tradition and place their copy in a mass-circulation newspaper, *The News.* By 1924 *The News* was carrying five million lines of advertising, ten million in 1927, fifteen million in 1931, twenty million in 1937. And since 1933 *The News* has carried more lines of display advertising than any other newspaper in America — with advertisers remarking, even in 1948, that *"The News* certainly tells it to Sweeney."

Leo E. McGivena, the famous creator of *"Tell it to Sweeney",* left *The News* to join Lennen & Mitchell, and is now head of his own agency.

"Mac" known as *The Old Maestro* among his friends in advertising, is one of the most gifted writers in advertising. His writing is free and easy, brilliant and colloquial at the same time.

He is a graduate of Loyola University, and has taken part in Loyola alumni activities. Mac is one of the book publisher's best customers. He says his major dissipation is buying books.

There is only one solution to an advertising problem:
Find the man!

FIFTEEN years ago nobody loved an alarm clock. But along came a Frenchman named Leroy and transformed this ugly household duckling into a family cavalier.

It took a lot of *finesse* to make a garrulous disturber of the morning peace seem like a cheery friend; a jolly old pal, even to the sleep-loving sluggard.

But Leroy was an artist in advertising.

Many men and several organizations have carried on this advertising since Leroy laid down his pen. And, to their credit, they have made no attempt to take out of it, that which Leroy inspired into it.

The manufacturer who hired Leroy settled his copy problem for many a year. *He found his man.*

◆

Two other men, H. P. Williams and George Dyer, put into clothing advertising twenty years ago the best that is in it today. Most clothing advertisers are still drafting their copy from the master patterns of these two advertising designers.

Thus, twice in succession, on its advertising problems, did the clothing business *find its man.*

A long while ago, Claude Hopkins created a certain type of *action* advertising which sent people into dealers' stores, while giving the advertiser an immediate *coupon count* on the number of these dealer-callers. Nearly every attempt that has since been made to put the coupon urge into national advertising has taken something from the Hopkins plan.

Here again, a great advertising need found its answer by *finding its man.*

For good advertising isn't *machine-processed;* it is man-made.

◆

The older and wiser an advertiser grows, the more he appreciates that "the man's the thing" in advertising successes. Finding the right agency service is largely a question of *finding the right man.*

And then making sure that he takes off his coat and does the job without delegating any part of it to sundry and supplementary Georges.

You may find *your* man on the pay-roll of a big agency. Or you may find him running an agency of his own, *selling himself* instead of a *hired staff.*

But the size and nature of his surroundings will have little to do with his usefulness to you.

His real power-plant lies within the man.

◆

The founders of this agency are wedded to the notion that the best advertising is, after all, a *personal service task;* not to be accomplished by *mass production methods.*

They concede the fine economic advantage of "group effort" in agency service. But they maintain that, in the final showdown, "conference copy" seldom holds a candle to the job done by the solitary worker who shuts himself up with his problem—and lives with it until he licks it.

The principals in this agency have been major executives in large businesses. Hence they are not awed by the detail-problems of large accounts. They are ready to cheerfully delegate that detail to their ample routine facilities.

But they will not delegate the responsibility for producing good advertising. That responsibility belongs to the principals and they assume it.

◆

To any national advertiser, spending one hundred thousand dollars a year or more in white space, who does not feel he is getting that vital spark in his advertising which only high-voltage personal service can infuse, *this is an open bid for an interview.*

Lennen & Mitchell, Inc., believe in *action* advertising.

Do you?

LENNEN & MITCHELL, INC.

An Advertising Agency in Which the Principals Do the Work

17 East 45th Street, New York

LENNEN & MITCHELL — *"Find The Man"*

I REMEMBER reading this ad and wishing I had a million dollar account to give its writer. I guess a few others must have felt the same reaction. Here's the story, straight from the man himself, Mr. Philip W. Lennen, Chairman of the Board of Lennen & Mitchell, Inc.:

"The late J. T. H. Mitchell and this writer opened up our shop . . . Lennen & Mitchell . . . on May 1st, 1924. I had resigned as Vice President of Erwin Wasey, out in Chicago, in order to team up with Jack Mitchell, a truly great all-around advertising man.

"At midnight, before hanging up our shingle, I made a rough draft of the basic principles under which we would operate the new agency . . . to differentiate it, if possible, from most other agencies in the field.

"Before sun-up the next morning, I had taken this code of principles and expressed it in the advertisement, *"Find the Man."* The advertisement was published in *The New York Times* a day or two later, and the following week in *The New York Herald Tribune, The Chicago Tribune, The Philadelphia Bulletin,* and several other large metropolitan newspapers.

"The effect of the advertisement was electric. It secured us leads on two very important accounts, which we subsequently landed and which are still in our house today.

"Incidentally, as you probably know, the *"Find the Man"* ad has been probably the most quoted ad ever written for an advertising agency. Usually agency advertisements are more or less institutional in character and the results from them can seldom be traced.

"But the fact that our little shop grew from practically zero in billing when we opened it up May 1st, 1924, to a volume of close to $12,000,000 by 1948, may be attributed to some extent to the principles we set forth in the 'Find the Man' ad."

If you don't like New York why don't you go back to where you came from?

WHAT a town this is!

From ocean to Bronx, East River to the Hudson, to the very borders of the hinterland, it is the civilized center of the new world.

Per capita it supports more drama (to be sure we still have our Abie's Irish Rose, but who hasn't?), more books, more magazines, more art, music, sports than any other city in America.

Its cultural appreciation attracts America's artistic expression.

It substitutes wisdom and enlightenment for blue laws (vide Philadelphia, Boston, et al).

Its philosophy represents the triumph of the individual. When we fight, it is for freedom of action.

· · ·

Art has always followed patronage. Horace had his Maecenas. Michelangelo, the Borgias.

For which reason our pride in New York goes so far as to include the denizens of the gold coast.

The gold coast, too, bears its share in making New York the center of America's creative activity.

Get Your Copy
Out today
15c

And we thrill that Manhattan is more than a place. It is a point of view.

· · ·

Understanding New York, THE NEW YORKER'S success is not so astonishing as it might appear.

It has merely spoken courageously and vividly for the New York point of view.

Tempered by brilliance, wit and satire, week by week it projects the happenings of this wonderful Island to fifty thousand bright Manhattanites.

In its ubiquitous roamings it distils the flavor of current happenings: in out of the way places, at the theatre, concerts, art galleries, on the Avenue, in clubs—wherever interesting people gather and say or do something worth while.

The mine is inexhaustible—here and nowhere else.

· · ·

A word to you who are in New York, but not of it—who are outlanders at heart: Leave New York alone.

You don't like New York. Very well.

You won't like THE NEW YORKER either. That's all right, too.

But if you don't like New York, why don't you go back to where you came from?

Every Friday
At all newsstands
15c

Welcome back!—hope you enjoyed your vacation

(we didn't take one)

While you were enjoying yours at mountain and seashore, we stayed here and worked.

Not that we complain about it. We have the sense that THE NEW YORKER was better than before vacation time.

At least, the public seems to think so. Notwithstanding the dog days and the absence from town of so many habitual New Yorkers THE NEW YORKER'S circulation is now at the peak—and gaining.

Perhaps *you* saw THE NEW YORKER while you were away? If you did, no need to tell you what's been going on. If you didn't, buy a copy of this week's issue and see what strides we've made.

(In advertising, too! 56 pages in this week's issue.)

THE
NEW YORKER

Twenty-Five West Forty-Fifth Street

THE NEW YORKER'S SEVEN HOURS OF SUSPENDED ANIMATION

"OUR first issue appeared in late February, 1925. By early May of the same year, after about eleven issues of the magazine, the balance sheet covering *The New Yorker's* operation looked very sick indeed. Not only had the original investment of $45,000 long since been used up, but the company owed me $65,000 'on the cuff.'

"It seemed clear that *The New Yorker* had not taken hold and that a long grim stretch of heavy losses faced the company. No outside capital seemed to show any interest in the business, and I felt unwilling to hazard what money I had.

"There had naturally been some discussion of whether to go ahead or not, and Harold Ross, our Editor, felt strongly that we should make up our minds one way or the other, as he felt an obligation toward some of the writers and artists who were contributing to us, lest they go ahead with a lot of work in advance and then find that *The New Yorker* had disappeared.

"Accordingly, to discuss the whole situation a meeting was called at the Princeton Club on a Friday early in May at 11:00 o'clock in the morning. There were four of us at this meeting, i.e., Ross, John Hanrahan (our publisher's counsel), Hawley Truax (one of our directors and a close friend of Ross and myself), and I.

"At this meeting, after studying the figures and rehashing what we had discussed for the past several weeks, it was decided to cease publication promptly so as to put an end to the loss of $5,000-$8,000 a week at which we were running.

"The meeting broke up in an atmosphere of no levity whatsoever, and the four of us walked up Madison Avenue together, Hanrahan to go to his office on East 42nd Street, and we to return to our office at 25 West 45th Street. I don't know with which of the other two men I was walking, but in a lull in the traffic I heard behind me Hanrahan's rather highly-pitched voice say "I can't blame Raoul for calling it off, but it surely is like killing something that's alive."

"Hanrahan's remark about killing something that was alive stuck in my mind and gave me no peace.

"That afternoon at 4:00 o'clock, up in Westchester County Franklin P. Adams and Esther Root were to be married, and Harold Ross and myself, both old friends of Frank's, were going to be there. Accordingly, that afternoon during the wedding reception, I suggested to Ross that he speak to nobody about our plans as yet, but that we meet again on Monday and see whether we possibly couldn't raise some outside capital to help carry the burden.

"We accordingly staggered along, and although we only raised $15,000, it was psychologically very valuable, and although it required approximately another half million dollars before we turned the corner, that one day in May was by all odds the closest the company ever came to a demise."

— RAOUL FLEISCHMAN

*　　*　　*

John Hanrahan's overheard remark gave *The New Yorker* another chance and his copy, of which the advertisement on another page is an excellent example, had the life that kept it living. *The New Yorker* needed, besides capital, *interpretation* — to readers and to advertisers, and John Hanrahan, one of the most gifted writers of publisher's promotion, gave to that job what was, perhaps, his finest and most effective work.

I am an alumnus of John Hanrahan's early days, and I have always been very proud of my association with this brilliant, kindly gentleman.

Big Ben

A National Alarm. Invented A°. D¹. 1908 by The Western Clock Co.

SEPTEMBER 24, 1910 $2.50 THE COPY

Life Size.

IT IS now two years since Big Ben was first designed by the Western Clock Company, a community of clockmakers founded two generations ago in the little town of La Salle, Illinois.

And with characteristic cautiousness these people have waited two years to put him out, two years of exacting tests and relentless efforts, two years of deliberate and undivided study.

There is no longer room for improvement nor need of secrecy. Big Ben is ready—selected jewelers will receive him from now on as quickly as consistent with manufacturing care.

Big Ben is a thin, beautiful and punctual sleepmeter with a silent motor that will not annoy you on your lie-awake nights and a deep musical voice that will call you on your sleepiest mornings.

Big Ben is mounted in a heavy, triple plated case, with large, strong, easy winding keys and a great open attractive face distinctly visible in the dim morning light.

There is a feeling of bigness and strength about him that you find in no other alarm. If he is oiled every other year there is no telling how long he will last.

$2.50

Sold by Jewelers only. Three Dollars in Canada.

BIG BEN — *"First He Whispers, Then He Shouts ..."*

HERE is a reproduction of the first ad ever to appear for that most famous of all alarm clocks BIG BEN. It was originally written by a Frenchman named Leroy, who went on to create many more of the most natural, readable, effective advertisements ever published in this country.

Consider Leroy's problem: an alarm clock is a prosaic thing. It is made of metal. It is mechanical. It gets us up in the morning when we'd rather sleep. Westclox had made BIG BEN pleasant to look at, even pleasant to hear. Now how could warmth be written into the advertising? Leroy reasoned that he could do it by *personalizing* BIG

BEN — referring to his product with the pronoun "he", never by "it".

"There is a feeling of bigness and strength about him that you find in no other alarm. If he is oiled every other year there is no telling how long he will last."

And so around BIG BEN was built up a warmth and a personality that made BIG BEN a member of more American families than any other clock of its kind. Remember the headline: *First he whispers ... then he shouts!* Remember it especially, and all this story, the next time somebody gives you a copy assignment for a "prosaic" product. There ain't no such animal — not to copywriters like Leroy, and advertisers like Westclox.

[91]

DALE CARNEGIE — *"How To Win Friends And Influence People"*

AS Victor O. Schwab, of Schwab & Beatty wrote in the November 1939 issue of *Printers' Ink Monthly,* "When an advertisement does a noteworthy job all of us can learn something from it, no matter what *it* is selling, or what *we* are selling."

Mr. Schwab had in mind the ad that sold a million books: *How to Win Friends and Influence People.* That is, it had sold a million books between December 1936 and November 1939. The sales to date aren't terribly important here; any ad that brings in *cash* for a million copies in three years solely via the coupon route, is one whale of a great ad!

But Vic Schwab writes great selling ads rather regularly. Remember *"The Man with the Grasshopper Mind"*? It was re-run so many times that it became an advertising landmark in the 30's — and they don't re-run couponed book ads for fun!

I'll simply say this for Mr. Schwab's copy-writing: study it carefully for it represents a peculiarly brilliant facet of advertising from which any copywriter can learn sound, inspiring stuff. Take the example at the left: physically, the advertisement stands out. It flags you. The general appearance gives you the feeling that here is something important, something well worth reading in terms of reader-benefits. The actual photographs of two persons indicate that there is going to be something factual in it — about them and what they may do for you.

Then go on and analyze the text paragraph by paragraph. Each one is written to develop the selling story a little bit more, firmly, logically. And if you want the whole story, go to a good library and look up that November, 1939 issue of *Printers Ink Monthly.* Your reward will be great indeed, and you'll pick up your pencil with renewed faith in the sales-producing power of well-built advertising.

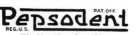

PEPSODENT — *Claude Hopkins' Film Campaign.*

ONE of the bewitching things about advertising is that everybody seems to be right! Everybody and everything — except dullness. Certainly there is no direct similarity between the *Jim Henry* campaign for Mennen's Shaving Cream, and Claude C. Hopkins' Pepsodent "film" campaign — yet both achieved notable success at about the same time.

You don't often learn when to use what from a text book. Experience creates an instinct in good advertising men — a philosophy, or a point-of-view, or what-have-you — and you turn to it as naturally as you like or dislike spinach.

One man believes heartily in testimonials and he uses them with repeated success. Another in inspirational, or emotional, indirect copy, and he goes to town with it, time and again. Still another bears down on straight "reason-why" and makes it pay-off beautifully, even fantastically. Some use

jingles, some humor, some narrative, some comic strips, some a profusion of captioned pictures, some no pictures at all.

Of course, the market, the competition, the timing, the product, and other factors are of vital influence — even so, what gets into print is largely the unswervable belief of the man or the organization producing it. Bewitching, I said; it's damn confusing! But aren't we glad it's so?

Claude C. Hopkins was the master of the reason-why school of advertising. The Pepsodent ad at left is an excellent example of Mr. Hopkins at his best. He believed in free trial offers, testing, coupons, and facts. And he was one of the most fabulously successful of all advertising men. Read this example of his work thoroughly. You won't be another Hopkins by reading this one ad, but if it induces you to investigate farther this particular school of advertising, it will have warranted inclusion in this book.

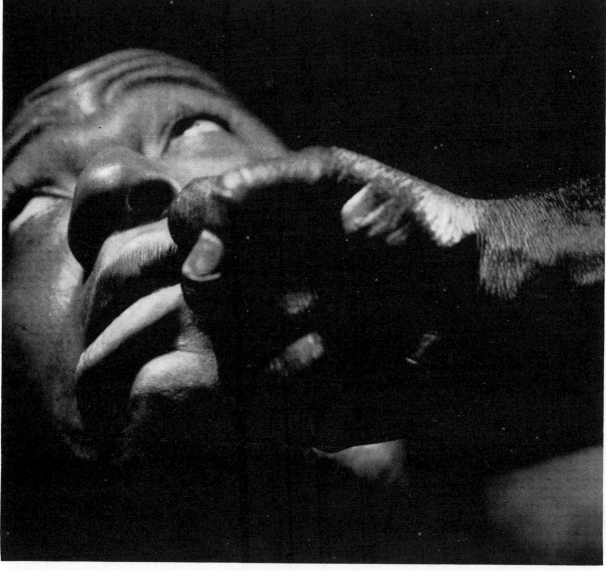

ACCORDING TO WEBSTER: The single instantaneous striking of a body in motion against another body.

ACCORDING TO YOUNG & RUBICAM: That quality in an advertisement which strikes suddenly against the reader's indifference and enlivens his mind to receive a sales message.

YOUNG & RUBICAM, INCORPORATED • ADVERTISING

NEW YORK • CHICAGO • DETROIT • SAN FRANCISCO • HOLLYWOOD • MONTREAL • TORONTO • MEXICO CITY • LONDON

YOUNG & RUBICAM, INC. — *"Impact"*

THERE is no doubt in my mind that the series of advertisements which Young & Rubicam began with the first issue of *Fortune* in 1930 was a powerful aid to the agency's success and growth. I had always wanted to advertise the agency, but to write copy for ourselves was just about the hardest assignment we had ever tackled, and we felt that we ought not to buy a schedule of space until we knew what we were going to say in it.

Then one day Harry Luce and Dussosoit Duke (then with Time, Inc.) came into my office with a dummy of a new magazine to be called *Fortune*. I was so struck with the idea behind the magazine that I immediately bought a 12 page schedule for Young & Rubicam. Duke, who was advertising director for Fortune, told me then and says now that ours was the first schedule bought in the book. Anyway, I know we were given our choice of position, which was the so-called Campbell Soup position — first page following reading matter. After buying the space we had to produce copy about ourselves no matter how tough the going might be. I tried one copywriter after another in the department, but could get nothing that satisfied me and finally sat down to write the series myself. *Impact* was the 5th ad in the series (which at this date has been running continuously since 1930). The whole series set a new style in agency advertising. For a time nobody imitated us and we stood alone . . . Times had changed a great deal since I had written the series for the Ayer agency, and my policy for Young & Rubicam reflected the change. Back in the early 20s, when I was doing the Ayer copy, a large segment of American industry was still unsold on the usefulness and value of advertising for their business. The Ayer's series undertook to help make advertisers out of non-advertisers. By the time Young & Rubicam began its series, however, the value of advertising to business was widely accepted. Manufacturers of consumers' goods were either using advertising or were anxious to us it. The question, Should I advertise? was largely answered. But new questions had arisen such as: How effective is my advertising? How can it be improved? What agency does the best job?

In each of the ads in the Young & Rubicam series I attempted to do two things: (1) to leave with the reader a valuable thought with regard to the effective use of advertising; (2) to make our own ad a forceful demonstration of our skill in presentation.

There were many effective ads in the series, but *Impact* made the greatest single hit. For this reason we repeated it periodically over many years. The proof I am sending you is a 1946 proof, which lists 9 agency offices as against the two we had in 1930. The ad itself is otherwise exactly as originally used.

The idea came to me this way. One day I showed John Orr Young a Postum ad which seemed to me to have an exceptional amount of wallop. When I showed it to him he said "it certainly does have impact". I said, "that gives me an idea for my next Young & Rubicam page in *Fortune*".

Vaughn Flannery, then our art director, Anton and Martin Bruehl, photographers, and I, worked long and hard to make that ad register as well as say *"Impact"* in every detail. Oddly, the very first picture idea that we rejected was a picture of two prize fighters, one getting a good sock in the jaw. Before we came back to it we tried at least 20 other ideas, none of them with sufficient *"Impact"*. It was only when Bruehl posed two negro fighters instead of two white fighters that the picture took on the fresh and dramatic character we wanted.

I had the same kind of trouble, but perhaps not so much of it, with the text. It had to be short, it had to be emphatic, it had to be conclusive. So I adopted the device of two definitions of the word *"Impact"*, and stopped there.

— Raymond Rubicam

THE NEW FORD CAR

An announcement of unusual importance to every automobile owner

by HENRY FORD

"NINETEEN years ago we made and sold the first Model T Ford car. In announcing it to the public we said:

"'We will build a motor car for the great multitude. It will be large enough for the family, but small enough for the individual to run and care for. It will be constructed of the best materials, by the best men to be hired, after the simplest designs modern engineering can devise. But it will be so low in price that no man making a good salary will be unable to own one.'

"If I were starting in business today, or asked to restate my policy, I would not change one sentence or one word of that original announcement. In plain, simple language it gives the reason for the very existence of the Ford Motor Company and explains its growth.

"IN THE last nineteen years we have made 15,000,000 Ford cars and added to the world nearly 300,000,000 mobile horse-power. Yet I do not consider the machines which bear my name simply as machines. I take them as concrete evidence of the working out of a theory of business which I hope is something more than a theory of business—a theory that looks toward making this world a better place in which to live.

"The Model T Ford car was a pioneer. There was no conscious public need of motor cars when we first conceived it. There were few good roads and only the adventurous few could be induced to buy an automobile.

"The Ford car blazed the way for the motor industry and started the movement for good roads. It broke down the barriers of time and distance and helped to place education within the reach of all. It gave people more leisure. It helped people everywhere to do more and better work in less time and enjoy doing it. It did a great deal, I am sure, to promote the growth and progress of this country.

"We are still proud of the record of the Model T Ford car. If we were not, we would not have continued to manufacture it so long. But 1927 is not 1908. It is not 1915. It is not even 1926.

We have built a new car to meet modern conditions

"We realize that conditions in this country have so greatly changed in the last few years that further refinement in motor car construction is desirable. So we have built a new car. To put it simply—we have built a new

and different Ford to meet new and different conditions.

"We believe the new Ford car, which will be officially announced on Friday of this week, is as great an improvement in motor car building as the Model T Ford was in 1908.

Smart new low lines and beautiful colors

"The new Ford is more than a car for the requirements of today. It goes farther than that. It anticipates the needs of 1928, of 1929, of 1930.

"The new Ford car is radically different from Model T. Yet the basic Ford principles of economy of production and quality of product have been retained. There is nothing quite like the new Ford anywhere in quality and price.

"The new Ford has exceptional beauty of line and color because beauty of line and color has come to be considered, and I think rightly, a necessity in a motor car today. Equally important is the mechanical beauty of the engine. Let us not forget this mechanical beauty when we consider the beauty of the new Ford.

"The new Ford has unusual speed for a low-price car because present-day conditions require unusual speed.

"The world moves more quickly than it used to. There are only so many hours in the day and there is much to be done.

"Fifty and sixty miles an hour are desired today where thirty and forty would have satisfied in 1908. So we are giving you this new speed.

Quiet and smooth-running at all speeds

"The new Ford will ride comfortably at fifty and sixty miles an hour. It has actually done sixty-five miles an hour in road tests.

"Since modern conditions demand more speed, they also demand better brakes to balance this speed. So we are giving you four-wheel brakes in the new Ford.

"The new Ford will be quiet and smooth-running at all speeds and you will find it even easier to handle in traffic than the old Model T Ford.

"The new Ford has durability because durability is the very heart of motor car value. The Ford car has always been known as a car that will take you there and bring you back. The new Ford will not only do that, but it will do it in good style. You will be proud of the new Ford.

"THIS new Ford car has not been planned and made in a day. Our engineers began work on it several years ago and it has been in my mind much longer than that. We make automobiles quickly when we get in production. But we take a long time planning them. Nothing can hurry us in that. We spent twelve years in perfecting our former Model T Ford car before we offered it to the public. It is not conceivable that we should have put this new Ford car on the market until we were sure that it was mechanically correct in every detail.

"Every part of it has been tested and retested. There is no guessing as to whether it will be a successful model. It has to be. There is no way it can escape being so, for it represents the sum total of all we have learned about motor car building in the making of 15,000,000 automobiles.

The new Ford will sell at a low price

"The price of the new Ford is low in accordance with the established Ford policy. I hold that it is better to sell a large number of cars at a reasonably small margin of profit than to sell a few cars at a large margin of profit.

"We never forget that people who buy Ford cars are the people who helped to make this business big. It has always been our policy to share our profits with our customers. In one year our profits were so much larger than we expected that we voluntarily returned $50 to each purchaser of a car. We could never have done that if this business had been conducted for the sole benefit of stockholders rather than to render service to the public.

"No other automobile can duplicate the new Ford car at the Ford price because no other manufacturer does business the way we do.

"We make our own steel—we make our own glass—we mine our own coal—we make virtually every part used in the Ford car. But we do not charge a profit on any of these items or from these operations. We would not be playing fair with the public if we did so. Our only business is the automobile business. Our only profit is on the automobile we sell.

"WE ARE able to sell this new Ford car at a low price because we have found new ways to give you greater value without a great increase in our own costs.

"We did not set out to make a new car to sell at such-and-such a figure. We decided on the kind of car we wanted to make and then found ways to produce it at a low price.

"The new Ford car, as I have said, will be officially announced on Friday of this week. In appearance, in performance, in comfort, in safety, in all that goes to make a good car, 't will bear out everything I have said here. We consider it our most important contribution thus far to the progress of the motor industry, to the prosperity of the country, and to the daily welfare of millions of people."

Henry Ford

FORD MOTOR COMPANY
Detroit, Michigan

FORD — *How The Tin Lizzie Became A Lady*

FOR sheer drama, attendance and sales, there has never been anything like the introduction of the Model A Ford in 1927.

The Model T Ford had come to the end of the trail after a long and useful career. Production was stopped. There were many rumors about what Ford was doing in the way of a new car.

Millions of people, and the whole automobile industry, were wondering what it would be like. For this was something more than a model change. It was a completely new car, a totally different kind of car for Ford, at one of the most critical times in the history of the Company.

Ford had lost sales leadership. Its car had outlived a pioneering era. There were many who said Henry Ford could never meet the new competition — could never come back. The very future of the company depended on the successful introduction of the new car.

N. W. Ayer & Son was selected as the advertising agency. George Cecil was assigned as copy writer and a whole staff of Ayer's most experienced personnel worked day and night to organize the unveiling of the new car.

That was in the spring of 1927. In June, Edsel Ford made a special trip to the Philadelphia office of the agency to look over plans and copy for the introduction of the car.

Few people realize that Edsel Ford had one of the ablest advertising minds of his time. He made his decisions quickly and had the courage to stick to a plan.

There was no fanfare on his arrival in Philadelphia. He was prompt, as usual. He disliked large meetings. So in the middle of the morning, when it came time to look over the advertisements in the Copy Department, there were just two other people — the head of the Copy Department and the copy writer.

"Shall we read you the advertisements, Mr. Ford?"

"No," he said quietly. "If you don't mind, I'd rather read them myself."

One by one he read all five of the full page advertisements that were to announce the car. Then he said —

"I think they will do all right. I have one change I'd like to suggest. In one of the advertisements I see you use the word perfect. I think it would be better to say correct. Nothing is perfect."

That was all. In less than forty minutes, Edsel Ford had approved something like $1,500,000 in advertising to introduce an important new car. The introduction of the car was later to justify his judgment.

Rumors scudded across the land like storm clouds on a winter day. The car would look like this! No, it would look like that! It would be 35 horsepower. It would be 135 horsepower. It would cost this, or that.

There were "secret" photographs purporting to be those of the new car. But the public was not sure and it waited eagerly for official news.

The advertising continued the pattern of suspense and built up to the final climax on introductory day, December 2.

The first advertisement was a full page signed by Henry Ford. It was illustrated only with his picture. The fifteen hundred words of text were written in Henry Ford's characteristic style. They spoke chiefly of Ford policies, told of the idea behind the new car, but gave no clue to appearance, specifications, or price.

The next day's full page lifted the curtain just a little and described the car in general terms.

Next day came the specifications of the car. But still no pictures. No prices.

Then came the fourth full page with pictures and prices.

This introductory advertisement had been furnished the newspapers without prices because even as late as a few days before introductory time the Ford Motor Company had not decided on what it would charge for the car.

Then, late in the afternoon of November 30, Edsel Ford took a little card from his pocket and read off the prices he'd written in pencil. (This card, autographed by Edsel Ford, has been framed and hangs in the Ayer offices.)

Immediately the prices were received, they were telegraphed to newspapers and dealers.

Newspapers everywhere were vigilant in their efforts to insert the right prices. They were careful to maintain the secrecy of the campaign.

December 2, the introductory day, was cold and rainy throughout most of the country, with snow in many sections. But bad weather could not dampen the interest of the public in the new car.

At 3 A.M., more than 500 eager motorists stood outside one Ford salesroom in New York City. By 9 o'clock the crowd was so dense that police reserves were called. Before the day closed more than one million people had called to see the car in New York alone.

Throughout the country similar excitement reigned. Before 6 o'clock more than 150,000 people had seen the car in Detroit.

Streets near the Ford branch in Dallas were crowded for three blocks. Factories closed so that workers could attend the showing. School children were taken to the exhibit in buses.

The stock market went up.

In Los Angeles one newspaper announced a 10,000 increase in circulation on the day of the announcement. In almost every city the new Ford was first page news and was spectacularly headlined.

Newsboys in many cities opened newspapers to the Ford advertisement and sold the papers with cries of *"Read about the new Ford." "News of the new Ford".*

Total attendance the first day of the showing was considerably more than 10,000,000 and within a few weeks orders for the car had reached more than 800,000!

It has been said that the whole trend of automobile advertising was changed by those early campaigns for the Model A Ford. The Ford advertising was purposely restrained and carefully avoided exaggeration and competitive attacks. The whole campaign was in line with the character of the Ford Motor Company and to the power of the simple truth, interestingly told.

Overnight, the Ford was given a new prestige and a new prominence. Senators, governors, writers, executives, people in high places everywhere sought to be the first to drive the new Ford. Having a Ford was a mark of distinction. *The Tin Lizzie had become a lady!*

Telephone service, a public trust

An Advertisement of the
American Telephone and Telegraph Company

THE widespread ownership of the Bell Telephone System places an obligation on its management to guard the savings of its hundreds of thousands of stockholders.

Its responsibility for so large a part of the country's telephone service imposes an obligation that the service shall always be adequate, dependable and satisfactory to the user.

The only sound policy that will meet these obligations is to continue to furnish the best possible service at the lowest cost consistent with financial safety.

There is then in the Bell System no incentive to earn speculative or large profits. Earnings must be sufficient to assure the best possible service and the financial integrity of the business. Anything in excess of these requirements goes toward extending the service or keeping down the rates.

This is fundamental in the policy of the company.

The Bell System's ideal is the same as that of the public it serves—the most telephone service and the best, at the least cost to the user. It accepts its responsibility for a nation-wide telephone service as a public trust.

AMERICAN TEL. & TEL.

"Telephone Service — A Public Trust" AND *"Weavers of Speech"*

THE Bell Telephone System has been one of the most consistent national advertisers for many years and its advertising is generally considered to be the finest in the institutional field. It is based on a firm belief that a business should be perfectly willing to tell the public what its policies are, what it is doing and what it hopes to do. This seems practically a duty.

It is not an easy duty to perform, because the people who make up the public are generally busy about their own affairs and are not particularly prone to take time off to read about the telephone business or any other.

The good-will of the public is not acquired overnight or laid on like a cloak. It comes only from long years of earnest, patient doing and telling. Public opinion may sometimes be fractious and it is often slow in coming to a fair conclusion. But given the facts it can be trusted to come up with sensible answers.

"Telling the public" is not something new for the telephone. It goes back a long, long way.

Some forty-one years ago, on April 6, 1908, the Ayer representative in Boston wrote this remarkable report to his headquarters in Philadelphia.

"Along the lines I have previously written, I wish to say that Mr. Vail the President of the American Telephone and Telegraph Company, has not yet given me a definite order for advertising in the publications, but we have had several conferences lately on this subject and I have laid before Mr. Vail an approximate suggestion of what an advertising campaign would cost with a list of spaces, papers, times, etc.

"The Telephone Company is giving this matter consideration and I fully expect that within a week or so, Mr. Vail will give me definite instructions to go ahead and place the advertising.

"The word 'advertising' to the Telephone Company means something different than it does to our ordinary advertiser of commercial products. They do not intend to use advertising to get subscribers — they have plenty of these and are getting more. They can get subscribers as fast as they can get the equipment. It is quite a problem to increase the

"Weavers of Speech"

To you, who each day
Take on anew your tasks
Along the lines that speech will go
Through city streets or far out
Upon some mountainside where you have blazed a trail
And kept it clear;
To you there comes from all who use the wires
A tribute for a job well done.

For these are not just still and idle strands
That stretch across a country vast and wide
But bearers
Of life's friendly words
And messages of high import
To people everywhere.

Not spectacular, your usual day,
Nor in the headlines
Except they be of fire, or storm, or flood.
Then a grateful nation
Knows the full measure of your skill and worth.
And the fine spirit of service
Which puts truth and purpose in this honored creed —
"The message must go through."

equipment and the question of getting new subscribers is not as important as the question of creating a more general atmosphere of satisfaction among the subscribers they already have on their books. "The Telephone company really wants to please the public and no one can tell the public this in so many words because they won't believe it. A great many people look on the telephone company as a big monopoly and they think as they have got a monopoly they are going to pursue a 'public be damned' policy, but this is not so. The telephone company is just as careful of details and want to please the public really more than some smaller corporations would ever think of doing.

"What we want to put in this advertising, if Mr. Vail should entrust us with it, is to write a series of advertisements which will sink down deep into the hearts of all classes of people who use the telephone — giving them facts and explaining all the troubles which are experienced in running a big telephone company in any part of the country and end it by taking the reader by the hand and leading him through the various intricacies which are confronted by the telephone company and after the public has made this trip through these intricate passages, they should have a great and more abiding faith in the good intentions of the telephone company.

"The more I think of this problem the more enthused I am with the idea that there is an endless opportunity to get in closer touch with the public and keep them in perfect confidence by giving them something interesting to read in these advertisements all the time, year after year. It would be a slow process perhaps, but I believe it is a sure way. "I will write you further along this line later on and I hope to report to you soon that Mr. Vail has given us an order to place the business.

"When we get as far as writing the advertisements for the telephone company we have a first class individual 'character' to identify their series in the use of a picture of the *bell*."

Ayer got the business. Two months after this report was written, the first telephone advertising appeared in national magazines and it has continued ever since.

The remarkable thing about that 1908 report is that it could be reprinted today, almost word for word, as the advertising policy of the Bell Telephone System.

There is no doubt that Mr. Vail concurred in that 1908 policy. Many other telephone executives, notably Walter S. Gifford, Arthur W. Page, Keith S. McHugh, Leroy A. Wilson and Clifton W. Phalen have carried it forward over the years. Ayer and A. T. & T. have made a good team.

When I wrote Ayer for some background material, my old friend George Cecil, who has been writing the telephone advertising for eighteen years wrote as follows:

"I have always thought that one of the great telephone advertisements, in its social and business significance, was written not by an advertising man but by Walter S. Gifford, the president of A. T. & T.

"In 1927 he made a speech at a meeting of the National Association of Railroad and Utilities Commissioners. "In July, 1928, his speech was made into an advertisement headlined *Telephone Service — A Public Trust*.

"One of the unusual points about the advertisement was the fact that it was one of the few instances where a major business publicly stated the base on which it hoped to serve the public. It was there in print for all the public to see. It was there in print for the Company to live up to. Mr. Gifford's Dallas speech is still the guide book and the Bible of the telephone business."

We've covered 1908 and 1928 in the telephone campaign. My choice among the recent advertisements would be *"Weavers of Speech"* which appeared in 1948.

This is an example of the friendly, human interest advertisements that give the Bell System advertisements so much character and effectiveness.

The Bell System thought so much of it that they made it into a short movie, with a narrator, sound effects and everything. That's the first time I ever heard of an advertisement turning up as a movie and it may have established something of a record.

TO THE MAN WHO IS AFRAID TO LET HIS DREAM COME TRUE

 YEARS AGO you heard of Rolls-Royce—later you saw one—and a dream formed in your mind . . . "Some day, when I have the money, I'm going to own that car!"

Now you have the money—and you waver. A dozen bogies buzz about your ears . . . "I can get along with a cheaper car" . . . "Is Rolls-Royce really worth the price?" . . . "Maybe folks would think I'm splurging" . . .

Yes, you can get along without a Rolls-Royce. You can get along without trips to Europe, or a fine piano in your home, without Oriental rugs on the floor, or sterling silver on the table. But you don't. Because the *actual value* you get out of these things makes them worth more than their cost. And your friends know that. These things you buy are above criticism. They are proof of your judgment, your good taste.

Now take Rolls-Royce. The protection it offers you and your family is alone reason enough for its purchase. For Rolls-Royce is the safest car in the world! No part on which the safety of the occupants depends has ever failed in this car. Ask your insurance friends—they'll tell you Rolls-Royce gets lower collision rates than any other car!

Then the comfort, the restfulness of Rolls-Royce —the solace it brings to nerves harried by business, frayed by the din of a noise-mad age. Rolls-Royce was built as a protest against noise—against not only obvious squeaks and rattles, but against even those tiny quavers and quivers that, seemingly negligible and perhaps unnoticed, wear you down, bring you up tired at the end of a long trip.

Prove that! Step into a Rolls-Royce, grumpy and weary from a day at the office. The car cradles your tired body like your lounge chair at home. The

ROLLS-ROYCE

roar of the city may be all around you—you move in a well of silence. Rough roads may lie ahead— you take them without a tremor. Instead of riding, *you float!* Restfulness almost as complete as dreamless slumber! You can drive 300 miles in a Rolls-Royce without fatigue!

Or say you're dawn-fresh, eager for a thrill. Take the wheel of a Rolls-Royce—*and get it!* See how the car hugs the road, holds its direction. That's balance! See how it levels out hills. That's power! See how it eats up the miles. That's speed! And try the brakes —foot-brakes that have brought a car down Pike's Peak with the clutch out and the motor off!

What do you pay for this comfort and quiet, this super-safety, the supreme joy of perfect motoring? No more than you pay for an ordinary fine car. True, the first cost of Rolls-Royce is high. Why? If we could take the car to pieces right here on this page, we would show you, gear for gear, shaft for shaft, why Rolls-Royce costs its price. But—and here is one of the sweetest points of the car . . .

You never realize it has gears and shafts. You drive it year after year, and the motor never flutters, the springs never complain. Rolls-Royce is *guaranteed* for three years—nine times longer than any other

car! Consider this 3 year insurance against failure of any mechanical part and compare it with your own experience!

Then compare the depreciation on your present car with that on a Rolls-Royce 10 years old. You're paying for a Rolls-Royce without ever owning one! But, you may say, "I don't want to keep a car ten years, because of changes in body styles." All right, change the coachwork on your Rolls-Royce every few years. You'll have an everlastingly new car—and you'll still be making the best fine car investment in the world! America's foremost bankers —163 of them—endorse Rolls-Royce as an investment by owning Rolls-Royces themselves!

But this page isn't big enough for the whole story. Rolls-Royce is the finest vehicle that a wizard age has offered to man. And you, with the purchase price in your pocket, hesitate to buy it!

No matter where you live, Rolls-Royce will gladly send a car to you for a 100-mile trial. Or perhaps you would rather see a representative—or secure printed matter giving more detailed information on Rolls-Royce. Make your request—we will fulfill it.

ROLLS-ROYCE DIRECT WORKS BRANCH: 58TH ST. AT EIGHTH AVE., COLUMBUS CIRCLE . . . TEL. CIRCLE 6385 IN NEWARK: 190 WASHINGTON ST. TEL. MITCHELL 1185

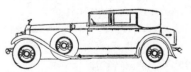

ROLLS-ROYCE — *"To A Man Who is Afraid To Let His Dream Come True"*

TO MOST of us who grew up in the automotive age the name Rolls-Royce has a peculiar fascination. It represents somehow the Ultimate! The car we'll own someday *when . . .*

Jack Rosebrook, long one of Young & Rubicam's star copy men and supervisors, best expressed this latent dream of men who know ambition best in this beautifully written advertisement which appeared but once — and which actually sold more automobiles off the floor than any other Rolls-Royce ad of record. In it, the man who is afraid to let his dream come true, finds out that, in the slightly paraphrased words of a famous statesman, the only thing he had to fear, was fear itself!

Read this copy for another extremely fine example of emotionalizing facts.

We travelled 2000 miles to save 65¢

LADIES, THIS WILL INTEREST YOU

SOME time ago we acquired a new handkerchief buyer.

A strange fellow who wasn't interested in bridge or football or politics, or in anything except handkerchiefs. He didn't even care if he never got his golf game under 100—his only ambition was to double our handkerchief business.

After inspecting the samples of every manufacture in the Red Book, he convinced us that to secure handkerchief values which would really pull people in off the street, we had to go straight to the source of supply, buy our own raw linens, hem them, monogram them and box them ourselves.

And then he persuaded the firm to send him to Europe (a trip which the advertising department has been vainly trying to wrangle for years) and he went to Ireland, to the flax fields, and he saw the spinners and weavers themselves, people who grow their own flax, and he placed an order for 15,000 yards of raw linen.

And when the linen was ready we sent it to our own finishers and they tore the linen into squares (costs more to tear linen than to cut it, but makes better handkerchiefs). And after they had hemmed the squares very neatly indeed, we again took the handkerchiefs away and sent them to our own embroiderers who added graceful initials.

And when we got all through we found that *the same handkerchiefs which we had always been selling for $2.50 a box could now be sold for $1.85 a box.*

Pure Irish linen, six in a box, with white embroidered initial, they provide a Christmas gift into which we have put months of effort, a gift worthy of any man.

Our $3 initial handkerchiefs (box of six) were made in the same way. We bought the linen at the flax fields in Ireland, did our own monogramming etc., and therefore the quality is the same as that usually found at much higher prices. These initials are cut out.

Other initial handkerchiefs $1.50 to $5 per box.

Weber *and* Heilbroner
14 stores in metropolitan area

WEBER & HEILBRONER — *"We Traveled 2000 Miles To Save 65¢"*

I GUESS this ad must have appeared thirty years ago. I know the tearsheet in my file is yellow with age and practically falling apart.

I remember saving it because I thought it was the greatest ad about handkerchiefs I have ever read — an opinion that still stands after about two hundred readings.

Imagine somebody saying to *you:* "Joe, give us something on handkerchiefs for Friday's paper."

Somebody must have said that to George Bijur years ago and because Mr. Bijur was a brilliant

creative man he wrote a piece of copy about handkerchiefs that is just as good as anything you ever read — a splendid example of what a good creative man can do with a commonplace assignment.

George Bijur rose to extraordinary heights in the profession of advertising. After holding down a number of jobs in agencies and retail stores, he opened up for himself, and in a few years was billing millions of dollars in business. At the outbreak of World War II he gave up his accounts, without strings, and went into the Army Air Force.

"Look at All Three!

BUT DON'T BUY ANY LOW-PRICED CAR UNTIL YOU'VE DRIVEN THE NEW PLYMOUTH WITH FLOATING POWER"

"It is my opinion that any new car without Patented Floating Power is obsolete."

THOUSANDS of people have been waiting expectantly until today before buying a new car. I hope that you are one of them.

Now that the new low-priced cars are here (including the new Plymouth which will be shown on Saturday) I urge you to carefully *compare* values.

This is the time for you to "shop" and buy wisely. Don't make a deposit on any automobile until you've actually had a demonstration.

It is my opinion that the automobile industry as a whole has never offered such values to the public.

In the new Plymouth we have achieved more than I had ever dared to hope for. If you had told me two years ago that such a big, powerful, beautiful automobile could be sold at the astonishing prices we will announce on Saturday ... I'd have said it was absolutely impossible.

I have spent my life building fine cars. But no achievement in my career has given me the deep-down satisfaction

A STATEMENT BY WALTER P. CHRYSLER

that I derive from the value you get in this 1932 Plymouth. To me, its outstanding feature is Floating Power. We already know how the public feels about this. Last summer it was news, but today it is an established engineering achievement.

It is my opinion, and I think that of leading engineering authorities, that any new car without Floating Power is obsolete. Drive a Plymouth with Patented Floating Power, and note its utter lack of vibration ... then drive a car with old-fashioned engine mountings and you will understand what I mean. *There's absolutely no comparison.*

We have made the Plymouth a much larger automobile. It is a BIG car. We have increased its power, lengthened the wheelbase and greatly improved its beauty.

In my opinion you will find the new Plymouth the easiest riding car you have ever driven. Yet with all these improvements we have been able to lower prices.

Again let me urge you, go and see the new Plymouth with Floating Power on Saturday. Be sure to look at all THREE low-priced cars and don't buy *any* until you do. That is the way to get the most for your money.

FIRST SHOWING NEXT SATURDAY, APRIL 2nd, AT DESOTO, DODGE AND CHRYSLER DEALERS

PLYMOUTH — *"Look At All Three"*

ALMOST everybody in advertising will admit that the late J. Stirling Getchell's advertisement for Plymouth *"Look at all Three"* is one of the all-time greats. In my book, the story behind it deserves the same classification. Here it is as written for *Advertising & Selling* by J. V. Tarleton, Getchell's talented partner throughout the brief, bright life of J. Stirling Getchell, Inc.:

"Sometime in March, in the Spring of 1932, the Chrysler, DeSoto and Dodge Divisions of Chrysler Corporation held a large regional dealers' meeting somewhere on Long Island (I believe in Flushing).

"The purpose of this meeting was to introduce to these Chrysler Corporation dealers the promotional, merchandising and advertising plans for the announcement of a new Plymouth automobile scheduled to take place the following month, April.

"At that time Plymouth was entering its third year, having been launched in 1929. It was naturally a very new and a very small contender in the low-priced field then dominated entirely by Ford and Chevrolet.

"J. Stirling Getchell, Inc., a new advertising agency, was an even younger baby than Plymouth, having started only the previous year. This agency was formed by Stirling Getchell and the writer, who themselves were pretty young too, being respectively, Getchell, 31, and Tarleton, 29.

"J. Stirling Getchell, Inc. had been appointed by the DeSoto Division of the Chrysler Corporation in November of 1931, and hence had worked only five months on that assignment, but with rather outstanding success.

"The one big fact that gave rise to the whole 'Look At All Three' idea was that Henry Ford, whose plants had been out of production for almost a year while he tooled up for the new V-8, was planning to introduce this radically new model in the very same week when Mr. Chrysler was planning to announce his new Plymouth.

"The automotive trade press and the newspapers had been giving a tremendous play to stories about the forthcoming marvelous new Ford. People had been reading about it for weeks and even months. You might say that the country was literally waiting with its tongue and its check book out for the new Ford to appear. In all this noise and excitement about Ford, it was quite obvious that hardly anyone knew or cared about

Mr. Chrysler's new Plymouth. Chevrolet was in a very good position, having out-styled and out-sold the old Model A Ford, and had obtained a very strong hold on the market while Ford had been out of production retooling.

"That's the background picture. Now to get back to our dealer meeting on Long Island. Byron Foy, who was then President of DeSoto Division of Chrysler Corporation, and hence the employer of J. Stirling Getchell, Inc., invited Mr. Getchell to attend this meeting with him just as a matter of courtesy and interest.

"The new car was presented and exposed to the dealers; likewise the announcement and promotion plans, including the advertising campaign (by a Detroit agency).

"This proposed advertising, in Getchell's opinion, was orthodox, dull, and without any particular imagination or distinction of any kind. In other words, it was simply the old Detroit formula stuff with not a kick in a carload.

"Getchell thought about it and stewed about it after he got home, and being the active and energetic young man that he was, he decided to do something about it.

"The following day he and the writer called on Mr. Foy, told him that it seemed to us Mr. Chrysler was missing the boat and a great opportunity if they printed the kind of advertising proposed, and couldn't we please on our own risk and responsibility take a crack at a brand new version of the Plymouth announcement campaign. Mr. Foy said to go ahead and if we came up with anything interesting, he would be glad to have a look. So we went to work.

"Getchell and the writer proceeded to bat their brains out for a day or two looking for unique and different way of announcing a new car — a way that would take advantage of the suspenseful situation created by Mr. Ford and get Plymouth through the swinging door on his push.

"This, in a nut shell, was the strategy of the idea and the credit for it belongs completely to Stirling Getchell. The method of executing it, however, proved to be a somewhat difficult nut to crack. Finally Getchell conceived what he thought was a good idea. It was this: Arthur Brisbane, the great Hearst editor and publisher who was then still alive, was a good personal friend of Walter Chrysler's. Getchell thought of having Mr. Brisbane write a series of full page newspaper ads in which he would announce and extol the merits of his friend's new Plymouth car.

"We wangled an appointment with Mr. Brisbane, outlined the idea to him and he said: 'Let me think it over'.

"Two days later, he sent a full page newspaper layout which he had made himself and a letter.

"In the layout, he had pasted up a large photograph of Billy Sunday, the famous extrovert Evangelist, in one of his more acrobatic poses. He had decapitated Mr. Sunday and pasted on a head of Walter P. Chrysler. I forget exactly what the headline said, but it was a first-person quote saying in effect: 'Come and see my new Plymouth automobile', and it was signed, Walter P. Chrysler.

"In his letter Brisbane said that he had thought the thing over and felt that while he would be an excellent authority for an advertisement about newspapers which he knew, he thought that Mr. Chrysler would be more convincing on the subject of automobiles, which he knew. His layout was, of course, home made, crude and would have been ridiculous in a newspaper, but it gave us our first real glimpse of what the announcement ad should be.

"We decided that he was right and proceeded to work on a series of advertisements, all of which were planned to show Mr. Chrysler with his new car and all of which would be written by him and signed with his own name. We worked for a day or two along these lines, but were handicapped in one important respect. We had no pictures of Mr. Chrysler. We emulated Mr. Brisbane and tried shooting photographs of models, pasting Mr. Chrysler's head on them. We hired artists to make drawings, but with no success. All of these attempts looked absolutely frightful and had no reality or conviction whatever.

"At about 7 o'clock in the evening, we were sitting over my drawing board in a somewhat sweaty and dispondent condition when Mr. Roy Peed, then General Sales Manager of DeSoto, dropped in unexpectedly.

"He said 'What the Hell are you boys doing?' And we told him. He said, 'Why don't you make some pictures of Mr. Chrysler?' We said, 'Hell, he doesn't even know who we are'. He said, 'I think I can get him for you'. We said 'When'. He said 'Tonight'. 'If you can get a photographer, I'll get Mr. Chrysler'.

"Mr. Peed then telephoned Mr. Chrysler's apartment from our office and found him in the middle of dinner. He explained, however, what we wanted and said that if Mr. Chrysler could drop down to the Salon in the Chrysler Building after dinner, we would be all ready with a photographer and a car and that it wouldn't take 20 minutes to shoot the pictures. Mr. Chrysler said he would be there.

In the next two hours, we had gotten the manager of the Chrysler Building show room back from his home in Astoria, Queens, a photographer with lights and models in case we needed them, and were all set up and ready to go and extremely nervous when the big boss showed up at 10 o'clock.

"As far as I know, Mr. Chrysler had never had the experience of being pushed around by a commercial photographer before under a battery of very very hot kleig lights. We were afraid he would put on his hat and go home any minute, but as time went on, it was obvious that the boss was enjoying himself tremendously. We kept him there until midnight and sent our photographer packing with about 50 negatives which he developed and printed over night.

"The following day, using these pictures, we laid out and pasted up 6 full page newspaper ads and that evening took them up to Mr. Foy's apartment after dinner and spread them on his library floor. One of these advertisements showed a large picture of Mr. Chrysler in a very informal pose with his foot on the bumper of a new Plymouth. The headline on this ad had originally read 'Look at All Three Low Priced Cars Before You Buy'. In the process of making the layout, the writer had boiled this down to four big words 'Look At All Three'.

"Mr. Foy's first inclination was to eliminate this advertisement from the series because, he said, (and I'm almost certain that we all agreed with him) that it didn't seem a good idea to invite inspection of our competitors' products.

"It was finally decided, however, to submit three of the ads, including this one, to Mr. Chrysler the following day.

"We spent the rest of that night finishing and producing those three ads. We had retouchings, plates made, type set and the following morning were able to lay on Mr. Chrysler's desk three complete full page newspaper ads finished and ready for the electrotyper.

"I should digress here for a moment to make one point. Most people now (including your good self) speak of the 'Look At All Three campaign'. The fact is, there never was such a campaign. It was only one ad — one of the three I have just described. The second headline said *Two Years Ago I'd Have Said It Couldn't Be Done*. The headline of the third ad I have completely forgotten myself, but it's obvious today that of the six advertisements we originally created and the three we eventually published, only one, 'Look At All Three' had that unusual quality of hitting the public's fancy and getting over a really fundamental strategic idea.

"Opinions on this point may differ, but I believe that essentially it was the sportsmanship of this appeal and the forthright tone of the copy that captured the public's imagination.

"To get back to chronological narrative: It didn't take Mr. Chrysler more than ten minutes to decide that he wanted to publish these three advertisements. Other executives and their subordinates summoned to the meeting were full of objections and reservations. They said 'How can we do it?' 'These boys don't even have the Plymouth account.' 'Who will be paid for them?' 'How can we ask our present agency to run the work of another?' Mr. Chrysler finally put an end to the discussion of smacking his big mechanic's hand on the desk and saying, 'I don't give a Goddam how you do it, but I want to run those ads!' That was the end of the meeting. The ads ran in the same week in April, 1932 as the announcements of the new Ford and Chevrolet.

"The day when 'Look At All Three' was published in newspapers all over the country, the reaction was unmistakable. Chrysler Corporation dealers reported that their doors started swinging early in the morning and didn't stop until late at night. Plymouth, over night, had become a real contender in the low-priced field, and as you know, has remained so ever since. I don't remember what Plymouth's sales figures for 1931 will show. You can get them, I'm sure, through organization channels. I do know, however, that sales in 1941, the last year before war-time restrictions, ran well over 600,000 and I believe were almost 700,000, including export sales.

"To wind up the story, I should say that J. Stirling Getchell, Inc. received no commissions whatever for this work.

"We were paid for our out-of-pocket expenses on production, such as photographic, engraving and typographic costs, and turned our plates over to Lee Andersen & Company for publication.

"After the ads had run, Getchell and the writer were summoned to Mr. Chrysler's office and were asked what we would like in payment for our work. We said 'Nothing — except the Plymouth account'. Mr. Chrysler asked us how we would like a nice 30-day European vacation with our wives and all expenses paid. We said, 'No thanks, Boss'. He said, 'How would you like to each have a custom Chrysler Imperial with a LeBaron body and your initials in gold on the doors'? We said, 'No thanks, Boss'. Then we went downstairs and kicked each other for a while.

"P.S. Four months later, we got the job. I mean the Plymouth account."

"Here's an Extra $50, Grace
—I'm making <u>real</u> money now!"

"Yes, I've been keeping it a secret until pay day came. I've been promoted with an increase of $50 a month. And the first extra money is yours. Just a little reward for urging me to study at home. The boss says my spare time training has made me a valuable man to the firm and there's more money coming soon. We're starting up easy street, Grace, thanks to you and the I. C. S.!"

Today more than ever before, money is what counts. The cost of living is mounting month by month. You can't get along on what you have been making. Somehow, you've simply got to increase your earnings.

Fortunately for you hundreds of thousands of other men have proved there is an unfailing way to do it. Train yourself for bigger work, learn to do some one thing well and employers will be glad to pay you real money for your special knowledge.

You can get the training that will prepare you for the position you want in the work you like best, whatever it may be. You can get it without sacrificing a day or a dollar from your present occupation. You can get it at home, in spare time, through the International Correspondence Schools.

It is the *business* of the I. C. S. to prepare men in just your circumstances for better positions at better pay. They have been doing it for 28 years. They have helped two million other men and women. They are training over 100,000 now. Every day many students write to tell of advancements and increased salaries already won.

You have the same chance they had. What are you going to do with it? Can you afford to let a single priceless hour pass without at least finding out what the I. C. S. can do for you? Here is all we ask—without cost, without obligating yourself in any way, simply mark and mail this coupon.

INTERNATIONAL CORRESPONDENCE SCHOOL — *Coupon Advertisements*

SOMETIMES the appearance of advertising, like the people who read it, doesn't change at all!

One of the oldest and most successful advertisers in the United States has learned that it isn't necessary to risk a thin dime on the tricks of the trade once you hit a formula that works. Phooey on the new stuff if the old stuff keeps on working. *"Here's That Extra $50, Grace!"* appeared in 1919.

There's a slight concession to the type faces employed today, and there's very definitely a third party influence in the modern text, but that old rugged cross of "fundamental appeal" in theme and layout, goes on like ole man river.

Because, like ole man river, man's desire to get ahead, to earn more money, to be admired, to get the gal, and to keep in the running, is as changeless as the orbit of the earth.

Another piece, "I got the job!" predated the "Grace" copy and was among the forerunners of the I.C.S. dramatic title and illustration combination that had such an important bearing on the phenomenal success of this advertising during the post World War I era. The writers responsible for this copy trend were G. Lynn Sumner, now head of his own agency in New York (see No. 68), W. Ross McKnight (present whereabouts unknown), and Paul V. Barrett, now Director of Advertising for I.C.S.*

"One thing", writes Paul Barrett, "perhaps more than any other, proves the strength of our current Third Party slant so well exemplified by the 'Many of our Key Men Owe their Success to I.C.S. Training' advertisement — and that is this: in magazines like *Popular Mechanics, Popular Science* and *Mechanix Illustrated* we run two advertisements in each issue. We have found, with few exceptions, the advertisement nearest the second cover does the best job for us. On a number of occasions 'Many of our Key Men,' in the position *farthest* from the second cover, has upset all calculations and actually outpulled the advertisement farthest front. As a result of this experience we plan to run testimonial copy, both Second and Third Party, on the farthest-back-from-second-cover copy in the hope of increasing the productivity of this position."

The "Many of Our Key Men" copy was written by Howard Wolf, an Ayer writer, with the help of the man who has been like a father to so much I.C.S. advertising: Paul V. Barrett.

He got the job, too!

B. ALTMAN & CO.

$2.50

We believe there
are at least 500 men in New York
who love their wives...and want
to give them flowers for Easter

So ... we've provided 500 old-fashioned
bouquets .. ready now and packed in
beautiful boxes. They're just inside the
Fifth Avenue entrance ... all at one price
and that one price very easy to afford.

$2.50

B. Altman & Co., Fifth Ave. at 34th St. MUrray Hill 2-7000

B. ALTMAN & COMPANY —

"We Believe There Are At Least 500 Men In New York Who Love Their Wives"

HERE'S an excellent piece of copy that sold 500 Easter bouquets for B. Altman & Company in about three hours. The advertisement is the work of Ruth Packard. This advertisement was selected by *Advertising & Selling* in 1934 as the best retail ad of the year. It gets my vote as one of the best retail ads of any year.

One amusing incident occurred in my not too fruitful search for data on this advertisement: I wrote to B. Altman & Company, giving the headline, and asking for background. B. Altman wrote back saying that I must be mistaken, the Company had never published such an advertisement. I hope somebody's face turns faintly red. It seems such a little price for such a lot of mistake!

When heaven was at the corner of Sycamore and Main

BACK HOME, when I was a boy, there was a place at the corner of Sycamore and Main that was as wonderful to me as anything out of a fairy tale.

For on that corner was the Packard showroom. Just about once a year, father would go there, and he always took me with him.

We never actually bought a Packard, for father's income was never more than modest. But we got a great kick out of feasting our eyes on those magnificent cars and imagining what it would be like to own one.

This year, my wife and I decided we needed a new car. As we passed the Packard showroom I said, "Let's go in, just for the fun of looking," exactly as my dad used to do.

Imagine our surprise when we found a Packard wasn't just something to dream about, but a car we could really afford. We found that—with the recent $100 price reduction on the Packard Six— we could have a Packard without paying a cent of cash. Our old car more than covered the down payment. And the monthly payments were only a few dollars more than we should have had to spend for one of the lowest priced cars.

So we're driving the car we've always wanted. And we're as thrilled as a couple of kids with it. Its lines tell the world we're Packard owners. And those same lines will keep our car smart and recognizable as a Packard over the many long years we expect to drive it.

Best of all, our Packard costs us no more to run—and less to service—than the car we used to own!

Moral: Get the facts—they'll lead you to a Packard.

Packard

ASK THE MAN WHO OWNS ONE

The new 1938 Packard Eight Touring Sedan

PACKARD — *"When Heaven Was At The Corner Of Sycamore And Main"*

THROUGH the years, Packard has been a consistently fine motor car with advertising to match. Written symbol of this dual achievement has been the famous Packard slogan *"Ask The Man Who Owns One"* which has appeared in every advertisement and every piece of sales literature since 1902.

The author was J. W. Packard, founder of the Company, who gave the slogan a rather casual birth in a letter to a prospect. Mr. Packard had great faith in the performance of his automobile, and when this particular prospect wrote in for proof of dependability, Mr. Packard simply provided the name of an owner in the vicinity of the inquirer and advised him to ask the man who owned one.

This phrase, like *"I'd Walk A Mile For A Camel"*, shone like panned gold through the commonplace circumstances of its birth — which leads this humble commentator to observe again that good ideas are everywhere, but, Lord, how important it is to know one when you see it, or hear it.

To those of us who grew up with the motor car, the Packard radiator, or shape, or lines, have always represented a sort of dream of princely things. The Packard to us was like the richest family in town, or the big house on the hill. It was a vivid, driving dream and its power was as certain as the great engine under its hood. Someday, we'd own . . . a Packard!

Jack Rosebrook, of Young & Rubicam, put this latent longing into one of the first nostalgic Packard ads a good many years ago: *Maybe you were that boy.* And maybe because *I* was that boy, and maybe just because the ads themselves are so beautifully, powerfully sincere and human — I don't know: I know only that I followed them religiously and consider them among the finest examples of I-remember advertising ever written.

The one chosen for this book is just about the best: *"When Heaven Was At The Corner Of Sycamore and Main."* But there were others — like *"I Wanted To Grow Up and Marry Mr. Washburn."*

These later ideas and headlines are Sid Ward's, Copy Director of Young & Rubicam. Stanley Jones wrote the marvelous text — and don't forget that the people at Packard okayed them!

EYE OPENER! With all its extra value, this Buick sedan lists at $51 *less* than last year!

ℰver hear the One *about* the Farmer's Daughter?

IT seems that one day a traveling salesman in a smart new 1939 Buick pulled up at the gate where the girl was standing.

"Nice day," said he, lifting his hat. "Wonderful!" she agreed.

"Nice sort of day to take a nice long automobile ride," he suggested."Wonderful!"said the farmer's daughter.

"Got a pretty snappy car here," said the traveling salesman. "Just about the handsomest thing to be seen in anywhere!"

Again the girl agreed — "It's wonderful!"

"It's got a swell engine," said the salesman. "Gets more good out of every drop of gasoline. A Dynaflash straight-eight! You ought to see it travel!"

"Wonderful!" said the farmer's daughter.

"Darned comfortable car too. Those BuiCoil Springs certainly do make the rough roads behave. Never driven a car that travels smoother."

Said the farmer's daughter: "Just wonderful!"

"And look! Big windows. You can see the country. Why there's 413 more square inches of safety glass in this sedan. It's a treat to travel in a car like this!"

"Wonderful!" agreed the girl.

"Well," said the salesman, "how about taking a little ride with me?"

"Listen, mister!" said the farmer's daughter. "Where you been? We've two Buicks in the garage. Want to race to town?"

Easy on the eye—easy to buy —on General Motors terms!

NO OTHER CAR IN THE WORLD HAS ALL THESE FEATURES

★ DYNAFLASH VALVE-IN-HEAD STRAIGHT-EIGHT ENGINE ★ BUICOIL TORQUE-FREE SPRINGING ★ GREATER VISIBILITY ★ HANDISHIFT TRANSMISSION ★ ROOMIER UNISTEEL BODY BY FISHER ★ TORQUE-TUBE DRIVE ★ TIPTOE HYDRAULIC BRAKES ★ CROWN SPRING CLUTCH ★ "CATWALK-COOLING" ★ OPTIONAL REAR AXLE GEAR RATIOS ★ FLASH-WAY DIRECTION SIGNAL ★ SELF-BANKING KNEE-ACTION FRONT SPRINGING

"When better automobiles are built Buick will build them"

"ℬuick's the Beauty!"
EXEMPLAR OF GENERAL MOTORS VALUE

BUICK — *"Ever Hear The One About The Farmer's Daughter?"*

THE late Hayward M. Anderson, of the Kudner Agency, Inc., wrote this advertisement. Besides being a wonderful piece of copy and a great selling ad, the story behind it is one of my favorites —

It started with a copy requisition for a farm paper ad. On that particular day Hayward's mind was completely blank as far as good farm paper ideas were concerned and he sat around for an hour or more trying to get started. (Don't we all?)

All he could think of was the familiar phrase: "Ever hear the one about the farmer's daughter?"

It kept coming back and back, and eventually penetrated deeply enough to make Hayward wonder if a good ad could be written in the form of the ordinary, humorous farmer's-daughter story.

Now, Andy (I can't call him Hayward any longer), set about to find out. *Ever hear the one about the farmer's daughter* kept bouncing around in his mind. He ran a fine old piece of yellow paper through the typewriter and when it came out it so amused him that he showed it to Jim Ellis, then copy chief of Kudner. Jim got a chuckle out of it and said, "Let's slip it into Art Kudner's copy folder and see what happens."

For a couple of days neither Jim nor Andy heard anything from Mr. Kudner so they naturally supposed that the boss had read it, gotten a chuckle, and had finally disposed of the whole thing by throwing it in the wastebasket.

Then one day Mr. Kudner dropped by Andy's office and said very seriously: "Andy where do you expect to run that farmer's daughter ad?"

Andy was a little taken back so he said off-handedly: "I thought we might run it in the *New Yorker* or some other magazine with a humorous touch."

"No," said Mr. Kudner, "that belongs in the *Post*. It's worth a page."

Photo courtesy Twin Coach Company, Kent, O.

Rubber keeps a motor bus singing in the rain

A typical example of B. F. Goodrich product development

A MANUFACTURER of the big passenger busses was in a quandary. On rainy days his new model bus would sputter and stall when moisture and dirt worked its way into the distributor cap. Trouble-shooters said that redesign and relocation of the distributor was the only answer; but that would set back production for months, and wouldn't do a thing for the busses already in service. B. F. Goodrich engineers were called in.

Within 48 hours B. F. Goodrich laboratories had produced a rubber cover (by the same Anode process used to make surgeons' gloves) that sealed the distributor from rain and dirt, resisted the grease and heat of the engine, and offered no weak spots for electrical leakage. Results: a bus fleet rolling through the rain with its fire dry; an automotive manufacturer's problem solved with speed, efficiency, economy.

In industrial fields B. F. Goodrich makes rubber products by every process known to the rubber industry — made in every conceivable shape and design.

Hundreds of businesses have learned that B. F. Goodrich rubber engineers are always on call to assist company engineering staffs in solving any problem that rubber can meet. *The B. F. Goodrich Company, Industrial Products Division, Akron, Ohio.*

B.F. Goodrich
FIRST IN RUBBER

B. F. GOODRICH COMPANY — *"Rubber Keeps A Motor Bus Singing In The Rain"*

THIS is not a "famous" ad. It probably isn't a "great" ad. It is, however, representative of one of the most *consistently competent* advertising campaigns ever run in American magazines.

For fifteen consecutive years this campaign has appeared every few weeks with *the same* layout, *the same* type faces, and *the same* kind of copy. That's a record.

The father of the campaign is H. E. Van Petten, Manager, National Advertising, for the B. F. Goodrich Company, and the writer was Kenneth W. Akers, an executive of the Griswold Eshleman Company, Cleveland advertising agency.

Frank T. Tucker, Director of Advertising, for B. F. Goodrich, says that "The basic reason for the outstanding success of this campaign is not the attention-arresting picture, nor the headlines which we think are pretty good, nor even the interesting narrative-style copy. The basic reason for the success of this campaign, in my opinion, is that it has been running for about fifteen years."

And Mr. Van Petten says of his offspring: "We know these ads are widely read and interesting. I recently made a readership check of 9 of them. In read most, 3 ranked third, 1 second, 1 third, 2 fifth, 1 seventh and 1 tenth. The number of ads in the issues checked ranged from 40 to 74.

"We know the people who are reading them are reading about B. F. Goodrich products, not about moving picture stars, dramatic world events, or far-fetched analogies. In most cases they are reading *performance stories* about our products.

"We receive many letters from people who simply want to tell us that they enjoy reading the ads. Many of these people are not users of our products. Our own salemen tell us that our advertising is constantly mentioned to them by engineers, production and purchasing men, and others called on.

"Recently, one of our salesmen made a $15,000 sale and was told that the interest in B. F. Goodrich products originated in this advertising campaign. We have no way of knowing how often this happens."

My hat's off to an advertiser who knows he's got something good — and *sticks to it.*

We hope we set a boy to dreaming

OUR Parade of Progress has come and gone.

The big silver trucks have packed up their shows and disappeared over the far horizon.

We enjoyed our stay and your hospitality; we hope that you enjoyed the things we had to show you.

If it gave you a clearer understanding of how General Motors links Science and Industry in the service of human needs, we are grateful.

We hope it accomplished one more thing: that somewhere in your city we have set a young boy to dreaming!

As we see our job, General Motors is not concerned alone with making good cars or fine products for today.

We are even more vitally concerned with preparing better cars for tomorrow and with providing even greater conveniences for future households.

For in so doing—in performing this task faithfully—we believe we are contributing toward a better country and a richer and more satisfactory future for our sons and daughters.

The real hope for continued progress lies in the spirit of individual initiative —in the methods and processes yet to be perfected and the discoveries still to be made.

That's why we hope that among the crowds who visited our exposition there were youngsters who found their imaginations stirred, who caught the glimmerings of a vision, who started in pursuit of that vision by turning to their home chemistry sets, their construction toys, their tool kits and workbenches.

The first purpose of the Parade of Progress is to interest, to enlighten, to entertain.

Through that purpose we hope to make clear the processes through which industry performs its share of the world's work.

But parades must sooner or later all reach their end. Progress is something that can never halt.

That is why we hope that somewhere we set a boy to dreaming—and set him on a road of usefulness and service to himself, his country and his fellow men.

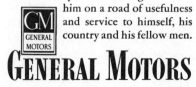

GENERAL MOTORS

GENERAL MOTORS — *"We Hope We Set A Boy To Dreaming"*

ABOUT twenty years ago General Motors had a very elaborate and effective traveling scientific exhibit called the *"Parade of Progress."* It was really quite a show, involving several huge trucks, a big silver-covered tent and a lot of interesting and informative exhibits and lectures.

The late Charles Lewis was in charge of the "Parade of Progress" and it was a project very close to his heart.

He had personally selected all the fine young boys who made up the Parade's personnel and he was very proud of them and the exhibit.

In connection with the exhibit, it was decided that there should be an ad to run after the Parade had left town thanking people for their interest and attendance.

The ad was to run only once in each city and was not what you would call a large copywriting assignment. The late Hayward Anderson, of Kudner, wrote one piece which could have been called adequate, but Mr. Lewis wasn't satisfied.

He came into Kudner's office one day and tried to tell them just why he didn't like the copy as submitted.

He frankly said that he could not put his finger on anything particular, and that there was no doubt that the copy, as written, would do all that General Motors could expect on the original specifications.

But as Andy listened to him talk, he realized that the "Parade of Progress" was something that meant a great deal to Charles Lewis. Andy realized that Mr. Lewis had a great vision and in his own quiet and persistent way, was doing everything he could to make that vision real.

After ten or fifteen minutes, Anderson began to catch fire himself. He began to see that the "Parade of Progress" was not simply a traveling side-show but possibly the way to open a youngster's mind to some pretty great and wonderful things.

So he excused himself from the meeting and went directly to his typewriter. Andy says there wasn't much to writing the ad except keeping it simple and giving it the sincerity of feeling which existed among those who were putting on the "Parade of Progress."

"I remember" Andy writes "bothering myself somewhat about the headline — *We Hope We Set a Boy to Dreaming.* It sounded a little awkward and colloquial, yet it was what I wanted to say so I stuck to it.

"The art director did a nice job of getting the photograph and giving me a simple straightforward layout. The ad was accepted and put on the schedule to run in each city where the 'Parade of Progress' appeared.

"The reception was quite wonderful.

"I never expected words of mine to come from Church pulpits but ministers read the ad and quoted from it literally. One city — I think it was St. Louis — asked for enough large reprints to put the ad in each of the city's schools. Newspapers wrote editorials and General Motors got so much favorable comment that the ad continued to be used for two years as a follow-up to 'Parade of Progress' stops.

"We got an award on it but to me the greatest satisfaction lay in the fact that I had caught and expressed Charlie Lewis' vision about a thing which could have been classified only as a promotion stunt.

"Since the ad ran, of course, we have had the usual requests to 'do another boy ad' and on one or two occasions we have tried. However, this is one of those cases where everything fitted together very nicely and I don't believe any of the second efforts have been quite as successful as this one.

"All of which illustrates one feeling I have about copy. There are moments of inspiration and strong feeling during which an advertising copywriter pretty much pours his heart out through the typewriter.

"These moments are rare and generally can't be repeated deliberately. Most efforts to do the same thing again fall short in some way and I think it is a mistake to ask or expect a copywriter to stay always on these inspirational peaks.

"One note of humor: I often regret that I ever wrote this ad because I have a neighbor who never fails to ask me when we happen to catch the same train: 'Well, are you going to set a boy to dreaming today?'"

"That's A H--l of a Way to Run a Railroad!"

BOSTON & MAINE — *"That's A Hell Of A Way To Run A Railroad"*

I AM indebted to Harold Cabot, president of the Harold Cabot Company for the story behind this outstanding statement:

"The advertising committee of the Boston and Maine then consisted of Mr. A. B. Nichols, chairman (vice president and clerk of corporation); Mr. H. F. McCarthy, passenger traffic manager; Mr. Pat Mullaney, freight traffic manager; Mr. H. L. Baldwin, publicity manager; Mr. Gus Munster, vice president in charge of purchases and stores; and Mr. Delmont Bishop, advertising agent.

"Advertising proposals by Harold Cabot & Co. were made before the entire committee which would approve or reject, and if it approved, would expect that the final proof would be initialed by Mr. Nichols, Mr. Baldwin and Mr. McCarthy.

"The committee meetings devoted part of the time to seeing the specfic proposals of the agency, and part of the time to discussion of railroad problems and possibilities which might be assigned to the agency for development, in addition to any ideas the agency itself presented.

"For many meetings prior to the publication of 'That's a Hell of a Way to Run a Railroad' the committee had discussed, and Mr. Nichols had separately discussed with us, the need of a statement which would explain some of the problems of the railroad in times of inclement weather. There were many staff reports of complaints from riders because of the delay of trains on route or delays in leaving the North Station whenever there was a severe storm.

"Mr. Nichols was determined in taking the stand that any such statement should not apologize. It was his opinion (at that time he had been in railroading for some 45 years) that only an explanation could be made that we could not anticipate the many difficulties which the operating people encountered, and therefore, no apology could be made or any promise that the difficulties could be brought to an end.

"In his mind, it is a very challenging public relations job. We distinctly recall him saying several times that no public statement should be made, ulness it was a forceful explanation and one that would result in sympathy for the operating people.

"Dick Holland, for Harold Cabot & Co., was assigned to keep closely in touch with the operating people through the winter and at the same time to do a certain amount of checking around the stations in order to judge the attitude of the public.

"On the afternoon of a particularly heavy storm, there was delay in trains leaving the North Station. Dick stayed at the station and joined in the waiting crowds for several hours. The following morning he met with Mr. Frank Rourke, the General Superintendent and discussed with him the specific delays and the reasons for them.

"After the meeting with Mr. Rourke, Dick met with Baldy and reviewed some of the comments he had overheard in the station the previous day. He also relayed the information Mr. Rourke had given him from the operating side. As there is always "conflict" between the editorial and advertising departments of a newspaper, so in a railroad there are considerable differences between the traffic, advertising and operating departments. Baldy made the usual sour comments reflecting his opinion of the operating department and added a stock railroad phrase taken from a cartoon which is believed to have originated in *Collier's* Magazine, 'That's a Hell of a Way to Run a Railroad!'.

"Holland returned to the office and under the caption, 'That's a Hell of a Way to Run a Railroad!' dictated a memorandum based on his conversation with Mr. Rourke.

"This was turned over to Harry Patterson and others in the copy department. Patterson inserted the refrain, 'That's a Hell of a Way to Run a Railroad!' between each paragraph and added the line at the bottom, 'But the Railroad Always Runs'. He and Holland then set to work to brief the paragraphs in the memorandum, and the result with the layout was shown to the advertising committee.

"Just prior to this showing, Holland again checked the information with Mr. Rourke to be sure that he had not misinterpreted it.

"The advertisement was unanimously approved by the advertising committee at the first showing. One member only, questioned the wisdom of spending the money on an explanation rather than to spend it on some definite selling objective. He approved the advertisement but preferred to spend the budget on direct selling. He was won over by the others. The committee was, of course, fully aware that the advertisement was entirely of a different sort than had ever been run in railroad circles, a radical change, and yet it accomplished exactly what Mr. Nichols had in mind originally.

"It was decided that because the advertisement was so radically different that the advertising committee should ask Mr. French, president of the Railroad, and chairman of its executive committee, whether or not it should be further approved by the executive committee. Mr. French agreed at once that it was an outstanding advertisement, and he suggested that while it might be wise to review it in the executive committee, nevertheless, if there was another snow storm prior to a meeting of the executive committee, the advertisement should be run on the judgment of the advertising committee. A snow storm came prior to the meeting of the executive committee; the advertisement was run without having been shown to that committee."

To men who want to Quit Work some day

THIS PAGE is addressed to those thousands of earnest, hard-working men who want to take things easier some day.

It tells how these men, by following a simple, definite plan, can provide for themselves in later years *a guaranteed income they cannot outlive*.

How the Plan Works

It doesn't matter whether your present income is large or merely average. It doesn't matter whether you are making fifty dollars a week or five hundred. If you follow this plan you will some day have an income upon which to retire.

The plan calls for the deposit of only a few dollars each month—the exact amount depending on your age. The minute you make your first deposit, your biggest money worries begin to disappear. Even if you should become totally and permanently disabled, you would not need to worry. Your payments would be made by us out of a special fund provided for that purpose.

And not only that. We would mail you a check every month during the entire time of your dis-

ability, even if that disability should continue for many, many years—the remainder of your natural life.

Get this free book

The Phoenix Mutual Company, which offers you this opportunity, is a 125 million dollar company. For over three-quarters of a century it has been helping thousands of men and women to end money worries.

But you're not interested in us. You are interested in what we can do for *you*. An illustrated, 36-page book called "How to Get the Things You Want" tells you exactly that. It tells how you can become financially independent—how you can retire on an income—how you can provide money for emergencies—money to leave your home free of debt—money for other needs.

This financial plan is simple, reasonable, and logical. The minute you read about it you will realize why it accomplishes such desirable results —not for failures, not for people who can't make ends meet, but for hard-working, forward-looking people who know what they want and are ready to make definite plans to get it. No obligation. Get your copy of the book now.

NEW RETIREMENT INCOME PLAN

Here is what a dividend-paying $10,000 policy will do for you:

It guarantees when you are 65
A Monthly Income for life of $100 which assures a return of at least $10,000, and perhaps much more, depending upon how long you live.
or, if you prefer,
A Cash Settlement of $12,000.

It guarantees upon death from any natural cause before age 65
A Cash Payment to your beneficiary of $10,000. Or $50 a month for at least 24 years and 8 months.
Total $14,823

It guarantees upon death resulting from accident before age 60
A Cash Payment to your beneficiary of $20,000. Or $100 a month for at least 24 years and 8 months.
Total $29,646

It guarantees throughout permanent total disability which begins before age 60.
A Monthly Disability Income of $100 and payment for you of all premiums.

Plans for women or for retirement at ages 55 or 60 are also available.

PHOENIX MUTUAL
LIFE INSURANCE COMPANY
Hartford Office: Hartford, Conn.   First Policy issued 1851

Copyright 1929, P. M. L. I. Co.

PHOENIX MUTUAL LIFE INSURANCE CO., 000 Elm St., Hartford, Conn.
Send me by mail without obligation, your new book, "HOW TO GET THE THINGS YOU WANT."

Name_____   Date of Birth_____

Business Address_____   City_____

Home Address_____   State_____

PHOENIX MUTUAL — *"To Men Who Want To Quit Work Someday"*

THE Phoenix Mutual advertisement *"To Men Who Want to Quit Work Some Day"* was the "key" ad in that advertiser's success as the outstanding coupon-puller in the life insurance field.

Mr. Cyrus T. Steven, Director of Public Relations for the Phoenix Mutual Life Insurance Company, has this to say about it —

"Readers of this book will be interested to learn that when Mr. J. L. Watkins, the author, was deciding to include the familiar Fisherman Advertisement of the Phoenix Mutual, he did not have access to the advertising records of that company. Consequently, in making his selection, he had to depend entirely upon judgment and advertising instinct. And yet he did succeed in choosing the one advertisement which, above all others, was a landmark of historic importance not only for the Phoenix Mutual, but also for other early champions of 'pretesting methods' who, then and since, have been alert enough to profit by Phoenix Mutual example. Here is the story:

"Because the 'product' was right and the need universal, the life insurance business grew to greatness with only modest use of display advertising. In fact, prior to 1923, only a few giant companies — notably The Travelers, Prudential and Metropolitan — were widely known for their advertising. But in July of that year, the Phoenix Mutual of Hartford, Conn., 'broke the ice' for the remainder of the industry. Like their neighbor companies, the Phoenix Mutual used a dignified, institutional campaign designed to promote prestige.

"But after 30 months, the author of these notes (then in charge of Phoenix Mutual advertising) was dissatisfied with results. The thin flow of inquiries was in such meager volume that it was impossible to judge the relative merits of the various appeals being used. But when the use of coupons was suggested (in the manner then being employed by a few venturesome book publishers, correspondence courses, and mail order houses), the advertising agencies were found to be unanimous in discouraging the idea.

"In those days, the life insurance business did not, of course, command the public esteem it now enjoys. And so, in all fairness, these advertising agencies should be commended for hav-

ing the courage of their convictions when they advised: 'Life insurance can't possibly be sold by coupon advertising, but only through agents. Furthermore, coupons would be too undignified for a financial advertiser to use. You would lose prestige!'

"But the Phoenix Mutual believed otherwise. Having used pre-tested letters successfully for more than 15 years in Direct Mail campaigns, it felt certain that similar methods could be used with display advertising. And it wasn't long before a prominent advertising authority was found who shared Phoenix Mutual convictions. His name is known to all: Bruce Barton!

"Thus it happened that in May, 1926, the Phoenix Mutual of Hartford, with Bruce Barton's enthusiastic support, became an early pioneer in the field of 'pretested' advertising, then in its infancy. And since no guide posts existed, each possible new trail had to be explored and exploited. Another fortuitous occurrence was the arrival on the scene of Mr. John Caples (who has since written several books on tested advertising methods and is now a vice president of Batten, Barton, Durstine & Osborn, Inc.). In fact, the Phoenix Mutual became the first client whom Mr. Caples served in the capacity of account executive.

"Our popular Fisherman Advertisement appeared in public print first on January 6, 1929, nearly 2½ years after our coupon advertising began. It had its test run in the Magazine Section of the New York Sunday *Times.* To our astonishment, it produced nearly 3 times as many inquiries as its 25 predecessors had averaged. But most important of all, its volume of sales was larger by 4 times!

"Small wonder that this Fisherman Advertisement gave us the 'key idea' which has dominated Phoenix Mutual advertising ever since. It paved the way for the decades of successful advertising which followed. Furthermore, the illustration is so basic it is still being used periodically in display advertising and is still appearing in all booklets on retirement income plans published for male readership. To countless thousands, this smiling old gent with rod, reel and creel has become symbolic of how it feels to 'get rid of money worries and retire on an income for the rest of your life!' — or to look forward to having 'six months' vacation, TWICE A YEAR!' "

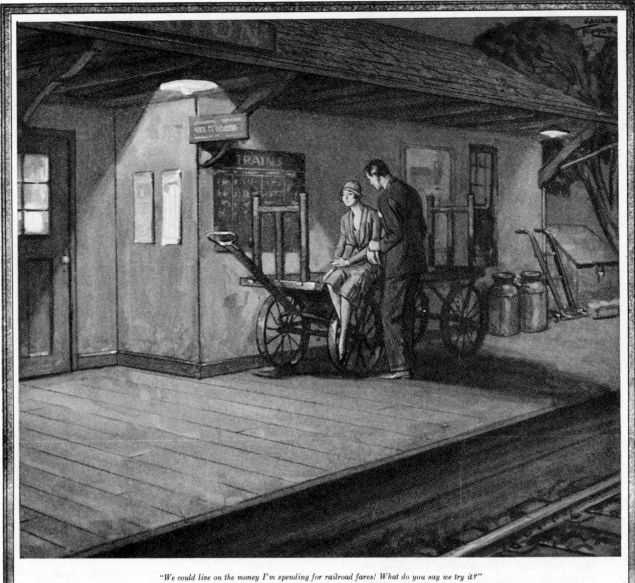

"We could live on the money I'm spending for railroad fares! What do you say we try it?"

The Greatest Reason in the World

HY did you buy life insurance?" I asked him.

"Well," he said, "it was because once I met a young person coming up the stairs of an apartment house with her arms full of packages, one of them dangling from a slender string. I didn't think she'd mind, so I offered to help her. At the door of her apartment, I saw that she was quite pretty. She still is.

"Because late one night, while she and I were waiting at a dimly lighted railway station for the Owl to take me home, I said, 'We could live on the money I'm spending for railroad fares! What do you say we try it?' We did, and it worked.

"Because one day I was offered a job by another company, and when I told my boss, he promised me ten dollars more a week if I'd stay. When I told *her* of the boss's generosity, she said, 'What do you mean, generous? If he knew you were worth that much to him, he should have paid it to you before he had to.' So I quit and took the new job.

"Because one night she woke me up and said, 'I think I'd better go.' We went, and the last I saw of her that night, she was being trundled down a long corridor in a wheelchair, in spite of her protests that she could walk. When I saw her the next morning, she was lying very still and white and with the sweetish smell of ether on her breath. A nurse came in and asked, 'Wouldn't you like to see him?' But I wasn't interested in babies just then—not even our own.

"Because one autumn evening, while we were driving leisurely along a country road, we came upon a small white cottage, its windows ablaze with the light of the setting sun. She said, 'What a place this would be for us!' Yes, what a place it has been for us!

"It's because of these memories, and many others that I wouldn't tell you and that wouldn't interest you even if I did, that I bought life insurance.

"And if the premiums could be paid in blood, instead of money, pernicious anemia would be a pleasure.'"

• • •

Moral: Insure in The Travelers. All forms of insurance. The Travelers Insurance Company, The Travelers Indemnity Company, The Travelers Fire Insurance Company, Hartford, Connecticut.

TRAVELERS INSURANCE COMPANY — *"The Greatest Reason In The World"*

WHEN this advertisement first appeared — nineteen or twenty years ago — I thought it was one of the best I had ever read. Certainly one of the best about life insurance.

I liked its frankness. It disarmed me at the start by saying: *"Why did you buy life insurance? I asked him."*

I liked the smile tucked in here and there.

I liked the way the guy talked about his wife and baby, and his home, and what they all meant.

And later, I liked the way the Starch Reports gave this copy No. 1 position in almost all classifications, but particularly in *Read Most*.

And still later, I liked the fact that this fine piece of copy was written by the client! George Malcolm-Smith, a member of the Travelers publicity staff, wrote it straight from the heart in 1938.

It was first used as a piece for a house organ (imagine it!), and later when suggested as a possible idea for a *Post* ad, Young & Rubicam, the agency, grabbed it and ran it, as was.

This particular advertisement has been read and re-read before different groups of life insurance men, advertising men, and plain ordinary life insurance buyers, and C. W. Van Beynum, Travelers' Publicity Director, tells me that requests for copies still come in. I wonder if you'll agree with me as to why — *somehow the public senses the ring of sincerity and truth when it appears in cold type, and is just as quick to challenge "emotional" pieces that are synthetic.* If you believe something in this world, it shines through whatever you select as a medium of expression.

And those are the greatest reasons in the world I can think of for loving this bewildering but wonderful business!

WHILE FIRE LOOKS ON AND SMILES

MEN who smoke, or carry lighted cigars, cigarettes, pipes or matches while handling gasoline are inviting Fire, and thousands of blackened ruins bear testimony to their unpardonable carelessness.

Fire is a public enemy against which we are fighting a defensive battle. We *must* be more careful. We must do everything in our power to protect our homes, schools, public buildings and places of business, and to safeguard the investment that they represent. The Hartford Fire Insurance Company will help you in your efforts to prevent fire and will make good your loss if fire does come.

There is a local agent of the Hartford near you. He will see to it that you are protected by the service and policies of a Company that has been serving property owners faithfully for 114 years.

HARTFORD FIRE INSURANCE COMPANY, Hartford, Conn.

The Hartford Fire Insurance Company and the Hartford Accident and Indemnity Company write practically every form of insurance except life

HARTFORD FIRE INSURANCE COMPANY — *"While Fire Looks On And Smiles"*

OCCASIONALLY, in advertising, a symbol is created that somehow, to coin a phrase, speaks louder than a thousand words. Such a symbol was Hartford Fire's famous red devil, later called the Hartford Hellion.

For years this black-robed, red-faced-and-red-footed figure gave the advertisements of the Hartford Fire Insurance Company a stopping quality that has seldom, if ever, been equalled.

The idea had its inception in the fertile, human brain of Mr. J. W. Longnecker, for thirty-five years Advertising Manager of Hartford Fire until his retirement in 1944. But to the late Richard M. Bissell, long President of the Company, must go the credit for recognizing the inherent values in that powerful, arresting figure, and for himself writing the first copy to go with it.

Besides Mr. Bissell and Mr. Longnecker, Calkins & Holden's Calkins, Spaulding, Sherman, Rene Clark and Ed Georgi contributed developing ideas which gave the Hellion its greatest fame.

My friend, Joe Holmes, is now a horse

JOE always said when he died he'd like to become a horse.

One day Joe died.

Early this May I saw a horse that looked like Joe drawing a milk wagon.

I sneaked up to him and whispered, "Is it you, Joe?"

He said, "Yes, and am I happy!" I said, "Why?"

He said, "I am now wearing a comfortable collar for the first time in my life. My shirt collars always used to shrink and murder me. In fact, one choked me to death. That is why I died!"

"Goodness, Joe," I exclaimed, "Why didn't you tell me about your shirts sooner? I would have told you about Arrow shirts. *They never shrink.* Not even the oxfords."

"G'wan," said Joe. "Oxford's the worst shrinker of all!"

"Maybe," I replied, "but not *Gordon*, the Arrow oxford. I know. I'm wearing one. It's Sanforized-shrink-proof. Besides, it's cool. Besides, this creamy shade I chose is the newest shirt color, *bamboo.*"

"Swell," said Joe. "My boss needs a shirt like that. I'll tell him about Gordon. Maybe he'll give me an extra quart of oats. And, gosh, do I love oats!"

If it hasn't an Arrow Label it isn't an Arrow Shirt

ARROW SHIRTS

Sanforized Shrunk — a new shirt free if one ever shrinks

Made by CLUETT, PEABODY & CO., INC.

ARROW COLLAR — *"My Friend, Joe Holmes, Is Now A Horse"*

IF you can read this Arrow Shirt ad without a warm glow and a wide grin, you probably won't agree either that books like this should have at least a couple of pages of laughs in them!

I've always loved this series of Arrow Shirt ads by George Gribbin of Young & Rubicam. This was the 4th or 5th of a series that ran in New York newspapers about eleven years ago. I don't know what the occasion was except that each ad was to point-up a particular feature of the shirt (in the Joe Holmes ad, the fact that Arrow Shirts don't shrink).

George says that here's how the idea came about:

Shirts have collars. Horses have collars, too. Horse collars fit loosely; don't shrink and choke the horse. Ought to be some tie-up there. Let's see if we can get an ad out of this . . .

And what an ad!

In fact, George was so fascinated by his chimerical visitation with his friend Joe Holmes, that he forgot to put the price of the shirt in the copy and didn't notice it until he saw the ad in the *Times* the morning it appeared. Too late. The price was $2 (1938, remember).

Aunt Meg . . . who never married

I REMEMBER the night Jim Foster went off to the war . . . that last brave flutter of the handkerchief . . . and the sigh of the whistle as the train crossed the bridge over Matthews' Falls.

Aunt Meg never talked about Jim Foster. She lived with us till we grew up, moving through all the golden memories of childhood . . . the sound of her voice reading in the dim room the time Jane and I had measles . . . her hands arranging roses in a silver bowl on summer mornings . . . the faraway songs she used to sing.

Aunt Meg never married. And the hopes that echoed in her smile departed with the flutter of the handkerchief, the train whistle sliding into silence behind the mountains.

Aunt Meg died ten years ago, gone to her memories, and leaving happy memories behind. And when we think of her we remember the beauty of all that made her life . . . the scent of roses, distant music, summer light and shadow . . .

When someone we loved has passed away, we face the problem of a suitable memorial — a memorial in keeping with the depth of our affection and the character of the person we wish to honor.

Immediate questions present themselves: What designs are available and where may we see them? What costs are involved? Which type of stone will assure *eternal* beauty?

Today these questions are best answered by one statement: look for the memorial dealer who features memorials sculptured from Select Barre Granite and approved by the Barre Guild. The Guild mark on a memorial is applied only to Select Barre Memorials created to the highest Guild standards of Design, Workmanship and Material. A Guild Certificate guaranteeing per-

manent satisfaction through every step of a memorial investment is supplied with each approved memorial. Behind the Barre Guild stands an entire industry, located in the Barre, Vt., district, *"The Granite Center of the World,"* and composed of nearly one hundred manufacturer-members of the Barre Granite Association, using granite from the following quarries: J. K. Pirie Estate, Rock of Ages Corp., E. L. Smith & Co., Wells-Lamson Quarry Co., The Wetmore & Morse Granite Co.

PERSONAL

Here are three suggestions which will help you when the selection of a memorial is your responsibility: First, choose a memorial dealer who features memorials sculptured from Select Barre Granite as approved by the Barre Guild, and insist on a Guild Certificate when you buy. Second, remember that only a monument manufactured *in the Barre, Vermont, district* is a genuine Barre Guild monument. Third, send today for the beautifully illustrated free booklet, "Barre — The Story of Granite." Address: Barre Guild, Dept. S-1, Barre, Vermont.

BARRE GUILD
Reg. U.S. Pat. Off.

Select BARRE GRANITE Memorials

BARRE GRANITE — *"Aunt Meg Who Never Married"*

IN 1937, the advertising of the Barre Granite Association featured shudderingly realistic photographs of tombstones, with such headlines as — FOREVER — ETERNITY — IN MEMORY'S GARDEN.

To me, this seemed decidely wrong end to. The monument business lived because someone worth remembering had died. The ads should be about *people*.

This seemed to make a lot of sense to the Advertising Committee of the Barre Granite Association, and the H. B. Humphrey Company, Boston, was eventually appointed the Association's advertising agency.

The "Aunt Meg" ad achieved a certain fame. It appeared in the *Saturday Evening Post* and *Fortune* in February 1939 and was followed each month by such successors as "Weddings always make me cry" — "When I hear a boy's choir singing the hymns my mother loved" etc.

All about *people*. People worth remembering.

In February 1940 the H. B. Humphrey Company, Boston, received the national Medal Award for Excellence in Copy — the first and only time this honor has gone to a New England agency.

As to results: our over-all objective was to acquaint as many people as possible with the fact that the Barre Guild seal was a trade-mark of unsurpassed significance in the monument field. Thorough readership of advertisements was therefore indispensable. The Starch readership ratings for 1939 proved how well we succeeded. We were always among the first ten in *Read Most* — and the Aunt Meg ad ranked first in *Read Most*. Demand for Barre Guild inspections by manufacturers in the Barre district increased about six hundred per cent that first year. Out in the field, monument dealers demanded the Seal on finished monuments from Barre more and more. They discovered, as many retailers before them have discovered, that merchandise marked by a recognized and accepted trade-mark is easier to sell. And the increasing demand for Guild-approved monuments goes on to this day.

Producing this copy was a team job. The slant was mine, as were the original headlines, but Miriam Dewey, one-time copywriter with Young & Rubicam, New York, did most of the copy.

Imagine Harry and Me advertising our PEARS in Fortune!

OUT HERE on the ranch we don't pretend to know much about advertising, and maybe we're foolish spending the price of a tractor for this space; but my brother and I got an idea the other night, and we believe you folks who read Fortune are the kind of folks who'd like to know about it. So here's our story:

We have a beautiful orchard out here in the Rogue River Valley in Oregon, where the soil and the rain and the sun grow the finest pears in the world. We grow a good many varieties; but years ago we decided to specialize on Royal Riviera Pears, a rare, delicious variety originally imported from France, and borne commercially only by 20-year-old trees. And do you know where we sold our first crop—and the greater part of every crop since?

In Paris and London, where the finest hotels and restaurants know them to be the choicest delicacy they can serve to discriminating guests. And they serve them at about 75 cents each! Our Royal Riviera Pears went to other distinguished tables too—to the Czar of Russia and to the kings and queens and first families of Europe. We got a great kick out of wrapping big, luscious, blushing Royal Riviera Pears in tissue and knowing they were going to be served on golden plates and eaten with golden spoons.

America's Rarest Fruit— Shall We Ship It Abroad?

But I'm getting away from my story. The idea that kept coming to Harry and me was this: Why must all this fruit go to Europe? Aren't there people right here in America who would appreciate such rare delicacies just as much as royalty? Wouldn't *our* first families like to know about these luscious, golden pears, rare as orchids, bursting with juice, and so big you eat them with a spoon? Wouldn't folks here at home like to give boxes of these rare pears to friends at Thanksgiving and Christmas?

So we made an experiment. We packed a few special boxes of these Royal Riviera Pears and took them down to some business friends in San Francisco. You should have seen their faces when they took their first taste of a Royal Riviera. They didn't know such fruit grew anywhere on earth.

Well, a banker wanted not only a box for home, but 50 boxes to be sent to business friends to arrive just before Christmas. A newspaper publisher wanted 40 for the same purpose, and a manufacturer asked for 25. And that gave us another idea. We sent 11 sample boxes to important executives in New York, and back came orders for 489 Christmas boxes for *their* friends.

A New Christmas Gift Idea

That seemed to indicate there were plenty of men looking for something new as a Christmas remembrance for friends who "have everything." The next year, orders came in for several thousand boxes of these rare pears, and you never read such letters as we got afterward—not only from the men who had *sent* the pears and made such a hit, but from folks who *received* them and wanted to know if they could buy more.

Well, that's how Harry and I got the idea that there must be *enough* discriminating people right here in the U. S. A. who'd like to do the same thing. So we talked it over the other night and said, "Let's put an ad in Fortune—and see." We got a shock when we found what it would cost us to do it, but here we are—and *you* are going to be the judge.

Right now as I write this, it is late September, and out here in this beautiful valley our Royal Riviera Pears are hanging like great pendants from those 40-year-old trees. We'll have to watch them like new babies from now until picking time — not a leaf must touch them toward the last —trained men will pick them gently with gloved hands and lay them carefully in padded trays. They'll be individually wrapped in tissue, nestled in cushion packing, and sent in handsome gift boxes lithographed in colors, to reach you— or your friends—firm and beautiful, ready to ripen in *your* home to their full delicious flavor.

I envy you *your* first taste of a Royal Riviera—every spoonful dripping with sweet liquid sunshine. And you can just bet that every one who receives a box is going to have the surprise of his life.

We hope that right now you'll make up your list of business and social friends and let us send them each a box with your compliments. We'll put in an attractive gift card with your name written on it, and

we'll deliver anywhere in the United States proper, wherever there is an express office, express prepaid, to arrive on the date you name. And don't forget to include a box for yourself! A "Medium Family" box (10 pounds) is only $1.85. A "Large Family" box (double the quantity) is $2.95. At these low prices these pears cost a mere fraction of what you would pay for them in fine restaurants and hotels. And here's how sure we are you'll be delighted. If, after eating your first Royal Riviera, you and your friends don't say these are the finest pears you ever tasted, just re-

turn the balance at our expense and your money will come back in a hurry. Harry and I have agreed you are to be the final judge—*and we mean it.*

Just one more thing—there are far more folks reading Fortune than there will be boxes of Royal Riviera Pears this year. So, if you want to be sure to get some, we hope you'll send your order right along. We are putting a coupon down below, but a letter is just as good. Only, if you write, please say you saw this in Fortune.

HARRY and DAVID
Bear Creek Orchards, Medford, Oregon.

BEAR CREEK ORCHARDS — *"Imagine Harry And Me Advertising Our Pears In 'Fortune'"*

I'VE never met G. Lynn Sumner* but I've heard about him all my advertising life — first as Advertising Manager of the International Correspondence Schools and later as President of his own agency in Manhattan. And everything I've heard about him has been good. A wonderful guy — a fine mind — an excellent copywriter.

When I asked him by mail to tell me the story behind IMAGINE HARRY AND ME ADVERTISING OUR PEARS IN FORTUNE he definitely lived up to all the good things I'd ever heard about him, for this is what he wrote —

"One day in November, 1934, we got a telephone call from a man who said his name was Harry Rosenberg and was in Room 722 at the Waldorf-Astoria, and that someone had given him our name the night before and he would like to see us. (Incidentally, we have never found out who gave him our name). A couple of us went over to the Waldorf-Astoria and found Harry with a real problem. He had brought along from Oregon fifteen boxes of comice pears and they were ripening on him very fast. He had been living with them in that room for a week and they had just about forty-eight hours to go.

"Harry told us that he and his brother, David, grew these pears out in Oregon and for years had been exporting them to France, England and Italy where they were known as a great delicacy and sold at very high prices. The variety was comparatively unknown in America. Harry and David had the idea that this rare fruit might be an appropriate Christmas gift for executives to send to their prospects and customers instead of the usual liquor and cigars. So he had brought along these sample boxes to New York and in the course of a week, talking to banks and express companies, had gotten exactly nowhere.

"Harry's problem intrigued us and we decided to take a crack at it. We did not tell him what we were going to do but we took back to the office all the Waldorf-Astoria stationery we could lay our hands on. That night we wrote a letter, putting ourselves in the place of these two boys on the ranch in Oregon. The next morning we ran off fifteen of these letters and arranged with Harry to deliver the fifteen boxes by messenger immediately

following the delivery of those fifteen letters which also went by messenger. They went to fifteen of the top business executives in the Grand Central district. In this letter Harry and David asked each recipient just to take a bite of one of these pears, then think what a joy it would bring to his friends to receive such a gift at Christmas time. They offered to send a box right from the orchard for $1.65. Within twenty-four hours Harry had received orders for 489 boxes from eleven out of the fifteen men.

"Harry beat it back to Oregon in hot haste and he and David started packing Royal Riviera Pears (a new name was created for them) and we started getting out direct mail to selected lists. The time was short but we sold about 6,000 boxes between then and Christmas.

"The next season their selling efforts were still confined to direct mail and they sold about 15,000 boxes. By that time we had a formula worked out for the operation.

"In May, 1936, David came on from Oregon to discuss plans for the Fall. We told him that they were now ready for national advertising. He said, 'Where would we advertise?' We told him the opening gun should be a full page in *Fortune*. David was looking out the window of our office. He was very quiet for a few moments and evidently was adjusting himself to the idea. Then he said, half to himself and to us, 'Imagine Harry and me advertising our pears in *Fortune*.'

"Of course we did not let on, but we knew right then that he had given us the headline for the first advertisement. The copy was written in the style that had made their direct mail successful. We illustrated the page with a Kodak picture such as might have been taken in the orchard by one of the boys. The advertisement ran in *Fortune*, November, 1936, and was tremendously successful. Naturally we were pleased when it won the Advertising Awards medal as the best magazine advertisement of the year. Probably the most significant thing about it was that it marked the beginning of the development of a whole new industry in America: selling fruit by mail. Today Harry and David must have at least one hundred competitors but they are still on top of the heap."

* deceased

The pause that refreshes

The Coca-Cola Company, Atlanta, Ga.

EACH busy day tends down hill from that top-of-the-morning feeling with which you begin. Don't whip yourself as the day begins to wear. Pause and refresh yourself with an ice-cold Coca-Cola, and be off to a fresh start. ▼ The wholesome refreshment of Coca-Cola has made it the one great drink of the millions. A perfect blend of many flavors, it has a flavor all its own—delicious to taste and, more than that, with a cool after-sense of refreshment. ▼ It is ready, cold and tingling, at fountains and refreshment stands around the corner from anywhere.

THE BEST SERVED DRINK IN THE WORLD A pure drink of natural flavors served ice-cold in its own bottle —the distinctive Coca-Cola bottle. Every bottle is sterilized, filled and sealed air-tight by automatic machines, without the touch of human hands—insuring purity and wholesomeness.

OVER 8 MILLION A DAY

IT HAD TO BE GOOD   TO GET WHERE IT IS

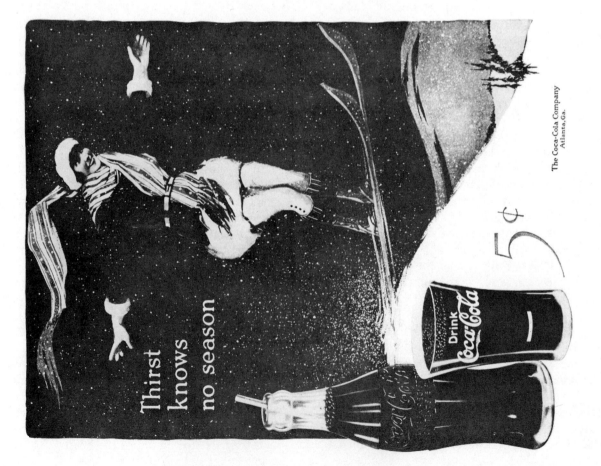

Thirst knows no season

5¢

Drink Coca-Cola

The Coca-Cola Company
Atlanta, Ga.

COCA-COLA — *Two Ads That Made History*

THE best known soft drink in the world is Coca-Cola and one of the best known advertising phrases is Coca-Cola's *"The pause that refreshes."*

Granting an excellent product, Coca-Cola is very definitely an advertising success. It started out just being Coca-Cola — and just selling in the good old summertime. A seasonal product if there ever was one. Big business one season; no business the other.

Faced with the problem of selling coke in the wintertime, the Company on December 9, 1922 ran the first full page ad of a straight-shooting campaign to remove seasonal valleys from the sales curve. You remember it: THIRST KNOWS NO SEASON. The line was repeated again and again and again — and it caught on. By 1930 Montreal was selling 66 million bottles of coke a year to New Orleans' 69 million! Today, Coca-Cola does more business in the winter than they used to do in the summer!

"Thirst knows no season" has become an accepted part of the public's attitude toward Coca-Cola.

Now many years ago these astute advertisers began the search for ways and means to make Coca-Cola fit into everyday life so as *to increase the number of occasions* when it could be served. Coca-Cola stopped thinking entirely about the product and considered only the behavior of people. Human beings, they reasoned, get along better when they pause in between spurts . . . when they pause and make a fresh start.

And there it was: THE PAUSE THAT RE-FRESHES . . . known 'round the world as Coca-Cola's very own. The idea was first featured in national magazines in September 1929 — one month before the stock market took a little pause that lacked refreshment entirely. And once again Coca-Cola sales plowed ahead.

The advertisement featuring the working girl is the first at-work variation of *"the pause that refreshes"* theme. Today, the at-work market is supported with its own advertising campaign.

These advertisements are considered milestones in Coca-Cola's splendid success.

The 2258th part

INTO THE MAKING of a Royal Typewriter go 2257 precision parts.

One *additional* ingredient, however, is greater than any of these. Because of it, the Royal has a reputation for all-round superiority, is known as the World's Number 1 Typewriter.

The name of that 2258th part is . . . Employee Co-operation. It is our proudest asset. For a typewriter is not run off on an assembly line, but it is the patient, meticulous product of many skilled hands.

And Royal is blessed with more than its share of Employee Co-operation. Possibly because of the security our people enjoy. Possibly because our free training schools help ambitious employees to advance. Or because all major executives at Royal have come up through the ranks.

Whatever the reason, Royal's 2258th part means a better typewriter for your money.

ROYAL

World's No. 1

TYPEWRITER

ROYAL TYPEWRITER — *"The 2258th Part"*

THIS is another fine example of institutional advertising largely because it appeared at a time when several of the leading typewriter companies were engaged in prolonged strikes and bickers — some of them of nearly two years' duration. The campaign, of which "The 2258th Part" is but one example, had a topical significance beyond its institutional character. An entire *Fortune* campaign was built around this slant and, as it appeared, salesmen wrote in to say that they found official doors opening to them that had never budged before.

Its author, Bill Tyler, long Vice President and Chairman of the Plans Board, Leo Burnett Company, Inc., Chicago; now Vice President and Director, Benton & Bowles, New York — also esteemed conductor of the famous "Copy Clinic" in *Advertising Age*.

"Off the bridge, you landlubber," *he yells!*

'Twas during one of those Northeast storms we have around here that Cap'n Ahab drives up.

"Ahoy, there," he howls, as I duck out into the storm. "Some gas for this infernal machine an' Oh! for the days of sail!"

"Didn't the 'Jennie Matthews' go down on a day like this?" I yells.

"That she did," he bellows. "An' a little oil on the troubled waters would've saved her!"

I know a fair wind when I feel one and I'm off —all sails set. "Skipper," says I, "on land or sea the right kind o' oil means a fair passage."

"None o' your steamin' tea kettles for me," he bellows. "Give me canvas!"

"Skipper," I tell him, "this Golden Shell Oil is tougher than the palm of a bosun's hand! An' it goes to work on your engine *fast*—faster than you could trim a stays'l."

"You're talkin' about speed now, son," he says.

"At 25¢ a quart it's a bargain!" I says, gettin' ready to drain an' refill.

"Off the bridge, you landlubber," he yells. "This oil of yours may be as smooth as your tongue—but you'll have to see the Chief Engineer!"

Sincerely,

Your Shell Dealer

P. S. *The Chief Engineer is his wife, an' she sure recognized a bargain the minute I talked to her.*

SHELL OIL COMPANY — *"Off The Bridge, You Landlubber"*

I CONSIDER these half-page Shell advertisements among the most effective of their kind ever written.

They ran in a number of magazines for about two years. This is how it all began and what it developed into — from the pen of the man who began it — Wallace Boren . . .

"It was the fashion at the time to glorify the service station operator. Copy about him and his alleged service to the public made him out a sort of composite of Little Lord Fauntleroy, the Good Samaritan, Sir Launcelot, and the Dean of English at Harvard. He was invariably pictured as handsome, beautifully groomed and tailored, young and suave.

"I had the feeling that this copywriter's version of the gink at the pumps didn't quite square with the public's everyday experience. I felt that service station operators had character, that they were very human, came in assorted shapes and in various degrees of erudition. I also believed that if the public knew them as they *were,* it would like them better than under the false front of the male models we were all using when an operator was called for.

"To illustrate the point, I did a piece of copy headlined 'SO I SAYS TO THE SALES MANAGER, YOU'RE NUTS!' The illustration was of two likeable mugs in conversation on the pump island of their station.

"The copy story was that the oil company sales manager had sent the station man a line of patter about his motor oil which was supposed to be delivered to the customer. The oil station man — totally unable to do more than parrot the spiel — had rebelled and was telling his customers a much simpler but more convincing and sincere sales story.

"A sense of humor (and of proportion) is not universal among sales managers, but Terry Kittenger, then heading Shell sales, apparently liked the idea of being told by one of his minions at the pumps that he was "nuts", and it was decided the campaign should run.

"For about two years, I believe, the ads appeared as half pages in a number of the magazines. Of course we were able to tell the story of the merits of the motor oil, in one way or another, in each advertisement, but always with anecdote and dialogue and in good humor, and with a cartooned illustration. If I remember correctly, at the time the readership of these half pages, according to Dr. Starch, surpassed all other national advertising and many times they were better read than the editorial content of the magazines in which they appeared. They may or may not have sold motor oil. In an operation as complex as that of a big oil company, it's pretty hard to trace sales directly to a given piece of copy. But there was ample evidence that the oil story was *exposed* to about 10 times the readership of the average advertisement and further evidence that there was a lot of good will and good humor and friendliness between the readers and the oil company.

"Editor William I. Nichols of *This Week* had been following the series, and he ferreted me out and asked if I could create a character for a home-spun column in his Sunday magazine. I picked the lunch wagon — the roadside hamburger joint — because it was the meeting place of all of society's stratums, it was nationally known, and urban in location — yet informal and free in spirit.

"The same technique was followed that had been used in the advertisements. We never patronized the customers, or the readers. We kept Wally, the proprietor, in a humble role but gave him and the other characters that come and go the freedom of spirit and of speech that all America seems to cherish. Art Director Burton Goodloe, who had laid out the Shell series, came along to do the drawings; and they and the writing are kept in the loose and comfortable dress of the everyday exchanges which go on between people who are not on dress parade or wearing their company manners. Hollywood sometimes calls this "corn." I guess it is. But Hollywood corn has to be stupendous or terrific, whereas Wally's variety is corn because he and his friends from the banker to the truck driver don't *know* any better.

"This experiment was my first on the editorial side, but apparently Bill Nichols' judgment of what his readers would like was pretty good because the high readership of the oil company ads continued in the 'Wally's Wagon' column. It's just nine years old now, and it has run unchanged except for one short period last year when we tinkered with the formula and tried to improve it. The "improvement" cost about 20 per cent of the readership, and we hastily put it back on the original track, where I suppose it will stay until someone comes along who can fill the space to better advantage for the magazine."

has been added! And of course *Borden's Evaporated* is good because *your* milk is so good in the first place."

"Borden's Evaporated? Did I do *that,* too?" wondered Elsie.

"Yes," he said, "and our Quality Control was right in there helping."

"Thank you," said Elsie, gratefully.

"Thank *you,*" he replied. "And thank you for doing your part toward making *Borden's Malted Milk*—which is so good, refreshing, and satisfying that Hollywood stars pick it as the mainstay of light luncheons that do right by trim figures. And that's not all . . ."

"Goodness," exclaimed Elsie, "what *else* have I done?"

"You furnished the milk that went into making *Borden's Chateau* and all the other delightful members of *Borden's Family of Fine Cheeses.* And, between us, they're the *finest* things that ever landed on a cracker!"

"That's nice—very nice," hesitated Elsie. "B-but—isn't anybody *drinking* my milk any more?"

"More folks than ever," chuckled the veterinarian. "I'm just explaining how our Quality Control extends its benefits way past *Borden's Milk,* to assure the wholesomeness and fine flavor of all the grand things Borden *makes* from milk. It's the reason that folks *know,* when they're buying any dairy product—*if it's Borden's it's got to be good!*"

• • •

More than 27,500 Borden employees work in behalf of 47,000 owner-stockholders, to provide the best of dairy products, to guard the goodness of all Borden foods, and to bring them to your home.

"Oh, Doctor, I bet you tell that to all the Girls!"

"NOTHING OF THE KIND, Elsie," the veterinarian answered briskly. "A *lot* of cows think I'm a fussy old crank. But I promise you I'm going to *stay* that way—just as long as I'm on this job of keeping you healthy. That's one way we make *sure* that *Borden's Ice Cream* is always pure and delicious."

"Ice cream? What have you and I got to do with *that?*" asked the puzzled Elsie, pointing a neatly turned horn at the tempting plateful.

"Nearly everything, my dear," he explained patiently. "If *any* food—like ice cream—is made from milk or cream, naturally *better* milk or cream will help make it a *better* food. My brother experts and I are solely interested in making sure that every drop of Borden's Milk always *is* better milk.

"We call this work of ours *Quality Control.* And another thing it does is to help folks do *magic* with your milk."

"Magic?" said Elsie, uneasily.

"Oh, it's only *after* you've given your milk to Borden's," he reassured her: "—and after it has been made into *Borden's Eagle Brand Sweetened Condensed Milk.*

That helps people make lovely cookies, candies, and cakes in almost no time. Then there's always soup . . ."

"I'd rather not talk about soup," said Elsie, sadly. "My poor brother—"

"I mean *cream* soups," he hastened, "and mashed potatoes and tea and coffee. *My,* but they all get a fine fresh, natural flavor when *Borden's Evaporated Milk*

THE BORDEN COMPANY — *Elsie*

THE most famous cow in the world is Elsie. Elsie made her debut in the austere pages of leading medical journals in 1936 and was immediately such a hit that doctors everywhere prescribed proofs for their office walls!

Stu Peabody used to have a framed copy of the first Elsie ad prepared for the medical journals on his wall. It was autographed by Helen Hoagland, who wrote the copy, and Jonel Jorgelscu (if we haven't spelled this name right, we are sure Jo will forgive us), who made the layout. Miss Hoagland named her.

From the medical journals Elsie proceeded into a small space newspaper campaign, a radio try-out, and the late World's Fair on Flushing Meadows. In each instance she stopped the show.

In May 1939 she went into four colors in leading national magazines and has been speaking her piece there regularly ever since. She says things for Borden that Borden could never say as well or as effectively without her.

Elsie's brilliant saga has been written with in-telligence and gusto by Stuart Peabody, Director of Advertising for The Borden Company. It appeared first in *Advertising & Selling* in June 1942 and was straightaway printed in condensed form in the August 1942 *Reader's Digest*. Few advertising campaigns have received greater or more deserved acclaim.

The reasons behind Elsie's phenomenal fame are many including complete coordination and tying in of the main idea to all promotion — publication advertising, store material, literature, exhibits and publicity. Another reason is the adroit use of a secondary spokesman to deliver the selling story in a human, friendly, smiling way — the way you and I like to experience in our own everyday relations.

Many writers at Y&R have contributed to Borden's Elsie copy. Ed Dexter started the magazine campaign and wrote it for the first two years. Ed was followed by Draper Daniels and Thelma Walker, but Elsie's personality was so overwhelming that no matter who put the words in her month they always seem to be distinctly Elsie's.

MANY PEOPLE DEFER SHOPPING UNTIL SATUR-
DAY, AND A SINGLE SATURDAY'S TRADE WITH US
OFTEN THRIBBLES THAT OF ANY OTHER DAY.
FOR THIS REASON, AND THE CONVENIENCE OF
VISITORS FROM THE COUNTRY, WE KEEP OPEN
TO-DAY AS USUAL, EXCEPT THAT WE SHALL OMIT
THE EVENING SESSION, AND CLOSE AT 6 O'CLOCK,
OR AS EARLY IN THE AFTERNOON AS TRADE IS
OVER; THEREFORE, TRY TO COME IN THE FORE-
NOON, IF POSSIBLE.

———

Rogers, Peet & Co.,

CLOTHES, HATS, AND SHOES,
569—575 BROADWAY,
Opposite Metropolitan Hotel.

OLD AND NEW CLOTHES.

" Off with the old, on with the new."

OUR NEW FALL SUITINGS ARE READY, BUT THE
FIRST INQUIRY IS FOR LIGHT OVERCOATS. WE
BEGIN THE ASSORTMENT WITH A FLAIN SER-
VICEABLE OVERCOAT FOR $5 AND END WITH THE
FINEST SILK-LINED GARMENT FOR WHICH $30 IS
A MOST REASONABLE PRICE. BETWEEN THESE
EXTREMES THE VARIETY IS GREAT ENOUGH TO
SATISFY EVERY ONE; NAME YOUR PRICE AND
WE'LL PRODUCE THE BEST COAT THE SUM WILL
BUY ANYWHERE. YOUTHS', BOYS', AND CHIL-
DREN'S LIGHT-WEIGHT OVERCOATS AS WELL AS
MEN'S.

THIS SHOULD BE A GOOD DAY FOR BOYS'
SCHOOL SUITS; ALSO FOR HATS, SHOES, AND
FURNISHINGS, MEN'S AND BOYS'. STORE OPEN
THIS EVENING.

———

Rogers, Peet & Co.,

CLOTHES, HATS, AND SHOES,
589—575 BROADWAY,
OPPOSITE
METROPOLITAN HOTEL.

THE ROGERS PEET STORY

I AM indebted to Robert M. Ferns, Vice President of Rogers Peet Company, for this lucid description of an advertising philosophy that hasn't budged an inch in more than seventy-five years:

The philosophy behind Rogers Peet advertising is basically the same as when Mr. Rogers and Mr. Peet opened the first Rogers Peet store back in 1874. It echoes, and amplifies, the principle of the Golden Rule upon which the policies of this Company were founded . . . policies which won the public's respect and confidence from the start.

The use of our now-famous Cartoons to catch and hold attention merely antedated the popular present-day appeal of the Comics to bank presidents and office boys alike.

Our messages are definitely *"The Friendly Voice of Rogers Peet,"* chatting with our friends and customers as if across the luncheon table.

In the beginning, Frank R. Chambers, one of the early partners of Rogers and Peet, wrote much of our advertising himself. He made it his business to know *all* the facts, and *all* the reasons, why men and boys should prefer our kind of clothes. When Mr. Chambers began to turn the chore of writing our daily messages over to younger men, he used to say:

"Just tell them the facts. Say what you say with a smile, and a bit of whimsy if you like, but always remember: men don't buy newspapers to read advertisements. All you can hope for is a glance.

"Keep your messages short and to the point, and if tempted to say too much, save it for another advertisement.

"Blessed is he who finds it difficult to recall what he wrote yesterday, even though it took him all day to write it. Therein is the secret of newness and versatility in telling the same old facts over and over and over again.

"Always remember," he admonished, "easy writing makes hard reading. Hard writing, easy reading."

Since about 1907, the writer has carried on, following in the steps of Mr. Chambers and his earlier associates.

Today, we believe that Rogers Peet Company is as well known for our Cartoon Advertising as for the Quality of our Clothes.

The Spirit of Progress, however, is always with us. In more recent years, we have augmented our daily cartoon series with larger space units, using style illustrations, to direct the younger generation's attention to the Modern-Smartness of our Traditional Quality.

Our cartoon advertisements, however, continue to symbolize "Rogers Peet" and like this good humor that is part of them, we believe, will long remain as young as the spirit back of them.

THE KID IN UPPER 4

It is 3:42 a.m. on a troop train.

Men wrapped in blankets are breathing heavily.

Two in every lower berth. One in every upper.

This is no ordinary trip. It may be their last in the U.S.A. till the end of the war. Tomorrow they will be on the high seas.

One is wide awake . . . listening . . . staring into the blackness.

It is the kid in Upper 4.

☆　　　☆　　　☆

Tonight, he knows, he is leaving behind a lot of little things—and big ones.

The taste of hamburgers and pop . . . the feel of driving a roadster over a six-lane highway . . . a dog named Shucks, or Spot, or Barnacle Bill.

The pretty girl who writes so often . . . that gray - haired man, so proud and awkward at the station . . . the mother who knit the socks he'll wear soon.

Tonight he's thinking them over.

There's a lump in his throat. And maybe —a tear fills his eye. *It doesn't matter, Kid.* Nobody will see . . . it's too dark.

☆　　　☆　　　☆

A couple of thousand miles away, where he's going, they don't know him very well.

But people all over the world are waiting, praying for him to come.

And he will come, this kid in Upper 4.

With new hope, peace and freedom for a tired, bleeding world.

☆　　　☆　　　☆

Next time you are on the train, *remember the kid in Upper 4.*

If you have to stand enroute—*it is so he may have a seat.*

If there is no berth for you—*it is so that he may sleep.*

If you have to wait for a seat in the diner —*it is so he . . . and thousands like him . . . may have a meal* they won't forget in the days to come.

For to treat him as our most honored guest is the least we can do to pay a mighty debt of gratitude.

THE NEW HAVEN R.R.

★ SERVING THE GREAT INDUSTRIAL STATES OF MASSACHUSETTS, RHODE ISLAND AND CONNECTICUT ★

THE STORY BEHIND "THE KID IN UPPER 4"

By NELSON C. METCALF, JR.

EARLY in World War II advertising's big job suddenly changed from hard selling to *selling in reverse.*

Food companies, soap makers, bus companies — all advertisers had to explain shortages and bad service to the people or endure a storm of complaints.

To the New Haven and other railroads this was a particularly critical problem. Train service is a very personal thing. Railroaders were working on man-killing schedules — and still their offices were besieged by angry passengers.

So we began a campaign in which the New Haven tried to explain the problem. We ran an ad which cited impressive war freight figures. It was called *"Right of Way for Fighting Might."* But people kept right on complaining.

In *"Thunder Along the Line",* I tried to tell the story of the fighting railroaders . . . the 24 hour hell they were going through. Tell it in a way that would rouse peoples' sympathy and understanding. *"Thunder,"* got *some* editorial notice — and *some* response.

But three weeks after the ad ran, the typographer who set the ad came to Boston by train. I met him shortly after he arrived. Almost in the same breath, he praised the ad — *and complained about the train service!*

That was the beginning of *"The Kid in Upper 4."*

I vowed I would write an ad that would make *everybody* who read it *feel ashamed* to complain about train service.

I decided the reason why the other ads had failed was that the subject matter was not personal, warm and close enough to them.

I asked myself: "What's the thing nearest to people's hearts today?" When I thought I had it, I pounded away on the story. I tried to make every word of it true and warm and personal — a sort of *emotional reason-why,* with truth that could not be denied.

Every writer has had the experience of an inspiration which takes his writing far beyond the ordinary. Suddenly something inside him strikes a universal chord. He *knows* it's right. That's the way I felt.

I spent three weeks of excited writing, rewriting and cutting the ad. Miss Mildred Damon, our secretary, put the "lump" in the Kid's throat. Bill Downes, my boss, supplied the "honored guest" in the last paragraph. I must have reworked "The Kid" 25 or 30 times before I was satisfied.

Don't think for a minute that "The Kid" was immediately okayed and rushed into proof form. Or that people at once recognized its promise.

"The Kid" almost didn't run at all.

There were seasoned advertising men who said: "Slush!" "Too much copy!" "Why not a YOU headline?" "Let's sell the idea straight!"

The art work by illustrator Ed Georgi was done and redone. At last it was decided to try it once in the New York *Herald Tribune.* I waited for the result with my heart in my mouth.

Finally, three days after the ad broke, the avalanche began and I knew I'd found the answer.

* * *

The avalanche Mr. Metcalf refers to was probably the greatest slug of publicity ever accorded any advertisement, anywhere, anytime. It was read on leading radio programs by the stars themselves, made into a song, pinned to thousands of bulletin boards, reproduced free in leading magazines and newspapers, read from pulpits, published in prisons, picked up abroad — more than 8,000 letters poured into New Haven offices, and Joseph B. Eastman, Director of Defense Transportation, asked the railroad to run it all over the country.

A rival railroad — the Pennsylvania — asked for 300 posters to display in its stations. MGM made it into a movie short, and it won the highest award for outstanding copy in 1942 — and in my book, for the war.

Metcalf himself was besieged with job-offers but wisely turned them down. You don't write kids in upper 4s every day for every kind of advertising assignment. Finally, after the war had run its course, Nelson Metcalf did make an agency change. He walked into McCann-Erickson cold and asked for a job, on the basis that he wanted more variety in his work and a better chance to learn!

AUTHOR'S NOTE: When publicity for this volume first appeared, I asked for suggestions and received many. Of the lot, many were war ads — some excellent indeed. But it was my feeling that to include all the really good war ads, or even say the best ten, would not only throw the book out of balance but open the way for even sharper controversy of a work that is bound to be controversial anyway. I stuck to "The Kid in Upper 4" as the most deeply moving of the lot.

— JLW

Cooling idea

IT WAS 7 years ago that America's most famous cake of ice made its first appearance.

Here it is once again, to remind you that a Four-Roses-and-ice-and-soda is *still* the most gloriously cool and refreshing drink you could ask for on a warm midsummer afternoon!

We're certain, once you savor the matchless flavor and mellow smoothness of a Four Roses highball, you'll thank us for not letting you forget what keen enjoyment awaits you.

For today, as through the years, there's no other whiskey with quite the distinctive flavor of Four Roses.

Try a Four-Roses-and-soda now — won't you?

•   •   •

Fine Blended Whiskey — 90.5 proof. 40% straight whiskies 5 years or more old; 60% grain neutral spirits.

FOUR ROSES

AMERICA'S MOST FAMOUS BOUQUET

FOUR ROSES

Frankfort Distillers Corporation, New York

FOUR ROSES — *Jack Rosebrook's and Henry Lent's Famous Campaign*

FOUR ROSES advertising is generally considered the most distinctive liquor advertising ever devised — and certainly the most consistently excellent. Almost *any* Four Roses advertisement could have been selected for this book. I've yet to find a poor one.

Product-name has had a lot to do with the effectiveness of this advertising. It gives you a head start creatively, but such a head start might have fallen flat on its face without Jack Rosebrook's (Young & Rubicam) copy styling and Henry Lent's constant competence in carrying on. *Ideas* and simple, direct expression are the secret of this distinguished campaign . . . the format of which is never noticeably changed.

The Four Roses ad shown here is Henry Lent's — the first, I believe, of that great series.

HAND WOVEN
BY THE MOUNTAIN PEOPLE
OF NEW MEXICO

New Christmas patterns in these unique ties.

Wearers say an exceptional value.* Sold only direct

from weavers to you.

For over 200 years the Spanish people who settled New Mexico have been raising sheep and weaving wool. Their looms and their craft have been handed down from father to son. And the colorful landscape in which these people have lived and worked has made natural artists of them.

Today I take the lovely fabrics these people weave and have them made up into such stunning ties as are shown here. These are as true reproductions as the modern color camera can get, made direct from the ties.

Well dressed men from all over America now send to me for these ties, because they say they can find no others, anywhere, so beautiful, unique, and durable at so low a price.

Fascinating texture

These ties are all wool—every thread of them—except an invisible silk seam along the fringed edge. **That is what** gives them their fascinating texture. And that is what gives the man who wears them that tweedy, out-of-door look.

That, too, is why these ties wear so well. When men learn by experience that these ties are cut and sewn so as always to tie right and hang right; when they learn that they can rumple them all they please and the wrinkles come right out; and when they find they can be sent to the cleaners again and again without showing wear—then they become fans for these ties.

My Christmas Offer

Yet—by selling direct from the weavers to you—I am able to give you these fine ties for only $1.00 each, postpaid. And for Christmas (until December 15th) I will send you any six of these ties for only $5.00, postpaid.

Can you think of any other gift so unique, so acceptable, so reasonable? Why not simplify your whole Christmas shopping by making selections for every man on your list now?

And you take no risk! For I sell every tie with this unqualified GUARANTEE: If any tie doesn't please you (or the one you give it to) for any reason what-

soever, send it back for exchange or get your money back without quibble. I must have satisfied customers, who repeat, to make this business successful.

How to order

Order by the number opposite each tie. Give me one or two second choices, in case I run out of some pattern you want.

Send payment by personal check, postal money order, or bank draft. *I cannot accept stamps.*

Orders from foreign countries cannot be filled—except Canada and Mexico—and of course all U. S. possessions and territories. Foreign customers must pay customs duties.

For Air Mail Service in U. S. (sent within four hours after your order is received) add extra postage as follows: 1 tie 18¢; 2 ties 24¢; 3 ties 30¢; 4 ties 36¢; 6 ties 54¢; and 6¢ for each tie above six.

Ties packed in an attractive gift box and wrapping for 5¢ extra. Mailed direct to recipient, if you wish, with your card or your name on our own unique card, without additional cost.

Please *print* all names and addresses. I am not much of a handwriting expert.

But order quickly, please

I must tell you that these weavers, in true Spanish style, start celebrating *El Natividad* pretty early in the month. So please send your order quickly if you want to be sure of Christmas delivery. I try to fill every order the day it is received, and usually do; but you know what the postal people are up against. For eastern states, in particular, let me have your order not later than Dec. 12th.

And remember: Every order filled with my GUARANTEE that if any tie I send you doesn't please you, for any reason whatsoever, return it for exchange or get your money back without quibble. Could I speak fairer than that?

SPECIAL NOTE: Tie No. 1006, in addition to maroon, can also be had in plain brown, rust, forest green, pearl grey, turquoise blue, light tan, black, blue-green, and light blue. Use this number and add the color you want.

WEBB YOUNG, Trader
203 Canyon Road, Santa Fe, New Mexico

* *For instance, George W. Engelmann, well known Chicago business man, writes: "Enclosed is my order for some of your ties. I would like to take this opportunity to tell you how well I like your ties. When I wear them they never fail to attract favorable comment. They are also the most durable ties and the best value I have ever seen."*

WEBB YOUNG — *"Hand Woven By The Mountain People Of New Mexico"*

THIS advertisement, written by James W. Young, sold more than 26,000 neckties straight from *one* November 1940 *Life* page.

It got trader Webb Young's necktie business off to a flying start.

*N. B. Watch for JWY's ads late every summer and through the fall on *Old Jim Young's Mountain Grown Apples* — *Every Bite crackles and the juice runs down your lips . . .*

How to Carry Fire in Paper

An EDITOR'S *Answer* *to the* ADVERTISING RIDDLE

Like the man who invented the Chinese lantern, the advertiser faces, day after day, the riddle, "How to carry fire in paper?"

How to so use words that in cold type they will set a flame to men's imaginations, and fill them with such warm desires as lead them on to action.

Here on FARM & FIRESIDE we have an editor who seems to have this knack.

With him, to entertain, to instruct, is not enough. He, too, is a salesman-in-print, and in his editing is that "itch for orders" which is always urging, persuading, his reader to translate ideas into action.

His simple methods

How he does it you may readily see in the current issue of FARM & FIRESIDE.

He uses, first, the stirring power of Example instead of Precept. FARM & FIRESIDE articles tell not what *ought to be* done but what *is being* done by other successful farmers.

He gets the warmth of man to man with pictures of his writers — homely pictures, often — and with many "I's" and "You's."

He sees the human side of every farming problem, and knows that optimism, encouragement and good humor are great fertilisers of dry facts.

He knows the quickening power that lies in headlines built of such words as How—Won—Success—Profits—Happiness.

His dynamic personality

So far his methods are communicable, imitable.

What cannot be so well described is the dynamic spirit of the man—his power to make every page fill you with a noble discontent, to warm again the ashes of forgotten good intentions, to fire you with new impulses toward what you, your home, your family may become.

A power to carry fire in paper that you will *feel*, as increasing evidence shows it is being felt in the 800,000 homes to which FARM & FIRESIDE is selling new ideas every month.

The Crowell Publishing Co.

381 Fourth Avenue, New York City

Farm & Fireside   Woman's Home Companion
    The American Magazine   Collier's, The National Weekly
       The Mentor

FARM & FIRESIDE

The National Farm Magazine

FARM & FIRESIDE — *"How To Carry Fire In A Paper Bag"*

I'M including this third selection from James W. Young's work, not alone because I consider it a well *thought-out* advertisement and a fine example of top-grade copywriting, but also because it contains a superb headline — of which there are all too few. And in those days: 1921 — hardly any.

Mr. Young wrote another advertisement for

Colliers about that time, and it, too, was off to a high-readership start with *Why Every Man Hopes His First Child Will Be A Boy.*

A good headline is the most important part of *most* advertisements. There's little reason for the reader to go on if the headline (and first paragraph) fail to excite his interest.

To *Peggy* - for marrying me in the first place...

for bringing up our children—while I mostly sat back and gave advice.

for the 2,008 pairs of socks you've darned.

for finding my umbrella and my rubbers Heaven knows how often!

for tying innumerable dress ties.

for being the family chauffeur, years on end.

for never getting sore at my always getting sore at your bridge playing.

for planning a thousand meals a year—and having them taken for granted.

for a constant tenderness I rarely notice but am sure I couldn't live without.

for wanting a *good* watch ever so long . . . and letting your slow-moving husband think he'd hit on it all by himself.

for just being you . . . *Darling, here's your Hamilton with all my love!*

Jim

HAMILTON WATCH — *"To Peggy — For Marrying Me, In The First Place"*

THIS is one my all-time favorites. Both the ad and the story behind it which I shall quote from a letter written by its author, Carl Spier, copy director of Batten, Barton, Durstine & Osborn —

"It had been our custom for years to do an emotional type advertisement for Hamilton Watch at Christmas time.

"Several years ago I was sitting at my desk trying to get some ideas for that year's Christmas attack. I think I must have tried about 40 or 50 approaches. Literally days went by.

"It is my belief that the best advertising of this nature sounds as though one person were talking to another and it has been my habit to often address a piece of copy to some specific individual. After days of struggling this basic truth reoccurred to me. If I were writing a letter to my wife what would I say?

"The first line that popped into my head was, *'To Peggy — For Marrying Me in the First Place...'* I think from then on I wrote the ad in seven minutes. If it's good it's because it was a searching of my own heart.

"In showing it to Robley Feland he added one thought that I think is the best in it. 'For a constant tenderness I rarely notice but am sure I couldn't live without.'

"When this ad first appeared something hap-

pened that is unique in my experience. At least 60 or 70 people took the time to sit down and write the Hamilton Watch Company thanking them for having published the ad. Again and again some man or woman in the hinterlands would say, 'You have put into words what I have long thought but have never been able to say.' Or someone else would write, 'I am copying it word for word to include with my Christmas present to my wife, changing only some petty details as applied to our lives.'

"I apologize for any element of vaingloriousness that runs through this note but it is impossible to give you what you ask without seeming to boast."

If there's any "vaingloriousness" or "boasting" in that description of the writing of a truly great advertisement, I fail to detect it.

The advertisement is repeated, I believe, each Christmas season. Only the art and the watches are changed; the copy you couldn't change. What in it could be said any better?

Please note that the Hamilton name appears only once in the copy, yet in the now *hundreds* of letters that the Hamilton Company has received, letter after letter ends with "My next watch will be a Hamilton."

You don't have to be knocked in the head to realize that this is one of the truly great selling advertisements ever written for watches.

A Hog Can Cross the Country Without Changing Trains—But YOU Can't!

The Chesapeake & Ohio Railway and the Nickel Plate Road are again proposing to give human beings a break!

It's hard to believe, but it's true.

If you want to ship a hog from coast to coast, he can make the entire trip without changing cars. You can't. It is impossible for you to pass through Chicago, St. Louis, or New Orleans without breaking your trip!

There is an invisible barrier down the middle of the United States which you cannot cross without inconvenience, lost time, and trouble.

560,000 Victims in 1945!

If you want to board a sleeper on one coast and ride through to the other, you must make double Pullman reservations, pack and transfer your baggage, often change stations, and wait around for connections.

It's the same sad story if you make a relatively short trip. You can't cross that mysterious line! To go from Fort Wayne to Milwaukee or from Cleveland to Des Moines, you must also stop and change trains.

Last year alone, more than 560,000 people were forced to make annoying, time-wasting stopovers at the phantom Chinese wall which splits America in half!

End the Secrecy!

Why should travel be less convenient for people than it is for pigs? Why should Americans be denied the benefits of through train service? No one has yet been able to explain it.

Canada has this service . . . with a choice of two routes. Canada isn't split down the middle. Why should we be? No reasonable answer has yet been given. Passengers still have to stop off at Chicago, St. Louis, and New Orleans—although they can ride right through other important rail centers.

It's time to pry the lid off this mystery. It's time for action to end this inconvenience to the travelling public . . . NOW!

Many railroads could cooperate to provide this needed through service. To date, the Chesapeake & Ohio and the Nickel Plate ALONE have made a public offer to do so.

How about it!

Once more we would like to go on record with this specific proposal:

The Chesapeake & Ohio, whose western passenger terminus is Cincinnati, stands ready now to join with any combination of other railroads to set up connecting transcontinental and intermediate service through Chicago and St. Louis, on practical schedules and routes.

The Nickel Plate Road, which runs to Chicago and St. Louis, also stands ready now to join with any combination of roads to set up the same kind of connecting service through these two cities.

Through railroad service can't be blocked forever. The public wants it. It's bound to come. Again, we invite the support of the public, of railroad people and railroad investors—for this vitally needed improvement in rail transportation!

Chesapeake & Ohio Railway · Nickel Plate Road

Terminal Tower, Cleveland 1, Ohio

C & O — *"A Hog Can Cross The Country Without Changing Trains — But You Can't"*

I AM indebted to Draper Daniels, Vice President in Charge of Creative Services, Leo Burnett Company, for the following on-the-spot report of how this ad got its start in life. And Draper can tell it better than anyone else I know —

"The late Robert R. Young, Chairman of the Board of Chesapeake & Ohio and later of the New York Central Railroad, was the best possible client for any advertising man who loved a two-fisted brawl and plenty of fancy work in the clinches. Back in 1945 Mr. Young set out to crusade for the improvement of the American railroad system.

"He seized upon the lack of railroad service through Chicago and St. Louis as a likely starting point. On August 27, 1945, Norman Stabler in a front page article in the *Herald Tribune* quoted this: There is no reason why transcontinental passengers should be shifted from car to car in midwestern cities when a carload of pigs receives every consideration going from east to west.' The many comments Mr. Young received as a result of that quotation led him to believe that he had hold of a public relations natural, and he began to make frequent use of it in speeches.

"James Eagan, Vice President and Copy Chief of Kenyon & Eckhardt who was personally handling the C&O campaign, received a transcript of one of these speeches in which Mr. Young had said: 'Hell, even a hog can cross the country without changing trains.' When he came to this quotation, Mr. Eagan got an idea for a headline which he carefully jotted down in the margin in the speech manuscript which was: 'A hog can cross the country without changing trains — but you can't!' One Friday morning he gave the manuscript of the speech and two proofs of previous C&O ads to a copy supervisor named Draper Daniels, who had just reported for work that

morning. 'Sorry to put you to work on your first day,' he said apologetically, 'but we need another ad for this series in a hurry. Like tonight.' By the middle of the afternoon he had his ad, which, after some discussion, he cleared with a few word changes. Copy was then submitted to Edwin Cox, Creative Director, who read it three times, laid down his blue pencil and said, 'Set it in type and make a layout.' It was mailed to Mr. Young about 7:00 that night with two other ads which had previously been prepared for a continuation of the C&O series. With it went a letter from Cox which said, 'This is one of the best headlines I have seen in 30 years in this business. If you never run another advertisement run this one.'

"Mr. Young was on the long distance phone the next morning. The hog ad was approved without change. From that day to this no one knows what happened to the other two ads.

"The effect of the advertisement upon consumers may have been questionable, but it hit railroad executives and newspaper men with staggering impact.

"Two or three weeks before it ran, the major railroads serving transcontinental travelers in and out of Chicago had publicly announced that through service was impractical. Before the hog ad was through running on a staggered schedule in major cities and in *Time* Magazine they reversed this position and announced that through service would be quickly instituted. The hog ad had inspired so much editorial support in the press and on the air and from a mailing of a proof to prominent businessmen that the pressure on the railroad executives was irresistible.

"Later on Mr. Young used to say that he had written the ad himself. He didn't. But he did have the big idea that inspired it and the courage to run it."

I'll never forget the first time he came into our shop about a year ago. He was a little man in a green elevator operator's uniform, oldish and very shy. We were quite busy that day, but he awaited his turn patiently and then asked to see some "fine sweaters." Now "fine sweaters" in this shop means twenty or thirty dollars, so I showed him some for ten, thinking that by so doing I could save him some embarrassment and still meet his requirements. He said they were "nice," but would I please show him our "best" ones. So I did, some Scotch cashmeres, in the meantime making a mental note never again to judge a man by his jacket. He selected one at $27.50 and then asked if I would "lay it aside" and accept "$2 weekly" until it was paid for. I said I would and he came in every Saturday for a month and lived up to his agreement. On his fourth payment he asked to see some more "fine sweaters," selected one at $25, and then asked if I'd lay this aside, too. He wanted still to pay $2 a week (not $4) and pick up both sweaters when the whole amount, $52.50, had been paid. I consented only after I had tried to dissuade him from spending so much money. I didn't know what his income was, but I suspected $52.50 was most of two weeks' wages. Believe it or not, after about six more payments he propositioned me again. It seems we had *four* English alpaca sweaters in our State Street window and would I please lay these aside, too! Well, this was obviously ridiculous. While we had nothing to lose (*all* his selections would remain in our hands until *all* were paid for, and this by his request), I felt I had to do something if my unusual client wasn't to go into hock for life. But it wasn't easy. This gentleman was obviously the sensitive type. I told him, and as gently as I could, that our arrangement was a bit top heavy, that there was no need to buy so many sweaters because the foreign markets were opening up again, that even prices might soon come down, and finally, I suggested something that was really none of my business—that he was spending too great a part of his income for things he could do without. He was very courteous. He listened intently

to everything I said but could he still have the sweaters? He said he didn't drink or smoke, that $2 a week was no hardship, and that if I was worried he could pay $2.75 or $3 weekly! I got nowhere. I asked him then if he would at least take out a couple of sweaters and enjoy wearing them while he was paying me. He said, "No, thanks," that he expected to pay his total bill by the following August, at which time he'd take them out in time for his two-weeks' vacation in Nova Scotia, his childhood home. Right after he left, Tim came up and informed me that, contrary to my belief, Mr. "C" now had *thirteen* sweaters in the "hold" department instead of the seven I had believed. It seems our little friend had bought half a dozen more in the weeks past while making his Saturday payments to other clerks!

So I called my boys together. What to do without offending our passionate friend. It was finally agreed I should go to his place of employment, and, as gently as possible, call the deal off and refund his payments or, if that proved too difficult, settle for the first three sweaters that were now paid for in full. Well, partly because I was very busy, but chiefly because I dreaded the job, I did nothing for a few weeks more. Finally, one Saturday afternoon, I asked my bookkeeper to give me Mr. "C's" account. It was—13 sweaters totalling $284, 39 payments totalling $78. Roxy also told me something that wouldn't be significant ordinarily but which was in this instance—no payments had been made these past four weeks. I walked up to the building where our friend worked, and, not seeing him about, asked the starter where I could find him. Possibly you have guessed the rest. Mr. "C" had died suddenly just four weeks before and was there anything he could do? No, there wasn't. I trudged back to the store and told the boys. Everybody felt low. About the only consolation we could find in the whole affair was my failure to deliver the ultimatum we had planned.

I shall be grateful for that failure as long as I live.

P. S.—What happened to the $78? Mr. "C's" heirs have been reimbursed in full.

ZAREH

IN the November 1947 issue of *Fortune* Magazine, in the *Shorts and Faces* Department, a certain name caught my eye — Zareh. A name like that would be apt to catch anybody's eye — especially anybody's eye in Boston. I've had permission from *Fortune* to reprint its neat profile about this advertising man who writes the kind of copy that gets itself read right down to the last letter. The example I've used, Zareh considers his best.

Zareh Garabed Thomajan

For about five years readers of Boston newspapers have been amused, intrigued, shocked, and even emotionally upset over a whimsical, brightly irreverent column, which, oddly enough, is an advertisement. The author, who calls himself "The Thief of State Street," is the proprietor of Zareh, Inc., a high-priced haberdashery in downtown Boston. He is a slim, dark-eyed, and disarmingly candid Armenian, Zareh Thomajan, who happened on a means to quadruple his yearly sales from $60,000 to $250,000 in five years and of earning considerable fame in advertising circles. His advertising cost: $3,500 a year.

After running the Harvardashery in Cambridge for eight years, Zareh opened his shop on State Street (Boston's Wall Street) "for the gentle in spirit and the rich in pocketbook." There he tried formal advertising, composing pontifical statements like "ready to don." There was no response at all, and he had decided to give up advertising for good when his cousin, Arlene Francis of stage and screen, suggested that he write his ads in the intimate vein in which he regularly wrote to her. So one noon hour he stopped over at Patten's restaurant, drank three martinis, and scribbled off an ad on the back of a doily. It simply told — in what Zareh calls his "loose" style — the story of his first customer, Joseph Morrill, a Boston lawyer and trustee, who entered the store back in 1934, bought three shirts at $7.50 each and three $3.50 ties, left rather abstractedly, then rushed back to shake Zareh's hand and say, "I like your nerve!" The day after this was printed, Zareh received twelve responses, which was as much a surprise to him as the column was to its readers.

Throughout most of his writing Zareh cleverly promotes quality against junk, small shops against larger competition, and frankly warns bargain hunters to keep away. One of his favorite topics is the sartorial conservatism of Bostonians. "In the field of men's wear," he wrote, "our fair city is the dumping ground for most of the merchandising mistakes of America." He also tells of the doings in his shop. He refers to his four clerks by their first names — Bob, Ara, etc., "who are too refined either to refute or rebuke you" — and discourses on such subjects as shoplifting, "which, like pregnancy, is something that isn't discussed in public too often"; the time he took Artie Shaw and a friend (they were both unshaven) for shoplifters; and the strangulation of mankind by undersized shirt collars. When his female bookkeeper left his employ, he advised that though the job didn't pay terribly well, two of his male employees were single, three were married "but trying to improve themselves." All his clerks were Armenians until he happened to hire an Irishman. This was a startling event, but "the place was beginning to look too much like a branch of Near East Relief. This Chetnik is momentarily beyond the need of alms."

Zareh started a Jack Benny-Fred Allen kind of feud with Neal O'Hara, columnist for the Boston *Traveler,* when O'Hara wrote a piece plugging Filene's basement. Zareh retorted: "I read that ad you wrote for Filene's basement last week and if you want my opinion it was terrible . . . Possibly you have never heard of the . . . antitrust laws that protect us small businessmen from the fat cigar fraternity . . . If you must direct us, must it be to a basement . . . are we moles?"

Zareh's column is probably the most widely read advertising copy in Boston and environs. At State Street he receives a steady stream of visitors who, if they do not come to buy, come to seek his advice in advertising their own products. A few of his fan letters are "scurrilous" like the one he got recently that began, "Zareh, you cur." Magazines and trade journals have run articles on his copy. The *New Yorker* reprinted one of his ads featuring a "positively insulting" scarlet corduroy loafer scat. Little, Brown & Co., publishers, asked him to write a book, and finally, he has been propelled into after-dinner speaking. He must have been the only haberdasher ever to address a group of 1,000 genuine Boston notables.

Reprinted from the November 1947 issue of FORTUNE Magazine by special permission of the Editors; Copyright TIME Inc.

Tonight, *at Midnight...*

we hand over our Tennessee Electric Properties *and a $2,800,000 Tax Problem*

AT MIDNIGHT, TONIGHT, The Commonwealth & Southern Corporation turns over to various public officials all of its electric properties in the State of Tennessee.

We have always believed, and still believe, that the interests of the public are better served by privately operated utilities than by publicly operated plants. Take our Tennessee properties for example:

The State of Tennessee and most of the communities we have been serving have depended, in no small part, upon the taxes they have collected from us to pay the cost of their governmental activities, including school, water, fire, health and other services.

Our Tennessee properties paid into local and state treasuries a total of $2,225,000 from electric revenues, for the 12 months ended June 30, 1939; with federal taxes, the total for this period is about $2,800,000. That is more than 20 cents out of every dollar received for electric service in Tennessee ... it amounts to over $7,670 in taxes for every day of the year.

All of our facilities in Tennessee have been built with the money of many private investors. The communities never had to increase their debts to build plants and distributing systems; they never had to pay out interest on bonds issued for electric service. The savings of thousands of citizens were brought, and would continue to have been brought, into this territory to help produce more industry, more local wealth and more steady jobs.

Our Tennessee operation has long given its customers one of the lowest average residential electric rates in the country ... as have our other operations in the North and in the South. Our rate has been reduced steadily to where, at the present time, it is much below the national average.

We have continually helped households to own modern labor-saving and convenience appliances, which have already placed the standard of leisure and living in our Tennessee territory considerably above the average in the country.

As result of our progressive merchandising and low electric rates, the average home in our Tennessee territory used far more electricity last year than was used by the average home in the entire United States.

. . . .

We have had to sell our electric properties and turn over a splendid organization to the Tennessee Valley Authority and other governmental agencies because we could not stay in business and compete with virtually tax-free and heavily subsidized plants.

Incidentally, our taxes have been multiplying and mounting for years. They are an ever increasing problem ... a veritable "headache", which other taxpayers can well appreciate. To be rid of any tax worries is, of course, always a relief.

We now turn over to government agencies, for about four-fifths of its real value, one of the finest public utility services in this or any other country ... one representing private investments of about a hundred million dollars.

Almost all the money we are receiving from this sale will be used to pay back the owners of the outstanding bonds and preferred stocks of The Tennessee Electric Power Company, at 100 cents on the dollar. A substantial percentage of these investors live in Tennessee. The common shareholders, principally The Commonwealth & Southern Corporation, are taking all of the loss.

To buy our properties, the municipalities are selling bonds largely tax-free and TVA is selling Government obligations which, in addition, will be a lien upon the incomes of all of us. These tax-free municipal and federal securities will be owned largely outside Tennessee. As a result, much income which citizens of Tennessee received from our Company will no longer benefit this community.

The incomes from all Tennessee Electric Power securities have, of course, been subject to taxation and have long helped to carry the costs of government. Whenever government takes over a private business, not only does the public lose the benefit of taxes paid directly by the business but also the substantial taxes paid by the owners of its securities.

. . . .

We sincerely hope that our former customers in this territory will continue to enjoy one of the best electrical services in the country.

To numerous friends and associates in Tennessee, many of whom have been most helpful and considerate, we are deeply indebted and very grateful. We wish them every success. Our hope is they will never be required to defend a business of their own against government subsidized competition.

Wendell L. Willkie, PRESIDENT

The Commonwealth & Southern System now comprises the following operations:	
	*Electric Customers**
Michigan	440,314
Illinois	69,538
Indiana	38,229
Ohio	197,749
Pennsylvania	49,697
Alabama	143,363
Georgia	211,461
Florida	17,818
Mississippi	44,012
South Carolina	29,411
Total	1,241,592

*On July 1, 1939.

The Commonwealth & Southern Corporation

This system's average residential electric rate .. in the North and the South : : now is 3.09 cents a kilowatt hour—26% *below the national average*
The average home served : . North and South .. now uses 1,200 kilowatt hours of electricity a year—37% *more than the national average*

COMMONWEALTH & SOUTHERN — *"Tonight At Midnight"*

THERE was a man a great many admired, and his name was Wendell L. Willkie. He came out of nowhere, it seemed, into the national spotlight and perhaps would have become President of the United States if he hadn't run into "The Champ" when he did . . .

So began my comment in this space when the first edition of *The 100 Greatest Advertisements* was published. I didn't realize how inadequate it went on to be, because behind this famous Commonwealth & Southern advertisement, is a very real story as to how many great ads are written . . .

I received two very fine letters — one from Mr. Silliman Evans, President and Publisher of Tennessean Newspapers, Inc., and one from Mr. John T. Harman, Jr., of J. Walter Thompson Company, New York. I think you will enjoy the quotes —

From Mr. Silliman Evans: "You did a grand job. You cost me a lot of money. I was so impressed with your collection of the '100 Greatest Advertisements' that I got on a special order, 200 of them and presented a copy to outstanding advertising managers in the city of Nashville and to various members of the staffs of our national representatives and to each and every member of the advertising department of *The Nashville Tennessean,* which comprises about sixty men. You would be flattered with the appreciation they have shown for my presentment to them of this fine book.

"May I say for your files of memorabilia that I am the cause of the Wendell Willkie ad.

"*The Nashville Tennessean* led the campaign in Tennessee for the TVA and the acquisition of the properties of Commonwealth and Southern, under the compulsion of the SEC. During that time and prior, Wendell Willkie and I knew one another quite well.

"I suppose you are perhaps what we Southerners call a "durn" Republican and were for Hoover once and against him last. Willkie was quite a remarkable fellow, however, despite his personal views. The TVA officials never intended to expropriate the assets of C & S on an unfair basis..

"After the deal had been consummated and the date set for the formal delivery of the assets of the Tennessee subsidiary of C & S in the TVA area, I had the idea that Willkie would like to make a graceful exit from the TVA scene. I wrote personally an ad which I thought was very good. I called Willkie and asked him to meet me at my hotel uptown in New York if he would do so, and if not, I would go down and see him. He said he would drop by the Ritz and see me.

"I sold him on the idea and showed him the copy. He hung his big right leg over the side of the chair:

"'Silliman,' he said, 'I am my own favorite author. You sold me the idea and I will write this ad the way I like it.'

"He re-wrote many paragraphs of it, using some I had written, but in the main it was his advertisement."

From Mr. Harman: "When Wendell Willkie was president of Commonwealth & Southern I was the assigned account representative (for J. Walter Thompson Company) at the time the Government was taking over his Tennessee electric properties. Willkie was of course a great mixer; it mattered not to him whether one was foe or friend, he enjoyed talking with everyone. Thus he had 'had a cocktail', as he told me, with the publisher of the *Nashville Tennessean* and this publisher (who had advocated Government ownership of Willkie's Tennesse properties) had suggested to Willkie that he 'take a page advertisment in the *Tennessean* and tell us good-by' when the deal was consummated. The publisher went on to say, 'Of course, I suppose, you wouldn't do that in view of the *Nashville Tennessean's* attitude.' Willkie replied, 'Sure I will. When we pull out down here, I'll take a full page in your paper and tell you good-by.' Then, Willkie apparently forgot all about it.

"The closing date was quite near when he remembered this promise. For, one day he put in a hurried call for me and told me the story. He said, I've got to make good that promise. Whip something up! I don't much care what . . . just say good-by to them and let it go at that!' I said, fine . . . will do . . .

"So I wrote a headline . . . *only a headline* . . . and got an art director to make a layout. The headline was, Tonight, at Midnight . . . we hand over our Tennessee Electric Properties *and a blank dollar tax problem.*'

"When Willkie saw it his eyes sparkled and he said, 'I think we've got something. Let's write the copy.' I then outlined to him my rough ideas all of which he accepted. He particularly wanted to make reference to 'the money of private investors' and the 'turnover . . . for about four-fifths of its real value.' Also, the sign-off, 'Our hope is they will never be required to defend a business of their own against Government subsidized competition,' are Willkie's words in their entirety.

"The final proofs looked pretty good to Willkie but he was not at all sure he had a 'good ad', he said. He put copies in his pocket and apparently showed them to some of his friends overnight who gave him varying opinions. However, in the end, he approved it and then I suggested we might publish it outside of Tennessee. He thought this was a good idea so a list of some thirty to forty dailies, coast to coast, was finally okayed. It was decided to publish in Tennessee on the day before the closing and elsewhere on the day of the closing. The little parenthetical note at the top did not appear in Tennessee papers . . .

"Unquestionably, Willkie's campaign for the Republican nomination dates from the appearance of this ad but the 'merchandising' of it was a big factor. I remember, after his nomination, one of the newsreels flashed the headline of the ad and gave it credit for starting the Willkie boom . . ."

So there you have the story from two authentic sources regarding what was perhaps the first advertisement in history to launch a major presidential candidate.

What everybody ought to know . . .

About This Stock And Bond Business

Some plain talk about a simple business that often sounds complicated.

WHY WE ARE PUBLISHING THIS INFORMATION

A little while ago we were talking with the editor of a big national magazine, a well-informed man. He said that he had never done business with a broker because he was afraid he wouldn't understand the "lingo they talk."

Since we are brokers, you can imagine that was something of a shock . . . made us think.

The financial business *does* use a lot of specialized words, but there really isn't anything complicated or mysterious about what those words *mean*. Because we've used them so long and so frequently, we've just assumed that everybody understood them.

That has been our mistake. And a big mistake. For if people don't understand what stocks and bonds are, they aren't likely to invest their money in them.

"So what?" you ask. Well, here's "what".

If people do not invest their funds in securities, American business and American government will not have the capital they need for growth — for new products, new plants, new jobs. That capital can come from just one place: People. Not just a few people with great fortunes — there aren't many of them any more—but from millions of people.

Or look at it from the social point of view. People who don't understand investments are easy prey for a wide variety of "get-rich-quick" artists.

Or look at it from the purely personal point of view. A lot of people might like to invest their surplus savings where they could earn a fair return on them. But if they are unfamiliar with securities, they aren't likely to invest their money in them.

For all these reasons, it is important that people should know as much as they can about this stock and bond business.

But where do you start?

Well, it would seem that a good place to start would be with the "lingo" that our friend the editor complained about. And we might as well go back to the most common words in the business. You may find a lot of this explanation pretty elementary. But the next fellow may not be wholly clear about the exact difference between a stock and a bond. So we'll start right there, in the belief that you'll be obliging enough to skip what you already know.

MERRILL LYNCH,
PIERCE, FENNER & BEANE

What Are Stocks?

The stock of a company represents the ownership of that company. If you own a share of stock in a company — let's call it the Typical Manufacturing Company — you own a piece of that company — a part of its plant, its production, a part of everything in that company. If the Typical Company has 1,000 shares of stock and you own 10 shares, you own one hundredth of the company, or 1% of it.

Some companies have only a few shares of stock and a few owners, while others — the big corporations like U. S. Steel and General Motors — have millions of shares of stock and hundreds of thousands of stockholders or owners.

Why Should Anybody Buy Stocks?

For the same reason that he might go into any other business for himself. To make money.

If you own 1% of the Typical Company, you own 1% of whatever it earns. Normally, some of those earnings or profits will be paid out to you and the other stockholders as dividends — so much on each share. The rest of the earnings will be put back into the business to do more work, make more earnings, more dividends.

How Big Are Dividends?

That depends on the company and how much it earns. Some companies pay out a substantial portion of their earnings as dividends. Other companies, particularly those that are expanding, may plow a greater proportion of earnings back into the business. Some companies pay no dividends. Of all the companies whose stocks are bought and sold on the New York Stock Exchange, about 90% are paying dividends. (That was the record last year.) The average dividend paid by these companies is a little better than 5% of what the stocks are selling at. Thus, if you bought one share of stock in each you could figure on making 5% on your money in a year. Some pay more. Some pay less.

Most companies try to pay dividends regularly. (The Pennsylvania Railroad has paid a dividend every year for more than a century.)

A company's board of directors decides what dividends will be paid and when. These directors are your representatives. You and the other stockholders elect them, each for a definite term. Ordinarily, you get one vote for every share of stock you own. The directors are the real heads of a company. The president and other officers are responsible to the directors for their management of the company.

What Do Stocks Cost?

The price of a stock, like the price of food or clothing, depends on how much other buyers are willing to pay for it, how cheaply those who own it are willing to sell. When a company first offers or "floats" its stock so that it can raise the money it needs to begin business, a specific price is set on that stock. But once the stock is traded in the market, its price is *not fixed or pegged by anybody or any agency*. It is determined by free and open bidding — by supply and demand.

That's why stock prices rise and fall constantly — sometimes rapidly. Some people who buy Typical Company stock do so not because they want to get the dividends that are paid on it but because they think the price of Typical stock will rise and that they will be able to sell it later at a profit. This is risky business for anyone who cannot afford to lose money, because the price of Typical stock may drop. Nobody ever knows for sure what's going to happen to the price of any stock.

What Are Preferred Stocks?

In addition to its common stock, some companies also have preferred stock, usually offered at $100 a share. This stock generally bears a set dividend rate, say of $4. Holders of preferred stock get those dividends before common stockholders get anything — that's one reason why it is called "preferred"—but if the company has a good year, preferred stockholders don't, as a rule, get anything more than the specified $4 dividend per share.

The stock is also called "preferred" because if the company is liquidated, holders of such stock get a first claim on whatever assets may be left after creditors' claims are satisfied. (Assets are property, such as plants or goods, that can be converted into money.)

Although preferred stocks differ widely in the *exact* terms of the preferred treatment which they provide owners, they always offer *some* preferences. Hence, the prices of preferred stock usually do not fluctuate as much as the prices of common stock over a given period.

Although preferred stockholders, like common stockholders, are part owners of the company, they often have no voice in management, no vote in electing directors.

What Are Bonds?

Bonds are a kind of promissory note. People who buy a company's bonds lend their money to that company, and the company agrees to pay them back at a set date, known as the maturity date. For the use of the money, the company generally agrees to pay a set rate of interest of, say, 3% per year. Bonds are usually backed by a mortgage on the company's property or by the general credit of the company.

Unlike stockholders, bondholders are *not* part owners of the company. They are *creditors* of the company.

Of course, as creditors their claims must be satisfied if the company goes broke, before stockholders — the owners — can divide so much as a dime's worth of the company's assets — if any.

Because bonds have this prior claim, they are regarded as the safest kind of security. That's why they appeal to conservative investors—widows, retired people, anyone who is willing to take a smaller return on his money, provided it's a surer one.

In times of economic uncertainty, bonds are always comparatively more attractive than stocks. Their prices do not fluctuate as much as stock prices, because they bear a fixed rate of interest and the element of risk is not as immediate a factor in the price.

Of course, the price of any bond is apt to be depressed, especially if there is any suspicion that the company is having a hard time.

In addition to corporate bonds, there are state, city, and government bonds. On state and city bonds, the revenue from taxes is frequently pledged as security for repayment. Back of U. S. Government bonds — the highest-grade investment there is — lies the integrity of the nation. Just that and nothing more, because nothing else is needed and nothing could add greater security. The integrity of the country is the standard of investment values.

State and city bonds are attractive to many investors, because the federal government does not tax the income from these bonds, as it does the income from company stocks and bonds or most U. S. Government bonds.

Bonds are usually issued in $1,000 units (sometimes $500), but as a matter of tradition they are usually quoted as though the price were a percentage of the face value. Thus, if a corporate bond is said to sell at 98½, it actually sells at $985.

Government bonds are quoted in 1/32nds. Thus a quote of 100.16 means 100 16/32 or in actual dollars, $1,005.

What Are Common Stocks Worth?

That depends on what people are willing to pay for them. And what they are willing to pay for a particular stock is largely determined by one factor — earnings. That includes what the company *has* earned (its past record), what it *is* earning (its present state of health), and what it *might* earn (its prospects for the future).

So you see it's not just a matter of figures. It's a matter of facts . . . knowledge . . . judgment. How aggressive is the company? How good is its management? How popular are its products? What part of earnings will have to be paid out as preferred stock dividends or bond interest? After all, these must be paid first, and what is available for common stockholders depends on how much is left.

Then you have to look outside the company and consider the whole industry in which it operates. Is its future bright? (The buggy industry once offered many good investments.) And what about competitors? Are they in better shape than your company? Might they take the market away from Typical Manufacturing?

Finally, you have to consider general business factors. For instance, will rising costs of labor and raw materials pinch your company?

These are just some of the questions to which the intelligent investor wants answers so that he can form a reliable opinion of what his stock is likely to be worth — *tomorrow*.

Investment values constantly change. That's why this firm has always urged stockholders to "Investigate — then Invest", and to keep on investigating afterwards.

Why Do Stock Prices Change?

At any given time, you may not agree with the price at which a particular stock is selling. You may think it is too high or too low.

There is a simple reason for that: What a stock is "worth" is a matter of personal opinion. But what it actually sells at is the sum total of a lot of individual judgments about it. The *price* of a security is nothing more than the collective expression of all the opinions of all the people who are buying or selling it.

If a number of people conclude at about the same time that a particular stock is overpriced, they may decide to sell it, and the price will probably fall. Or they may think it is selling at bargain prices and decide to buy it. Their combined orders may cause the price to rise.

That's why stock prices sometimes fluctuate sharply. Instead of changing by an eighth or a quarter of a point — which means an eighth or a quarter of a dollar — the price may change by several dollars, either up or down, in a short time.

Whenever there is a sharp price movement in either direction, it may pick up momentum and continue for a little while. That's because such a price movement is likely to attract other buyers or sellers.

For instance, if the price of Typical Manufacturing were suddenly to advance from $25 to $27 a share, others might notice the advance and quickly conclude that it was a good buy. So they might decide to buy it too, and that would lift the price still higher, perhaps to $28 or $29. At that point, some of those who originally bought Typical stock at, say, $25 might decide to take their profit of $3 or $4 a share and sell out. Then the price might start down again.

What Are Bull and Bear Markets?

Sometimes a great many people will decide more or less at the same time, perhaps just on the basis of the general business outlook, that it is a good idea to buy stocks—all kinds of stocks. Such general buying action raises the average price of all stocks. If the price rise is big enough and lasts long enough, we have what is called a bull market.

A bear market is just the opposite. The average price of all stocks drops because of widespread selling. To be bullish or bearish simply means to believe that stocks are going up or down.

Incidentally, it is a simple business to keep track of whether the market as a whole is moving up or down, because almost every major newspaper in the country publishes daily the average price of some group of key stocks and reports whether that average is moving up or down. The Dow Jones Averages are the best known of these indexes.

When Should You Buy or Sell Stocks?

Deciding when to buy or sell is often just as important as deciding what to buy or sell. This matter of timing is particularly important to the speculator.

But first, what is a speculator? And what useful purpose does he serve?

A speculator is a man who buys securities, expecting the price to rise so that he will make a profit on his purchase, usually in a short period of time. Or he may sell securities expecting the price to drop. The important point is that he doesn't buy securities as investments — for the sake of the dividends that they pay.

The speculator performs a valuable service in the stock market because he is willing to take risks — and risk, the risk of a sudden price change, is an inevitable part of any free market, whether it be a market for securities or foodstuffs or any other commodity.

Suppose you own stock in Typical Manufacturing, and suppose you want to sell that stock because you think the earnings outlook is bad. You might not be able to sell at anything like a fair price if it were not for a speculator and his willingness to assume the risk that you want to dispose of.

But no one should speculate unless he can afford to take risks. We've said that repeatedly in public advertisements and in counseling our customers. Nevertheless we are realistic enough to recognize the fact that there's enough desire for gain in even the most conservative investor so that he naturally wants to buy as low as he can and sell as high as he can. He doesn't want to lose an unnecessary dollar by an ill-timed purchase or sale. That's why we are always urging stockholders to make close and continuous study of the markets, for it is only through such study that one can reduce the risks in deciding *when* to buy or sell.

That point is especially important with respect to the *sale* of stock. If you own a stock which has risen to such a high price that you wouldn't consider buying it, it is only good sense that you at least consider selling it.

Too many people make the mistake of buying stocks, then putting them away and forgetting about them. That's bad business. If you want to invest successfully, you've got to pay attention to your securities and be always alert to new investment opportunities. What may have been a good buy last year or even last month may not be a good buy next year or next month.

Like everything else in this world, "securities are perishable."

How Are Stocks Traded?

There are thousands of different stocks and bonds — they are both called securities—but the ones that are bought and sold most frequently are those that are traded on the floor of the New York Stock Exchange. The securities of more than 1,100 major companies are "listed" on that Exchange, which means that they have been accepted for trading there.

All buying and selling on the Exchange is done between the hours of 10 A.M. and 3 P.M., New York time, Monday through Friday, and 10 A.M. to noon on Saturdays except in the summer.

What is the New York Stock Exchange? Physically, it is a large area, about two-thirds the size of a football field, in the Stock Exchange building at the corner of Wall and Broad Streets in New York City. Functionally, it is an organization consisting of 1,375 members who have bought memberships (commonly called "seats") on the Exchange.

Many of these members represent brokerage firms whose primary business is carrying out the orders of other people, the public generally, for the purchase or sale of securities. They are paid commissions for executing these orders for their customers. To provide service for investors throughout the country, these firms maintain many branch offices. All told, there are 609 member firms of the Stock Exchange that operate 936 branch offices in 370 cities. *This* firm alone has 98 offices in 96 cities.

What Is the Stock Exchange?

The Exchange is a voluntary association, as it has been since it was established 157 years ago, and it functions as an open auction market.

Before the Exchange agrees to list the securities of any company, it must be assured that the company is a substantial concern, that its securities are legally issued, that those securities are widely owned, and that the company agrees to issue regularly adequate public statements of its financial health.

Only member brokers can execute orders to buy or sell listed securities on the Exchange. If you give an order to someone who is not part of a New York Stock Exchange broker's organization, he turns that order over to a member broker. In such circumstance, you may be charged a small commission or service fee over and above the commission to the member broker.

What About Unlisted Stocks?

The New York Stock Exchange or "Big Board" is the biggest formal market for stocks and bonds, but there are thousands of security issues which aren't traded on that Exchange. Many are traded on the 24 other exchanges, such as the New York Curb Exchange, the Chicago Stock Exchange, or the Los Angeles Stock Exchange.

Still other stocks and bonds aren't listed on any exchange. These securities are called unlisted or off board securities; they are traded in what is popularly called the over-the-counter market. Government and municipal bonds are mainly traded in that market. So are the stocks of most banks and insurance companies, as well as the securities of many big corporations such as Time, Inc., Texas Eastern Transmission Corp., and the Weyerhaeuser Timber Co. By and large, however, unlisted securities are those of small companies that are apt to be better known locally than nationally.

They are bought and sold not only by many brokers who are members of the New York Stock Exchange but also by thousands of local security dealers.

Suppose a man in New York owns some stock in an Ohio machinery company and he wants to sell it. He doesn't know what it's worth because there is no regular market for that stock, and its price may not be published in the newspaper, as New York Stock Exchange prices are in many papers.

He goes to his broker, and the broker may ask for a price quotation by phone or wire from other brokers or security dealers who trade entirely in unlisted securities. He may find that the best bid for the stock is $23, while the lowest that anybody else is willing to sell it for is $25. If the stock is traded very frequently, the difference between bid and offer prices may be less. If it is almost unknown, the broker may have a hard time finding a market at any price. In this transaction, the broker acts as an agent and is paid a commission. However, in many over-the-counter transactions, the broker or dealer will buy the security himself, or he will sell such a security out of the supply of such stocks that he owns. In such trades, the dealer acts as a principal instead of as an agent, and the customer and the dealer agree on what is a fair *net price*, which includes a return to the dealer in place of a commission. In the end, the dealer may gain or lose on such transactions.

Merrill Lynch handles over-the-counter transactions either as a principal or an agent *as the customer chooses*. If a transaction is handled on a *commission* basis, it is the policy of this firm to charge commission rates that are even lower than those that now prevail on New York Stock Exchange transactions. If we handle such transactions on a *net* basis, we believe our price will be as low (if you're buying) or as high (if you're selling) as any you are likely to find. Further, we will trade only those stocks on a *net price* basis whose quality has been approved by our Research Division.

Who May Buy Stocks and Bonds?

Anybody — or perhaps we should say any honest and responsible citizen. For their own protection, brokers have to be sure about the responsibility of their customers because they accept oral orders to buy or sell. You'll find it a relatively simple matter to establish your reliability with a broker and to open an account.

Many potential investors haven't bought stocks and bonds simply because they don't know how to go about it. Some may have hesitated simply because they don't know a broker. They may even have thought of him as a somewhat unapproachable individual. He isn't. You can walk into any brokerage office in America without leave.

Finally, a lot of people probably have the idea that brokers only do business with people who invest thousands or tens of thousands of dollars at a time. Well, in our 98 offices we're proud to do business with people who talk in hundreds of dollars as well as people who deal in four and five figures. Last year, we found that 41% of our customers had incomes of less than $5,000 a year. At the other end of the scale were some who counted their income in hundreds of thousands. So you see, regardless of how big a customer you are, you'll always be welcome in any Merrill Lynch office.

But not everybody should buy stocks and bonds. We have consistently said that nobody should invest in the stock market unless he has savings sufficient to meet an emergency. And he should have insurance to protect his family. Then if he has surplus funds, he can probably invest them in stocks or bonds to his advantage.

You can tell your broker just as little or as much as you want to about your money problems, but whatever you tell him will be held in strict confidence.

Frankly, we hope you will want to tell us enough so that we can help you work out an investment program that will best fit your needs.

Does that mean that we will tell you how to invest your money? This is a point we want to make absolutely clear, for it involves a fundamental Merrill Lynch principle. Certainly, we'll try to help you if you want us to — if you *ask* for our advice and counsel. But we will not give you *unasked* advice; we will not foist our opinions or our recommendations upon you. What you buy or sell is your own business. We don't want to be accused of trying to make up your mind for you.

This firm spends about a million dollars a year in preparing and distributing to investors factual information about securities.

We'll give you all the facts and figures we have on any stock or bond you are interested in. There'll be no charge for them. We *want* you to have them — before you buy and *after* you buy. If you ask us, we'll even tell you how we think those facts and figures add up in terms of your own investment needs.

But in the end, the *decision is yours.* That's what we mean when we say

"Investigate . . . then Invest."

How to Buy and Sell Securities

How Do You Do Business with a Broker?

Here is what actually happens when a customer — let's call him Kenneth Smith — comes into our office, at 70 Pine Street to place an order for a hundred shares of Typical Manufacturing Company.

Mr. Smith goes directly to the desk of the man who regularly handles his business. (We'll call him John Ross.) Ross is registered with the New York Stock Exchange, which means that he is qualified as a man of good character and has passed an examination on the operation of the securities business. He is an employee of ours, with the title in our firm of "account executive." He's a man who thoroughly knows his business.

Smith might ask Ross for information about Typical Manufacturing from our Securities Research Division, and discuss the findings with him. But in this instance Smith has already checked on the company and knows that he wants to buy 100 shares of common stock. So he gets right down to business.

"What's Typical selling at now?" he asks.

If Typical Manufacturing were one of the major companies, Smith wouldn't have to ask, for he could look at the big electric quotation board which automatically shows the price at which the last previous sale was made. It also shows the high and low prices for the day and the closing price on the preceding day. The quote board in our 70 Pine Street office provides that information on 209 leading stocks, but Typical isn't among them.

"Sorry, I don't know the quote", says Ross, "but I'll let you know in a minute". Ross knows he can get that quote by a quick phone call, and the account executives in any of our 96 out-of-town offices can give equally good service by using the leased teletype wires that connect direct to our New York headquarters.

While Smith waits, he looks at the Trans Lux screen on which the ticker tape is projected to see if any sales of Typical are being reported right then. When a stock is sold on the Exchange floor, that transaction is reported on the tape. The price is shown and the number of shares involved in the sale. Because there are so many transactions, it is necessary to use a kind of shorthand, and the various stocks are referred to by initials or combinations of letters, such as C for Chrysler Corporation, CP for Canadian Pacific, and CGW for Chicago Great Western.

"Typical is quoted at 25 bid, 25¼ asked", says Ross in a minute or so. By that he means that $25 a share is the highest price that anyone is then willing to pay for it and that $25.25 is the lowest at which anyone is willing to sell it.

"Shall I place your order at the market?" he asks. A *market order* is one for immediate execution at the best price that prevails when the order reaches the floor of the Exchange, regardless of how the price may have changed — up or down a fraction of a point, sometimes more — in the interval between the time the order is placed and the time it can be filled.

Smith agrees. His order is immediately phoned over to one of our booths on the floor of the Exchange. There one of our floor brokers goes to the trading post at which Typical is bought or sold. There are 18 such posts on the floor of the Exchange, and at each of them a certain number of stocks are regularly traded.

At the trading post, our broker asks what the market is. Other brokers with orders to buy or sell Typical Manufacturing make their bids or offers in an audible voice. Secret transactions are not permitted on the Exchange floor.

Our broker immediately fills Smith's order at the lowest price at which the stock is offered, and Ross is advised by phone that the order has been filled.

The whole operation may have taken only two or three minutes. Smith may still be in the office. If he is, Ross will tell him that the purchase has been completed. If he is gone, Ross will telephone him.

As a matter of fact, most of our customers are apt to place their orders and handle all their business on the phone. Others do it wholly by mail. *It isn't necessary for a customer to come into the office at all to place an order.*

A customer can, if he wants, set the price that he is willing to pay. This is called a *limit order*. Smith might tell us, for instance, to buy Typical only if it could be bought at 24½. Further, he might say that any such order is good for a day, a week, a month, or indefinitely. Then if Typical is offered at 24½ within the time that Smith has set, his order to buy is executed, unless there are other similar orders on file that have precedence. Of course, the price of Typical might move right on up to 26 or 27. In such case, Smith would have lost his chance to buy at 25 or thereabouts. That's why any decision to buy that turns exclusively on the probable gain of a fraction of a point is apt not to be a good decision for most investors.

Limit orders can also be used in reverse — in selling stock. Thus, if Smith *owned* Typical, he might tell us to sell his stock for him, if we could, at 26.

How Big Does an Order Have to Be?

One hundred shares — a "round lot" — is the usual unit of trading on the New York Stock Exchange. But that doesn't mean that a customer can only buy or sell a hundred shares at a time. Many people want to buy only 5 or 10 or 25 shares at a time. These are called odd lots.

Suppose Smith wanted to buy only 10 shares of Typical. When we get that order we would fill it through an odd-lot dealer whose business it is to buy or sell in less than 100-share units. Such odd-lot dealers do business only with other brokers on the Stock Exchange floor, not with the public.

For rendering their service they charge one-eighth of a point or 12½c for every share of stock that they buy or sell to fill odd-lot orders for the customers of other brokers.

Apart from that extra eighth, odd-lot dealers don't charge any more for the stock that they sell than the price prevailing in the general market. On a 10-share order for Typical, Smith would pay that price which prevailed on the *next round-lot sale* after our broker gives Smith's order to the odd-lot dealer. Suppose the next sale was at 25. Smith would pay 25 per share, plus ⅛ for the odd-lot dealer, or 25⅛. If Smith were selling the stock, he would sell at 25, less ⅛ for the odd-lot dealer, or 24⅞.

What Does It Cost to Buy or Sell Stocks?

All transactions on the Stock Exchange are handled by member firms at reasonable commissions. The rates vary with the size of the order, being a little less proportionally on big orders than on small ones. At the present time, however, commissions on stock transactions average only 0.85 of 1%. On bonds the average commission is even less.

New York State and the federal government also levy transfer taxes on security sales or transfers, but these involve only a few pennies a share.

When Smith gets our bill the next day, it will state exactly what he bought, what price was paid, what commission is due, what postage or a tax, if any, is incurred, and what total amount is due. We do not make any charge for special services, such as research or information or carrying an inactive account or safe-keeping of securities, etc.

After Smith pays his bill — probably by check — he can obtain his stock certificate which shows that so many shares of Typical Manufacturing Co. have been registered in his name and that he is entitled to all rights, privileges, and dividends due stockholders in that company. But Smith, like an increasing number of our customers, may find it more convenient to leave the certificate in safe-keeping with us. That way he has protection against losing the certificate, and it is right here whenever the time comes that he wants to sell the stock. He will thus be relieved of the responsibility of personally delivering it at such time.

"WHAT'S THIS? . . . WHAT'S THAT?"

This isn't the *complete* story of how to buy stocks and bonds, of course. That would take volumes.

All we have tried to do here is set down answers to some of the most common questions that are asked us. And we have excluded a lot of things many people are curious about but that bear little relation to a program of prudent investment for *most* people.

For instance, there's "short selling", which simply means reversing the normal procedure — selling a stock first in the belief that it is overpriced, then buying it back at what you hope is a lower price.

Or maybe you'd like to know about buying "on margin", which means buying partly on credit.

In the main, these procedures are not important to the investor. But we'll be glad to tell you anything more you want to know.

Other market terms such as "rights", "ex-dividend", "stock splits", "debentures", "noncumulative preferred", "stop orders", and dozens of others we've had to omit simply for lack of space, but an understanding of them isn't likely to be important to most investors, except in occasional cases.

Again, for lack of space, we have not defined a whole host of financial terms that you are likely to encounter when you begin investigating various companies.

These terms are defined in a booklet, "How to Invest", which we have just published. A basic guidebook for all security owners, this new publication develops in greater detail the story of how this stock and bond business works. It reviews the basic principles of sound investing, such as the analysis of market trends, the diversification of holdings, and the management of a portfolio. We will be glad to send you a copy.

Copies of this advertisement in pamphlet form are available on request.
No charge, no obligation. Just write or phone . . .

MERRILL LYNCH, PIERCE, FENNER & BEANE

Underwriters and Distributors of Investment Securities
Brokers in Securities and Commodities

10 Post Office Square
BOSTON 9

Telephone: HUbbard 2-5700

MERRILL LYNCH, ETC. — *"Too Long?"*

People won't read long copy!

HOW many times have you heard that one? Well here's one more than 6000 words long, an all-text page, broken only by two boxes and scattered subheads, that will probably turn out to be one of the most thoroughly read advertisements ever published. Early readership research, by an absolutely impartial source, has definitely established that possibility.

For the advertisement appeared first in the New York *Times* last year, and though the page was neither created nor designed to pull inquiries, two varied write-in offers were made. One month after publication 5,033 requests for 20,000 copies of either or both of the items offered had been received — 4,000 of them the first week.

3,534 requests came by mail, 947 by telephone and 552 from visitors to one of the Merrill Lynch offices.

As Carroll J. Swan, Assistant Managing Editor of *Printers' Ink* wrote in his two excellent articles on Merrill Lynch advertising, "About 10% of the letters received were more than requests for literature. They commented on the ad, asked why they hadn't been told about the stock and bond business before, expressed a desire to invest money, and lead directly to new business from people who had been keeping away from the stock market because of poor management or misinformation . . ."

The advertisement is principally the work of Louis Engel, Advertising Manager of Merrill, Lynch, Pierce, Fenner & Beane. He wrote the copy, he says, to help clear up the stock and bond business in his own mind. He did that all right — for himself and a good many thousand others.

If a moral is needed, it may be this, never be afraid to tell the full story if it helps clarify the issue and gives people information they can use to advantage. People will read long copy just so long as it interests them.

Merrill Lynch feels that its advertising job is to create new investors. Only 49% of the people who have an annual income of $7,500 or more are investors, according to a recent Federal Reserve Board study. In the opinion of Mr. Engel "the greatest deterrment to investment in this country is simply ignorance. People — many of them successful or professional businessmen are uninformed about stocks and bonds. These same people don't like to admit their ignorance — nor their consequent distrust of the stock market. We make it easy for these people to learn what our business is all about, and the first thing you know they're writing us letters asking our advice on what to do with $5,000 or $50,000 of unproductive capital . . ."

This, incidentally, is about the only full-page ad ever used by Merrill, Lynch, Pierce, Fenner & Beane. Almost all of their copy runs with great regularity in seventy and forty line space. Each of the smaller ads, unlike the whopper, is created to pull inquiries — and in this respect, too, according to Mr. Engel, Merrill, Lynch, Pierce, Fenner & Beane, is very successful.

LADIES' HOME JOURNAL — *"Never Underestimate The Power Of A Woman"*

THERE are several major magazines superbly edited for women. But for the past several years only one has achieved fame in another part of the forest — the *Ladies' Home Journal*.

Its advertising promotion based on the theme *"Never Underestimate the Power of a Woman"* is an outstanding example of publishers' promotion at its best. In a field grown calloused and deadly dull through long years of humorless statistical straight and double talk, "Never Underestimate" is as fresh as an off-shore breeze and as telling as a rifle shot.

Gordon Page, formerly with N. W. Ayer & Son, and now with Marschalk and Pratt, New York, wrote this amusing letter about "Never Underestimate's" birth —

"Never Underestimate the Power of a Woman came off the back burner of a creative range where ideas simmer while the front burners are preoccupied with meeting closing dates. "In those days, sprightly advertising writing was being lavished on the *Ladies' Home Journal* by some of Ayer's best folk. 'The Magazine Women Believe In' was being inspiringly documented in paid space. The fact that 'Women Are Different' (vive la difference!) was being pointed up in elegant editorial advertisements. It was being fully demonstrated that 'Things Happen When The Journal Comes Out!'

"But always, when the time came to ask for the order, Journal editors linked arms with the Journal advertising department and forbade any lumping of four million women and their loved ones to be delivered to hungry advertisers.

"This was as it should be, except it caused a kind of advertising nightmare. One of the lush advertising buys of the time was having to be sold *between the lines* of some long advertising gems. Anything *direct* was outlawed. This, in turn, made a lot of people restless.

"It isn't possible to say or write *Never Underestimate the Power of a Woman* today and have it twitch in naked uneasiness the way it did the first time it was pencilled on a sheet of yellow paper.

"It was just a more direct way of stating the case for the leading woman's magazine of the day. But always believing you can do things with a twinkle that you can't do with a straight face, it was trotted down to Leo Lionni. I suggested to him that whimsey in the manner of Jimmy Hatlo might make it sing.

"It was with feet on Lionni's desk that I watched the thing take *Ladies' Home Journal* form. It's largely *his* fault that you can't say 'never underestimate the power of *anything*,' today, without echoing the *Ladies' Home Journal* line. Bless him!"

Now in its eighth year, "Never Underestimate" is demonstrating all the vitality that a great idea must show. No little part of the success of this series is Leo Lionni's art, and the fact that he comes up with many of the ideas himself. It takes about six to get one.

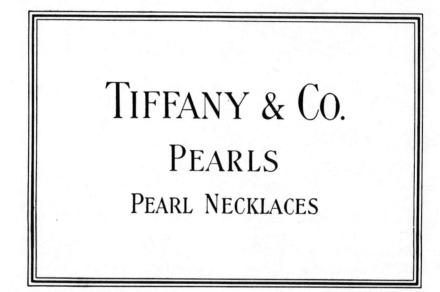

TIFFANY & CO.
PEARLS
PEARL NECKLACES

TIFFANY

IF you are old enough to know what the names STUTZ and MERCER mean — if you sang "Over There" in the days when over there was really quite a trip — or if you looked upon F. Scott Fitzgerald as a sort of Jazz Age god and "This Side of Paradise" as a kind of testament — you'll look upon this Tiffany advertisement, which so truly reflects the fabulous age of great names and princely fortunes, with a filling throat.

Tiffany!

Probably no name in America inspires such instant recognition and acceptance.

The advertisement shown appeared in 1915 when this famous store was located at Fifth Avenue and 37th Street and the name Tiffany & Co. didn't appear over the entrance or anywhere on the building — nor did the address appear in the advertising.

Mr. Milton Towne, long a leading light in Alley & Richards, New York, has handled the Tiffany account for many years, and when I asked him for the philosophy behind his client's famous advertising, Milt said: "I doubt that anybody knows. So many people took Tiffany quality for granted that copy just seemed superfluous! It's a little different now though — we use illustrations, prices, and even the zone number in the address!"

Things sure are changing!

"I pray the Lord my soul to keep"

Whatever our creed or language, we have all felt the impulse to pray. We may worship in various forms . . . we may call our God by various names . . . but, somehow, most of us express our faith in a Higher Power. When our loved ones are spared, we give thanks. At times of confusion or danger we call for guidance. When confronted by a mighty mountain, or the perfection of a tiny snowflake, we are awed by the wonder of life. We teach our children our faith, so that they will not be alone as they face the world.

FAITH is a _family_ affair!

Faith unites families for greater happiness

Faith is not just for holy days. Faith is for every day . . . at work, at play, in the quiet times the family has together.

We *need* faith—and never so desperately as today. The world is filled with voices of confusion. It is easy to feel helpless and alone. But faith in a Power outside ourselves can be a bedrock of family unity, a shield for family happiness.

A return to faith can give men and women a broader view of life—a sense of perspective. Then they are better pre-

pared for the give-and-take of family living. Small disputes have less chance of growing into serious quarrels which may tear marriage apart. The family united in faith has a strong and lasting bond.

Children naturally turn to faith when it is a daily part of the family life. And when they know the real meaning of faith, they will be tolerant of those who express *their* faith in other ways.

The home atmosphere is far different when a family stops trying to walk alone,

when it sees its place in the bigger scheme of things. It works together for the things it can control—and trusts its God for guidance in problems beyond its control. Such a family can't help feeling closer together, more sure of itself, happier!

To keep alive the family's faith calls for a positive plan—just as you plan for your family's material welfare. *How* your family expresses its faith is a matter of choice. What is important to you is that you *do* express it!

The Life Insurance Companies and their Agents

60 EAST 42nd STREET, NEW YORK 17, N. Y.

INSTITUTE OF LIFE INSURANCE — *"Faith Is A Family Affair"*

I SUPPOSE the less said about an advertisement with a religious theme, the better off I'll be. A controversial subject in a controversial book is surely asking for it! Nevertheless —

When I first saw this fine advertisement published by the Institute of Life Insurance, I read it word for word, tore it out of the magazine and thumbtacked it to my display board. I thought at the time, and without my knowledge concerning its general reception, that it was truly a great idea with copy to match.

So I wrote to Mr. Walter E. Schneider, Director of Press Relations and Advertising for the Institute, for background. Mr. Schneider was a most friendly and cooperative gentleman — one of the best — and as our correspondence progressed I became more and more impressed with the fact that the *"Faith is a Family Affair"* ad was perhaps a little bit greater than any of us can either analyze or appreciate.

In the December 31, 1948 issue of *Printers' Ink* Mr. Schneider wrote as follows:

"It's not news to be against sin, as Calvin Coolidge once sagely observed. But it was really a breath-taking surprise to learn from an advertising experience this year how many, many people are *for* such simple things as prayer and faith in the home.

"Cynics to the contrary, it seems that 'God Bless Our Home' is still an unwritten motto tacked invisibly over the doors of countless millions of American homes."

It is difficult to say whether the art or the message itself made this advertisement the most successful piece of copy published by the Institute of Life Insurance during the last seven years. It was probably both. The religious theme was delicate to start with but as it turned out the message pleased all faiths alike and not a single letter criticizing the advertisement was ever received.

Within a day after the advertisement first appeared requests to reprint rolled in. They came from various national, state and local religious organizations, from clergymen, from school teachers, mothers and others representing all major faiths. They came from foreign countries half way round the world and from Y.M.C.A.'s just around the corner.

That part of the ad which quotes from the famous childhood prayer . . . "I pray the Lord my soul to keep" . . . has been requested for publication in children's books and religious pamphlets.

The theme behind the "Faith" ad was suggested by Holgar J. Johnson, President of The Institute of Life Insurance. Maury Hanson who was then the Account Executive for J. Walter Thompson Company, New York, worked with Adrian Head who was Supervisor of Copywriters on the account, and as a team they came up with the copy and worked through its several revisions with the Institute's Planning Committee. Mr. Head says that David Kennedy, then a Thompson copywriter, contributed a great deal. The point is, it was a fine team job.

Frank Stephenson, Art Director of J. Walter Thompson Company and Frances Hook of Philadelphia, the artist, are responsible for the fine visual presentation.

The case of the crumpled letter

SCENE: *First floor of the Hastings home*

TIME: *The evening of August 1, 1944*

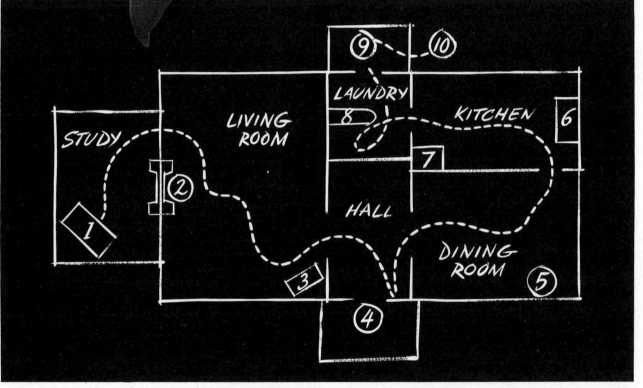

1. The desk at which Mr. Hastings opened his monthly bills and wrote an indignant letter to the electric company, protesting against their advertising that the average family gets twice as much electricity for its money as it did fifteen years ago.

2. The electric clock at which Mr. Hastings looked to see if he had time to mail his letter before dinner.

3. The family radio, with Junior parked close beside it, listening to "Jerry and the Jeeps."

4. The porch light which Mr. H. switched on to guide the dinner guests.

5. The percolator, ready and waiting to do dinner duty.

6. The electric range, filling the kitchen with appetizing odors.

7. The refrigerator, from which Mrs. H. was taking trays of tinkling ice cubes.

8. The iron, with which Nancy was pressing a dress for her date.

9. The back porch, on which Mr. H. paused to think things over—realizing that his family *did* use a lot more electricity nowadays, and maybe the company was right.

10. The trash can into which he tossed his crumpled letter.

Don't Waste Electricity Just Because It's Cheap and Isn't Rationed!

160 ELECTRIC LIGHT AND POWER COMPANIES*

SELF-SUPPORTING, TAX-PAYING BUSINESSES   *Names on request from this magazine.

ELECTRIC LIGHT & POWER ASSOCIATION — *"The Case Of The Crumpled Letter"*

"THE Case of the Crumpled Letter" was the *second* best-read advertisement in the history of the 160 Electric Light and Power Companies' advertising program. The first best was so definitely a war ad that I had to eliminate it, for reasons already given in this book.

This highly imaginative, dramatic, well written and flawlessly laid out advertisement is the work of an old friend at N. W. Ayer & Son in Philadelphia: Ken Slifer, Vice President and Manager of the Copy Department. Ken is a thoughtful craftsman. A couple of his Ford advertisements won medals in the Annual Awards, and he has written much American Telephone and Telegraph stuff since 1928.

So ponder this advertisement thoughtfully. Everything about it, from idea to final period is a fine performance. It should be an inspiration to anybody interested in producing human, readable advertising — as natural as a quiet evening at home with a good detective story.

Postscript

As popular as when first published in 1944, this ECAP ad (updated) got its third repeat last year (1958). This updating is interesting, and I am indebted to Ken Slifer of N. W. Ayer & Son, Inc., for this information — "The original diagram showed a two-story, center-hall house. In 1958, the most popular house is all on one floor. Copywriter Edward A. Kandle used the floor-plan of a one-level house for his revised diagram. Second major change was with the appliances listed. Many appliances had been invented in 14 years so the 1944 assortment fell far short of a reasonable collection for 1958. A new home-owner, Mr. Nelson, now looks at his hi-fi set, air conditioning, TV, hair dryer, all-electric kitchen including dishwasher, clotheswasher and dryer, as well as the conveniences standard in '44. Same result, though, as his indignant letter hits the trash can."

"I knew he'd forget...all he can think of is our new PLYMOUTH"

Modess .... *because*

Modess .... *because*

PLYMOUTH ... AND MODESS

YOU'LL never read much shorter copy than this, nor see much better advertising of its kind.

On the surface these advertisements seem to break a lot of the rules in the — what book? You certainly can't learn *how* to produce this sort of idea, nor exactly *when* to use it. Yet these advertisements are outstanding because they are basically sincere and beautifully done. There's nothing phony here — one is eminently human, the other confident and reserved. Their readership and identification ratings were tops. The monotonous grist from the daily and weekly advertising mills is immeasurably sharpened by the appearance of great advertisements like these.

Charles Coiner, Ken Slifer and a group at N. W. Ayer & Son, Philadelphia, did the Plymouth ads; Miss Ross Williams, Young & Rubicam, New York, did the Modess beauties.

HONEYMOON AT SEA ISLAND, GA. Sand, sea, and southern clime, and the
lush beauty of semitropical flowers make this a fascinating spot.
Painted by Andre Girard for the De Beers Collection.

How fair has been each precious moment of their plans come true ... their silent meeting at the altar steps, their first waltz at the gay reception, and now, these wondrous days together in a world that seems their very own. Each memory in turn is treasured in the lovely, lighted depths of her engagement diamond, to be an endless source of happy inspiration. For such a radiant role, her diamond need not be costly or of many carats, but it must be chosen with care. Color, cutting, and clarity, as well as carat weight, contribute to its beauty and value. A trusted jeweler is your best adviser.

De Beers Consolidated Mines, Ltd.

One-quarter carat $90 to $205

One-half carat $250 to $450

Two carats $1400 to $3335

One carat $600 to $1185

a Diamond
is forever

The prices above for unmounted quality stones were averaged
from a great many stores in May, 1948. Add Federal tax.

DeBEERS DIAMONDS

DIAMONDS are millions of years old, but man has known how to give them sparkle only for a few centuries. To paraphrase a bit: advertising, too, is many years old, but N. W. Ayer & Son was the first to give *it* the sparkle it needed to grow into a full-sized industry.

Ayer has produced many lustrous campaigns but none more beautiful nor more successful than the campaign for DeBeers Consolidated Mines, Ltd.

"When this campaign started in 1939, the prestige and emotional connotation of the diamond had slipped. Unwise publicity and advertising had caused the intrinsic values long associated with diamonds to deteriorate, and other gifts, such as automobiles, watches, and furs were replacing the diamond as engagement tokens. Diamond advertising was undertaken to strengthen the diamond engagement ring tradition. From the time the campaign started until 1947 the sale of diamonds in the United States enjoyed a steady and impressive sales climb. They fell off, along with many other luxury items, in 1947, but the first nine months of 1948 showed higher diamond sales than in any previous full year.

"Also indicative of the success of this campaign is the fact that recent surveys among engaged young women showed that 85% of them had engagement rings.

"And all this has been accomplished with a client whose offices are a mere 9000 miles away!

"The story behind the DeBeers—N. W. Ayer relationship is a significant story of mutual confidence, skillful planning and perfect execution. The Curtis Publishing Company in its Education Services has written-up this campaign as Advertising Case History #8. If you can get hold of a copy, by all means do it.

"The original DeBeers copy was written by the late B. J. Kidd (Mrs. Elizabeth Kidd) from 1939 to 1944. Since that time it has been the work of Frances Gerety. I imagine Paul Darrow did the layouts — which are superb."

SALADA TEA

What could be simpler —

"*SALADA Is Delicious Tea*"

ADD TO this the wide and constant use of small newspaper advertising space, put it on the back of the stove and let it cook for about sixty years . . . and maybe you'll have another success as great as SALADA TEA!

I don't know how to explain it. SALADA completely confounds all the, theorists and practitioners. It seems to break all the rules but one — consistency. It gives you no reasons for buying except perhaps the word "delicious." In fact, there's nothing much more to it than there is to any bold face logotype.

In 1948 all sales records were broken—SALADA is the largest selling brand of tea and tea-bags in North America. The Company announced there would be no change in advertising policy. I can see why, can't you?

HOLEPROOF HOSIERY — *The First Use Of Cheesecake In Advertising*

THE advertising experts will tell you that sex rates high on any list of fundamental appeals. Good.

Here it is: (sex) striking a fine blow for Holeproof Hosiery way back before the Varga girl was even born.

A year or so ago, no less an authority than *Fortune* Magazine credited Coles Phillips, the artist who created the Holeproof Hosiery girl, with initiating cheesecake. Good.

To the cotton and lisle-limbed world of thirty years ago the Coles Phillips' Holeproof Hosiery advertisements so glorified the female leg that not a maid anywhere could possibly get along without silk stockings. Sales sky-rocketed . . . and so did dresses. The flapper era came along and then we had knees — and now we're ready to start all over again. But somehow it will never be the same. There was a daintiness to Phillips' sex — a pleasant titillation; he never threw the book at you.

There's a little more to the story than this. Holeproof Hoisery has been consistently advertised since the early 1900's, and today, fifty-eight years more or less, later — the long-wear-satisfaction-guaranteed theme (plus sex) *still sells the goods.*

SALVADANO BASCOFIGLI

THERE IS POSITIVELY

NO PHOOL-IUM

IN STRYKERS Granulated SOAP

An Honest Confession from G. Stryker Suddsfaster, the Old Soapmaster:

Strykers does not contain phool-ium, hooey-um, hotair-ium, baloney-um or any other mysterious ingredients you can't understand. It's just good soap.

FOLKS SAY IT'S SWELL FOR WASHING CLOTHES and DISHES!

Read this SHOCKING UNCENSORED LETTER *(for adults only)*:

I must confess that Strykers will not make your things white for life. This is 'specially true of things that are blue, black or purple in the first place.

And maybe Strykers is old-fashioned, but it won't make things so white that you'll get the blind staggers from the dazzling glare. Strykers does NOT make things 23½ times whiter than new. The way I figure, if you didn't like the shade of white your pillowslips were when you first got 'em, then why did you buy 'em?

YOU DON'T GET IN A LATHER—Strykers does.

Unlike most all other washing products today, Strykers does not claim to be super-marvelous, astounding, dumbfounding or even flabbergasting. We don't expect you to get in a lather over Strykers ... but Strykers will get in a lather over you!

ROMANCE IN THE RINSEWATER?

I will also frankly admit that Strykers won't help you snag a new husband ... in fact, it won't even do much to improve the one you may have now. Much as we regret it, I cannot claim that Strykers is the granulated soap of romance. It just makes *soap* bubbles ... not *hope* bubbles. Strykers won't help you look any younger—but on the other hand—I guarantee it won't make you look even 1 day *older* than you really are.

THEN WHY BUY STRYKERS?

For folks who just want a *darn good washing product* (not a miracle), Strykers is as fine a granulated soap as can be made. Independent laboratory tests prove Strykers is *really* ten to fifteen per cent soapier than other leading brands. That means Strykers actually does give you *more suds with less soap.*

IT MAKES SENSE TO SAVE CENTS

Your box of Strykers has more actual soap by weight than nearly all other washing products that cost the same ... or even more! Compare weights and see how much you *actually* save when you buy Strykers.

PUSSYCAT - SMOOTH HANDS!

There's no phoolium, but there IS glycerin in Strykers. Ooodles of it. Nothing mysterious about glycerin. It's the same stuff you get in hand lotions that cost scandalous prices. Yes, ma'am. Hope you'll try Strykers soon!

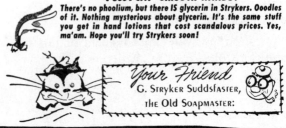

Your Friend
G. Stryker Suddsfaster,
the Old Soapmaster:

STRYKER SOAP COMPANY — *"No Phoolium"*

IN his introduction to this volume Raymond Rubicam says in part: "... current advertising style can be as monotonous as current automobile style, and preoccupation with it merely sets up the need for a strong antidote, lest the pressure of standardization ruin the youngster (young copy-writer) for life ..."

To me there is something decidedly monotonous about current soap advertising. It's so expertly done that it looks like Madison Avenue and Radio City laughing at Main Street and Brown's Grocery Store.

I suppose it's based on all the facts money can buy — and it must be successful — and if all these things are true ... God help us ... we're going to run out of superlatives sometime, and I'm sure romance is eventually going to abandon the soap dish and go back to the parlor sofa where it belongs.

That's part of the reason I've picked this unusual exhibit of soap advertising by a small company in California. You may not call this ad one of the greatest of all time, but in this book it serves exactly that purpose, for it is indeed a very sound example of about the only course a David-small soap company can take in a field of Goliaths. The august *Reader's Digest,* in its *Advertising Cum Laude* department, quoted from a couple of Strykers Soap ads in its September 1949 issue —

and that's where I saw it. My heart filled with joy because about twenty years ago, I submitted a campaign to a very large soap company and my first advertisement was titled: NO KISSES GUARANTEED!

It was a deliberate attempt to reverse the field and after reading it carefully with smiles of appreciation spreading across his jowls, the big soap executive said, (wistfully I thought): "We've spent too much money doing it the other way. But if I was a small soap company this is exactly what I'd do ... pan the hell out of the big fellows advertising ..."

So I wrote to the Stryker Soap Company for facts, and I take the liberty of quoting in part from a letter by vice president, Mr. A. Haas, Jr., —

"You inquire about the origin and success of our advertising campaign. As small soap manufacturers, we were convinced that since all the superlatives had long ago been used by our competition, we could only hope to be effective by being different."

You will find other examples of refreshing, original thinking in this book — something you should always dare to do, whether you get it okayed or not. Advertising will lose its effectiveness and its opportunities when it surrenders to inflexible formula.

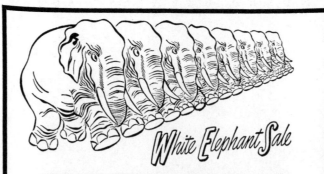

White Elephant Sale

ANNOUNCING SOUTH BEND'S MOST HONEST SALE

**The Best Assortment of Out-and-Out Junk Ever Offered.
We're Stuck With It, So We'd Like to Unload It On You.
If You're a Brave Person, Read On**

IN THE BOOK STORE WE OFFER:

Box Stationery

Dirty boxes, and we don't mean just soiled. Some war-time butcher paper like you paid fancy prices for. Some awful colors you wouldn't use on your cupboard shelves. You can't imagine unless you see 'em. Prices? 10c up.

Gift Wrappings

Paper, ribbons and Seals, ugly colors, shelf-worn, etc. You ladies can use the ribbons to hold up your slips, or tie up old papers. Some Xmas stuff in here, and awful nice for kindling. Limit 1,000 per person.

Black Ink

Sheaffer Skrip and Parker Quink. Black for writing V-Mail. We must have thought the war would last forever. 25c size 25c—15c size 15c.

Greeting Cards

Misfits of all kinds—they look like kids made 'em, but we bought 'em for fancy dough. Your choice, 6 for 5c, but don't send 'em out; burn 'em.

Books

How we ever got so many junkers, you'll never know. Our buyers should be shot. You wouldn't have 'em for a gift, so give 'em to somebody else for bridge prizes. If this stuffs sells, try writing a book yourself; it must be easy. All prices.

South Bend Pennants

With Indian head pictures! Can you imagine? Swell for patching broken windows, etc. Ideal for Mishawaka tourists. 9c each.

Junk

Telephone gadgets by Rube Goldberg; celluloid steno's cuffs for credit managers; photo album gadgets; games dating back to grandma's time; rubber cement like bubble gum; book ends, book plates and book matches; if we sell it all we'll be lucky—if we don't you will.

IN THE CIGAR STORE WE OFFER:

Fox-Hole Lighters

Remember the darn things? Flameless? No flame, no light. Sold for $1.50 complete with embalming fluid. Buy one just to show Junior you were in a fox-hole once. 49c and don't say we didn't warn you.

Tobacco Pouches

When we bought these they said there'd be a leather shortage; after we bought 'em there was. Make nice marble bags or moccasins. Overpriced to begin with, so we're selling them at what they're worth. 50% to 66⅔% off.

Cherry Wood Pipes

Corn cob substitutes, for smoking, that is. Worth only 5c each. We're asking 10c.

Briar Pipes

Supposed to be briar roots; might be sassafras or dogwood. Two grades: low grade, 99½c; extra low grade, 39½c.

Cigarette Rolling Machines

Remember the darn things? O.K. once but K.O. now. One free with each pkg. cigarettes.

Poker Chips

Paper, faded, wonderful for uneven table legs. Two buyers: .00009 inch thick, 19c box; .00048 inch thick, 39c box.

Razor Blades

All kinds, nice for ripping seams, but no good for beards even with these new shaving creams. 5c to 35c, no trade-ins.

Tobacco

Pounds and half-pounds of good brands like Bird's Nest Blend and Old Chaff and Irfsano, all with strictly home-grown worms. Make us an offer, one can or 20.

Toiletries (?)

Shaving lotions by Vitriol & Co.; shaving creams by Iran Oil Co.; shaving bowls by C. Ment Products Co.; tooth pastes by Carl Borundum; cigars by Hemp-Jute Co.; junkers by the carload.

At the price we're offering these gifts, we can't afford to wrap them, but we will. Just try this stuff and learn how we lose friends and alienate people. Jesse James carried a gun and rode a horse, but all we have is personality and an honest face. Remember we warned you. If you're a glutton for punishment, this is it.

Book Store Open Until 8:30; Cigar Store Until 11.

Walk In — Stagger Out — Convenient Exits

BRUGGNER'S
SOUTH BEND, INDIANA.

127 W. Washington   **110 N. Main**

"In the J.M.S. Bldg."

BRUGGNER'S — *"White Elephant Sale"*

PERHAPS the most interesting thing about the copy for Bruggner's White Elephant Sale is the story behind it. Why in the world would a book about great advertisements include the copy of a relatively obscure South Bend, Indiana, retail store? *Why?* Here's why —

Dear Mr. Watkins:

The matter of my case report on our "White Elephant Sale" just cannot wait any longer . . .

Is the idea original? Definitely not. Macy's is said to have used the idea; Jack Benny's success came from poking fun at himself; and I had on my desk for a year or more a similar advertisement reproduced in a trade journal I came across, and used as I remember by the Cunningham drug stores of the Middle West.

Who wrote the ads? I did. I believe I am not being egotistical in saying that not everyone can write such an ad. I started out in life as a newspaperman, and the knack of using the correct word is important, so that when I read two similar advertisements mailed to me from other cities since we ran our sale, I felt that these fell short of the mark. Maybe it's a sense of humor. Maybe it's the knack I speak of. Maybe it's the fact that I am owner of the business and therefore had no inhibitions in writing my copy.

The conviction that the idea was sound was strong in me ever since my experience with radio advertising more than ten years ago. For more than a year I sponsored a 15-minute program on our local radio station, "Behind the Scenes in Magazines", in which I wrote the copy, dug up the material and myself presented it each week with the help of my announcer. I gave it up eventually because it was just too confining, along with my store duties. At first it was just so-so. My friends were kind enough to say complimentary things about the program, but I felt they were being polite. One day my announcer did some ad-libbing in his commercial and referred to my store as a "joint". The next day a customer said he had heard the "joint" advertised on the air. We gradually experimented with the technique and eventually used nothing but humorous copy in the commercials. From then on we had a steady customer reaction.

People want to laugh. Knowing that our store had nothing to sell which our competitors did not also have — *except ourselves* — became a valuable piece of knowledge. It has become evident that people like honesty in advertising — I burn up listening to "no other soap has

what we have" — clothes get softer, whiter — up to 50% more of this or that — doctors say our cigarettes let you live longer, etc. — phooey. So you tell them the truth; make yourself look stupid and let them feel superior; and they go for it.

Was it successful? Supremely. There is no way of giving you exact figures, if I wanted to. We simply took merchandise as we found it and dumped it on the counters, without any preliminary mark-down accounting. I can tell you that we had daily sales increases during the seven business days we ran the sale, and that the ratio of advertising expense to sales and to cost of sales was something like this: advertising 2½ sales increases 10, cost of goods sold 20 to 30 (I can only guess at the ratio to cost of goods sold). So from a dollars and cents figure the sale was very costly, but I believe that the customer goodwill was worth ten times what it cost.

Customer reaction was terrific. The ad ran on Sunday morning and while we were occupied that morning in getting stock arranged for Monday morning, the telephone rang several times by persons wanting to know if we were open on Sundays — they wanted to come right down! One of my friends said he entertained his family at breakfast Sunday reading the ad aloud; many others echoed similar experiences. We had several mail replies from nearby towns — something we never get from straight copy, unless it is a coupon ad. All this summer we had requests from out of town places for copies of the ad, and one local resident, moving to Florida and later entering the retail business, wrote back for help in running a similar sale. A newspaper, anonymously mailed from Douglas, Arizona, in July, carried a used car "White Elephant" advertisement patterned after ours. During the sale we gave away about 50 tear sheets of our ad and we know of a dozen cases in which local residents mailed the ad to friends out of town. In one case a personal friend of mine, whom I hadn't seen in a year, told me in August that he was at the home of a friend of his in Cleveland, and this friend pulled out of a drawer a copy of our advertisement, which still another friend had mailed to Cleveland, and so the advertising came full circle back to me. You can't buy that kind of advertising!

Thank you, Mr. Louis V. Bruggner, for an excellent story in a sort of late-at-night, between-us-guys style that simply increases its significance as a warm, human lesson in advertising fundamentals.

FELS NAPTHA — *"All Right, Ann Ward"*

THIS was one of the most talked-about advertisements of 1928. I include it because there is a certain amount of creative daring involved that is admirable anytime. It violates many of the rules (why do I keep saying that) of copywriting and yet, it enjoyed tremendous readership success.

The idea and copy are the work of Sid Ward (H. S. Ward) Vice President and Copy Director of Young & Rubicam, New York . . . "There is no inside dope on the Ann Ward ad" writes Sid,

"I'd been going over a lot of letters women had written in about Fels Naptha. These letters were fresh, convincing and, above all, intimate. It occurred to me that a more intimate form of advertising might be worth trying. Hence the Ann Ward approach. The client liked the idea and okayed it without urging.

"The most remarkable thing about the ad, as far as I am concerned, was the mail. It drew letters like a radio program — so many we had to work up a form letter to answer them."

THE CURSE OF TOO MUCH MONEY!
(A SLIGHTLY TALL TALE)
by Mr. Friendly

We saved him so much money
He couldn't even fold it . . .
He hired 40 trucks
And they couldn't even hold it!
He cried, "Since you cured
Our production ills
Even my dollars have
Little dollar bills! . . .

"With all the mink coats
My poor wife has got . . .
She wears 5 at a time
Which is Ritzy, but hot!
If you save me more dough,
I'll burst into tears.
You've saved me so much now
It comes out of my ears!"

Maybe we've stretched a point . . . But honestly, we can show business after business, big and small, where American Mutual has reduced accidents and premium rates to way below the average for the field!

When you figure we still give you the chance to save 20% through dividends, we're only exaggerating slightly when we say you'll save so much you'll hire people to spend it!

AMERICAN MUTUAL
. . . the first American liability insurance company

The biggest extra in insurance . . . that's I.E. Loss Control,* a special service, at no extra charge with every industrial policy. Ask your American Mutual man to show you the "40 Convincing Cases." Write for free copy of "The All-American Plan for Business" or "The All-American Plan for the Home." American Mutual Liability Insurance Co., Dept. D-106, 142 Berkeley St., Boston 16, Mass. Branch offices in principal cities. Consult classified telephone directory.

Accident prevention based on principles of industrial engineering.

AMERICAN MUTUAL — *"You'll Have To Stop Glowing"* said Mr. Friendly

PERHAPS the finest thing that can be said about American Mutual's Mr. Friendly series is that since the series started American Mutual has risen from fourth to second place in sales and has increased its dollar volume more than 20% in the last year (1947-8).

The copy is the work of Mr. Don Calhoun of McCann-Erickson, New York — and here's the story —

"I was frightened by an insurance agent at the tender age of 29!" says Don.

"The fellow proved rather conclusively that I was just about to be run over, burnt to a crisp, poisoned or drowned!

"Shortly after this, I read some insurance ads with screaming mothers, weeping widows, flaming houses, and wrecked cars . . .

"Insurance, I concluded, was just a little jollier than the undertaking business . . . and who wants to see an undertaker!

"When the American Mutual people came to our agency, McCann-Erickson, and asked us to prepare a campaign, I figured it would at least be novel to write some pleasant insurance ads . . .

"Why try to scare people to death . . . Why not sell the positive side of insurance . . . the wonderful feeling of reilef when you know you're protected and everything's taken care of!

"To build up a warm, friendly feeling toward the company I developed a trade character. I wanted him to be amusing, likeable and helpful . . .

"My good friend, art director Jack Tinker, read some of the copy I'd written and drew a tall, skinny, old fashioned looking fellow with a derby hat . . . and that was Mr. Friendly.

"At first I named him Mr. Pinkham . . . but the American Mutual people pointed out that Pinkham was the name of a pill or something and couldn't we do better . . . We did.

"The first Mr. Friendly ad was entitled *'You'll Have to Stop Glowing!'* . . . *said the Air Raid Warden.*

"When Mr. Hodges, President of American Mutual, saw it, he said, 'I like it. It's fresh and different. The founding fathers of our conservative New England company will probably spin in their graves when we run it . . . but run it we will!' . . .

"American Mutual had the courage to try something new. And it seems to have paid off well!

"Other advertisers might take a lesson from this . . . relax a bit . . . and act like human beings!"

Oh darling—you shouldn't have

SOME TIME LAST NIGHT Macy's gave the last bow on the last package a loving pat, entrusted it to a tired delivery man, and locked up the store for the week-end.

New York looked very much like a small town at that hour. The business district was dark and quiet and deserted. The streets were almost empty. But everywhere where people lived and had their homes, there were lights . . . candle lights . . . Christmas lights, small, soft lights to help good children catch a glimpse of Santa Claus . . . big blazing lights that spelled music and laughter and good cheer.

And of course (like any small town merchant), we started to think about the light in her eyes when she scolds you for being so dear, so sweet, so foolishly generous. Honestly, we were so nervous 'way last Summer when we picked out the gift for you to give her. Tell us frankly, did she *really* like it? Is Junior playing with his electric train? What did grandma say about the scarf? Goodness knows we stand ready to forgive and forget, to exchange, to substitute.

But . . .

We hope with all our hearts that this is the sort of Christmas you've always dreamed of—a Christmas with someone you love, where the gifts are all magically the right size and the right color, where the children can't be pried loose from the toys or vice versa, and where the "Merry Christmas" wish is a joyous harbinger of the happy New Year to come.

MACY'S

MACY'S 1948 CHRISTMAS AD — *"Oh, Darling — You Shouldn't Have!"*

MY friend, Bill Tyler, moderator of *Advertising Agency's* COPY CLINIC called this Macy masterpiece his "favorite Christmas ad". I suppose he referred to 1948's Christmas ads. I'm using it as the favorite Christmas ad of all I ever remember reading.

It's just plain *grand!*

Sincerity, naturalness, friendliness, stick out all over it. Macy's Barbara Collyer wrote it — and gave every copywriter in the United States, present and future, a brilliant example of sheer competence in human interest copy. Advertising could do with a good deal more advertising like this.

People wrote in about this ad, called up, came in personally — as never before.

Hard-selling copy?

Who said that?

U. S. STEEL — *"He Came To A Land Of Wooden Towns And Left A Nation Of Steel"*

IT was the biggest advertising news in years — back in 1935 — when the story broke that Batten, Barton, Durstine & Osborn had acquired the account of the United States Steel Corporation.

Somehow everything about the United States Steel Corporation seems *big!* It sounded like the biggest account in the world. Actually, it wasn't at all; it was just a good healthy account with excellent reasons for adding the power of advertising to its gigantic power as our number one heavy industry.

Bruce Barton and Roy Durstine* made the original presentation and it was made on the basis that no big corporation could afford to ignore the public — especially in that particular political era when business was not only pretty definitely in the doghouse but was actually facing more and more Government regulation and competition.

Then again while the Steel Corporation had done no advertising as such, practically all of its subsidiaries had. There was little or no uniformity in any of the advertising and little over-all identification with the parent company.

The Corporation readily recognized that there would be economy in combining all advertising in one place, and by so doing, assure uniformity and appearance so that no matter which subsidiary advertised there would be a definite tie-up with all other subsidiary advertising, and with United States Steel. This was the first step in unifying all Steel products with one label or trade-mark.

To the public at large U. S. Steel Corporation was simply a symbol on brokers' boards and ticker tape — something for politicians to attack because it had happened to be successful enough to grow big. So the original campaign was designed to show how the Corporation had contributed to the progress of the country.

While the trade-mark was played up from the very beginning, the use of it as a label to identify products made from U. S. Steel did not actually get under way until about 1939 and has been in use ever since.

Since the very start of the campaign all Steel copy has been supervised by Bruce Barton. The original ad featuring Mr. Carnegie was probably written by George Bushfield of BBD&O with a strong assist from his boss.

This kind of advertising is a very definite credit not only to advertising itself but to a clearer understanding by the public of our entire economic system. There should be more of it.

*Roy S. Durstine, now President of Roy S. Durstine, Inc., Advertising, New York.

Wonder what a Frenchman thinks about

Two years ago a Frenchman was as free as you are. Today what does he think—

—as he humbly steps into the gutter to let his conquerors swagger past,

—as he works 53 hours a week for 30 hours' pay,

—as he sees all trade unions outlawed and all the "rights" for which he sacrificed his country trampled by his foreign masters,

—as he sees his wife go hungry and his children face a lifetime of serfdom.

What does that Frenchman—soldier, workman, politician or business man—think today? Probably it's something like this—"I wish I had been less greedy for myself and more anxious for my country; I wish I had realized you can't beat off a determined invader by a quarreling, disunited people at home; I wish I had been willing to give in on some of my rights to other Frenchmen instead of giving up all of them to a foreigner; I wish I had realized other Frenchmen had rights, too; I wish I had known that patriotism is *work*, not **talk**, *giving*, not getting."

And if that Frenchman could read our newspapers today, showing pressure groups each demanding things be done for them instead of for our country, wouldn't he say to American business men, politicians, soldiers and workmen —"If you knew the horrible penalty your action is bound to bring, you'd bury your differences now before they bury you; you'd work for your country as you never worked before, and wait for your private ambitions until your country is safe. Look at me ... I worked too little and too late."

WARNER
&
SWASEY
Turret Lathes
Cleveland

YOU CAN TURN IT BETTER. FASTER. FOR LESS ... WITH A WARNER & SWASEY

WARNER & SWASEY — *"Wonder What A Frenchman Thinks About"*

IN a campaign distinguished by consistently excellent copy, this Warner & Swasey selection *"Wonder What a Frenchman Thinks About"* is one of the best of the lot.

It appeared in September 1941 — just before World War II involved the United States — when Americans were wavering between a fear of Germany and an inclination to appease Hitler. If you will remember, we were in the midst of serious labor harangues, and that was the time when some rabid leader in the East said he didn't care how many Americans lost their lives in any war that might be coming due to lack of equipment, so long as the Union got the wage increase it demanded.

There was uncertainty, confusion everywhere — and France suffered. When this advertisement appeared, Warner & Swasey received immediate requests for permission to reprint. A rough record was kept of the number of reprints asked for and those alone totaled 4,400,000. Every known form of communication was used to distribute them—newspaper editorials, newspaper advertisements paid for by others, radio commentators, pay envelope enclosures, plant posters, house organs, folders, broadcasts by companies and individuals, etc.

Letters flooded in from people in practically every walk of life and from every part of the country. The theme of the letters was that at least one American manufacturing concern really understood the approaching war and its underlying causes.

Or, shall we say — one copywriter?

As an example of fine industrial and management public relations advertising, you'll look a long way before you find another as good as this.

A short course in Railroading
...for Airline executives

Airline executives are mighty proud of their airlines and we don't blame them. The airlines have been progressive and they have their place in the transportation scheme of things, just as the railroads have theirs.

But we wish they wouldn't spend so much time talking about the railroads in their advertising. They seem to know so many things about railroad service that aren't so!

They may know the airline business very well but they're a little hazy about the railroad business.

We don't like to mention a competing service in our advertising but now we're rather forced to talk about the airlines in order to inform the airlines (and the public, too) about some of the facts of the *railroad business*.

The airlines compare their fares with railroad fares and come to the conclusion that air travel is cheaper. But they always compare the one way fares. Since airlines make no reductions on round trips for travel in this country, the airline people apparently think the railroads don't, either. As a matter of fact, railroads make substantial reductions for round trip tickets. We figure most people have to get home sometime.

Here are some round trip fare examples:

	AIRLINE FARE	RAILROAD Coach	RAILROAD 1st Class
New York–{San Francisco / Los Angeles}	$236.60	$101.50	$153.35
Chicago–{San Francisco / Los Angeles}	170.90	71.50	99.35
San Francisco–Los Angeles	30.30	11.90	21.90

The airlines, in comparing fares, always add in the cost of a Pullman *lower* berth. A comparison of a seat in a plane and a berth on the train is the same as comparing a chair with a bed. The airlines aren't operating sleeper planes so the services aren't comparable on that point at all.

The airlines don't seem to know about our *Daylights*, so they don't mention the fact that you can go from San Francisco to Los Angeles and back on these luxurious streamliners, the fastest trains between the two cities, for $11.90 round trip or $3.25 less than the one way fare by plane.

And while we're talking about economy of rail travel we'd like to mention that we carry children free (accompanied by adults) when they're under 5 years of age, and at half fare when they are 5 to 11 inclusive. And children get seats for their individual use. Most airlines charge full fare for children except for a babe in arms.

In comparing their service with the railroads', the airlines forget to add in the bus fares to and from the airports (and bus travel time as well). Also they overlook their limited baggage allowances, which increase air travel cost with a normal amount of luggage. These added costs, we think, overbalance the pleasant free meal furnished air travellers when aloft.

We accept the fact that airplanes have one primary advantage—*speed*. But we think trains have a lot of advantages, too, including economy and plenty of room to move around.

CLAUDE E. PETERSON
Vice-President, SYSTEM PASSENGER TRAFFIC
SAN FRANCISCO 5, CALIFORNIA

NOTE: *Fares shown are subject to the 15% federal tax which applies to all forms of transportation.*

S•P The friendly Southern Pacific

Southern Pacific, route of the streamlined *Daylights, Lark, Sunbeams* and *City of San Francisco*, now has finer, faster trains than before the war and is building more streamlined trains for 1947 delivery.

SOUTHERN PACIFIC RAILROAD—"*A Short Course In Railroading For Airline Executives*"

THIS advertisement was intended to be a good natured rebuke to several airlines which were at that time (1946) stating that air travel was cheaper than train travel. It appeared first in San Francisco newspapers, where it attracted so much attention that it was run nationally at the request of the Southern Pacific Board of Directors.

Seldom has an advertisement caused such a stir. Officials of the railroad received several hundred letters, and in addition there were a great many newspaper editorials, as well as comment in the advertising trade press — all favorable.

Most important of all, the advertisement apparently accomplished its purpose, for shortly after it appeared comparative advertising by the airlines ceased.

The copy was written by Mr. F. Q. Tredway, General Advertising Manager of the Southern Pacific Company. The headline was written by Mr. Herbert K. Reynolds, of Foote, Cone & Belding, San Francisco.

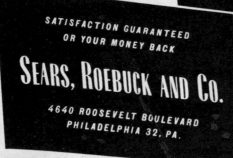

Spring & Summer 1949

With this book, Sears brings you the first good news about prices we have been able to present in many years.

True, some items are higher, in spite of all we could do, and many others are the same. But as you go through the book, you will find thousands of prices lower than last fall.

So, when you think of shopping, think of this catalog first.

Buying the catalog way is easy, convenient, safe. You choose from broad assortments in style, colors, sizes, materials and prices. You can do it comfortably in your own home—and save money besides.

*　　　*　　　*

Shop from this catalog by mail, by telephone, at Sears Catalog Order Offices or in Sears Retail Stores. For Easy Terms, see inside back cover.

SATISFACTION GUARANTEED
OR YOUR MONEY BACK

SEARS, ROEBUCK AND CO.

4640 ROOSEVELT BOULEVARD
PHILADELPHIA 32, PA.

THE SEARS, ROEBUCK CATALOGUE!

NO BOOK on great copy would be complete without this most famous of all salesmen in print!

More than a thousand pages of the strongest selling copy ever written — any page, any item, any year. Study the style! Read it often.

"We now have more customers than at any time in our history . . ." Significant, indeed.

"When you buy from this catalogue, you get facts . . . You buy with confidence because you buy with knowledge. Our merchandise is photographed . . . just as it will look . . . Our descriptions are simple, honest, straightforward statements of facts. We do not misrepresent. We do not "oversell". There is no pressure exerted on you, so you can select our highest priced . . . or our lowest priced . . . without anyone influencing your decision." Significant, indeed, indeed!

Who writes the descriptions of Sears merchandise? No one person, of course, for the task of writing adequate, factual, interest-compelling copy for over 100,000 items of merchandise is far beyond the powers of any single individual. Yet it is interesting to observe how exactly each description in Sears Big Catalog tallies with the statements made in the preceding paragraph. "Simple . . . honest . . . straightforward statements of facts". No misrepresentation . . . no overselling . . . no pressure to buy exerted on the customer. Why, then, do more than 12,000,000 Sears customers continue to order by mail each year from this huge book, in preference to shopping in stores?

To obtain an answer to this question we must go back to the early days of the Company when its founder, Richard W. Sears, first discovered people will order merchandise by mail if and when assortments are complete, prices are low and the advertising "message" in the catalogue follows this formula of simplicity, honesty, sincerity and adequacy. Mr. Sears learned this by actual trial and error, during the time when he was personally able to write every word of every description in his small watch catalogues. He proved to his own satisfaction and for all time to come that the more you tell the more you sell, and truth well told was worth a thousand fanciful or imaginary claims for superiority. Nor has time disproved what Mr. Sears was one of the first to discover. For a recent study revealed that advertising containing 10 facts as against 4 facts is 44% more effective! Yet you will not find the copy in a Sears catalogue dry and uninteresting. For so skillfully does the copywriter combine facts with similes, metaphors, pictorial nouns and lively, active verbs that he is able to weave into his description, simple, direct and factual though it may be, an irresistible allure few customers can resist.

Advertising men acknowledge the writing of good mail order advertising copy as one of the highest forms of the art. Certainly it is one of the most directly resultful and effective. And they will quickly admit that more well-rounded, seasoned and successful writers of advertising have come from the ranks of mail order copywriters than from any other field.

How to tune a piano!

The piano is out of tune. So we'll chop it up. Then we'll get a tin horn instead.

Sure, these men are crazy.

But they're using the same kind of thinking a lot of people have been using on the American economic system lately.

Our American way isn't perfect. We still have our ups and downs of prices and jobs. We'll have to change that. But even so, our system works a lot better than the second-rate substitutes being peddled by some countries we could mention.

It works better because of a few simple things. We are more inventive, and we know how to use machine power to produce more goods at lower cost. We have more skilled workers than any other country. We believe in collective bargaining and enjoy its benefits. And we Americans save—and our savings go into new tools, new plants, new and better machines.

Because of this, we *produce more* every working hour...and can *buy more* goods with an hour's work than any other people in the world.

We can make the system work *even better,* too: by *all of us working together* to turn out *more for every hour we work*— through better machines and methods, more power, greater skills, and by sharing the benefits through higher wages, lower prices, shorter hours.

It's a good system. It can be made better. And even now it beats anything that any other country in the world has to offer.

So—let's tune it up, not chop it down.

**THE BETTER WE PRODUCE
THE BETTER WE LIVE**

Approved for the
PUBLIC POLICY COMMITTEE
of The Advertising Council by:

EVANS CLARK, Executive Director, Twentieth Century Fund
BORIS SHISHKIN, Economist, American Federation of Labor
PAUL G. HOFFMAN, Formerly President, Studebaker Corp.

PUBLISHED IN THE PUBLIC INTEREST BY:

(SPONSOR'S NAME)

THE ADVERTISING COUNCIL — *"How To Tune A Piano"*

THE Advertising Council "is a private, non-profit, non-partisan organization supported and operated by advertisers, advertising agencies and the advertising media groups, for the purpose of utilizing Advertising in the solution of national problems."

The quotes are from the sixth annual report concerning the Council's work, and the advertisement is one of the most successful from the Council campaign promoting a better understanding of the American Economic System. In fact, *"How to Tune a Piano!"* attracted more favorable attention and comment than any other advertisement in this important series. Advertisers had sponsored it in 44 different publications up to press time, with more orders coming in.

"America's Economic System has brought more rewards to more people than any other system the world has ever known. We outproduce all other nations — turn out more goods and services for every hour we work — enjoy the highest standard of living in all civilization.

"Yet many Americans haven't the faintest idea of what makes our system work or how to make it better. They magnify its imperfections and seem blind to its benefits. They are open to attacks on the very foundations of our system because they do not know the answers.

"To resist the underminers — to maintain our high standard of living — to raise it even higher for our children, everyone should have a better understanding of what has made America what it is — and should realize the fact that the better we produce the better we live."

That is the quoted goal of this particular Advertising Council campaign. It gives all Americans the knowledge that is needed to appreciate our system, and the ammunition that is necessary to stop the "crackpots."

This may not be a "great" advertisement (though it is rapidly proving to be the best in this series), but the idea behind it, is the greatest in the world.

And it demonstrates very capably indeed advertising's potential in the field of ideas.

Results from the Advertising Council's major campaigns for 1948 are significant: The Red Cross goal in 1948 was $75,000,000. It was 99.4% subscribed long before the books were closed. The Council's Traffic Safety campaign began in 1946. Traffic fatalities dropped more than 1,000 in 1947. And for the first 10 months of 1948, the traffic death toll was approximately 8,000 fewer lives lost than over the same period in 1947. And the mileage death rate per 100,000,000 vehicle miles dropped to a new low in 1948, and it's still going down. 43,373 young women enrolled in schools of nursing during 1948 as a result of the Student Nurse Recruitment campaign conducted by the Council in cooperation with the American Hospital Association. This is the highest enrollment of any peacetime year — nearly double the number enrolled during the same length of time prior to the war years.

Despite the continued high cost of living, the sale of Savings Bonds in 1948 was the highest in peacetime history. The purpose of the Council's campaign was to maintain a balance between maturities and redemptions and sales. Sales were estimated at $7,200,000,000 with a net gain over maturities and redemptions of $2,500,000,000. Some 75,000,000 Americans still hold about $85,000,000,000 worth of bonds, of which some 33,000,000,000 are "E" bonds. Treasury officials give full credit for this remarkable result to the advertising support American business has been giving to the campaign.

The Council's campaign for Forest Fire Prevention resulted in a 20% reduction in the number of man-caused forest fires in one year. And still another Council effort has lifted Armed Services Prestige to a new high in enlistments — more than 1,700,000 volunters which is a record unduplicated by any other nation in the peacetime history of the world.

SUPPLEMENT

When the clock swings 'round to four~
COFFEE

Right at the peak of the day's duties it pays to pause for a chummy, cheery cup of Coffee.

It is a stimulus to effort in the office or in the home—it coaxes cheerful spirits and clear-thinking for the rest of the day.

As regularly as the clock swings 'round to four, drink an appetizing, reviving cup of Coffee. Not very far from wherever you are, there is a coffee house, soda fountain, restaurant or hotel which makes a feature of Afternoon Coffee.

This advertisement is part of an educational campaign conducted by the leading COFFEE merchants of the United States in cooperation with the planters of the State of Sao Paulo, Brazil, which produces more than half of all the COFFEE used in the United States of America.

This is the sign of The Coffee Club. Look for it in dealers' windows. It will help you find good coffee.

JOINT COFFEE TRADE PUBLICITY COMMITTEE, 74 Wall Street, New York

COFFEE ~ -the universal drink

This advertisement will appear during the week ending October 8th.

JOINT COFFEE TRADE PUBLICITY COMMITTEE —

And The Coffee Break Was Born

YOU are in on the birth of one of the biggest and best sales ideas ever to be delivered of a fine campaign.

If you don't think so — try to find your secretary about that time in the morning or afternoon.

That's why George Cecil of N. W. Ayer & Son, Philadelphia says: "I hesitate to get too brash about claiming credit for this. For there are, according to my best research, some 864,518 executives who are looking for the author with blood in their eyes and a determination to shoot on sight . . ."

"Of course, most ideas are born quietly, without fanfare, and often without realization of their possibilities.

"Frequently there is only a typewriter or a pad of yellow paper and a pencil in the delivery room. Time has a way of washing out the vital statistics.

"There is, however, considerable evidence to show that the first advertising of a coffee break on a national basis was in the campaigns for the Joint Coffee Trade Publicity Committee as far back as 1921, 1922 and 1923.

"The advertisements were inserted in a number of newspapers throughout the country. Local roasters were encouraged to pick up the idea and use it in their own advertising.

"There were, in fact, a number of advertisements on the idea of pausing for a chummy, cheery cup of coffee in the office or in the home or at soda fountains, restaurants, etc.

"We weren't brave enough to suggest it in mid-morning but we did lay great stress on the idea — and the pick-me-up benefits — of a break for coffee at four o'clock in the afternoon.

"The idea took hold in a limited way during those early years. But it wasn't until World War II that it left the simmering stage and really got to boiling in business offices as well as factories throughout the country. And it's been practically epidemic in recent years. That's why those 864,518 executives could very well be gunning for me.

"There wasn't anything sensational about the words or illustrations and they wouldn't win any prizes for fine writing or design.

"The all-important thing, as in all campaigns and sometimes missing these days through lack of digging, was the copy idea.

"And that, as it has turned out for the coffee business, was a lulu!" Definitely, a lulu!

Cake: Betty Crocker White Cake Mix. Frosting: new Betty Crocker Fluffy White Frosting Mix, tinted pink.

All the rest of your natural life

The first birthday. And the first step. And the first word. And the first day of school. And the first mumps. And the first bumps too big to kiss away. And the first date and the first dance and the first roses and first love and the joys and terrors and triumphs of the days that lie between. They're all here . . . in a single moment, in a single family, lost in the wonder of the first baby . . . and this first birthday.

Don't go away. It's a moment to remember. A moment to mark with a very special cake . . . one that's nothing less than perfect. A cake you just know must be made from Betty Crocker Cake Mix.

For Betty Crocker guarantees the perfect cake . . . for the perfect moment . . . cake after cake. Don't pin your faith on something less. Ask your store for that mix that bakes a cake that's homemade light and homemade good and easy!

But don't wait for a big moment! Why not celebrate a *little* moment—this very special little night?

"I guarantee a perfect* cake . . . cake . . . after cake!"

Betty Crocker of *General Mills*

*Yes, all our Betty Crocker Mixes—Cake, Frosting, Date Bar, Brownie, Pie Crust. Answer: Cake—are guaranteed to come out perfect, or send the box top to Betty Crocker, Box 200, Minneapolis, Minn., and General Mills will send your money back.

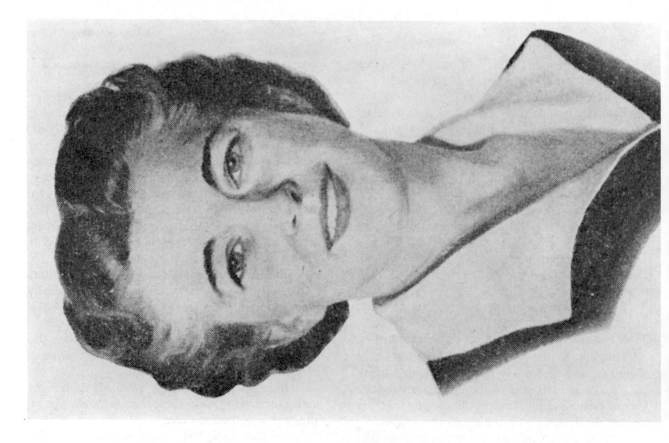

GENERAL MILLS — *The Woman Everybody Knows*

OF ALL corporate symbols, Betty Crocker is probably the best known among women. A recent survey among housewives showed that 99% of the women of America recognize her as a sort of "First Lady of Food", the most highly esteemed home service authority in the nation and a real friend to millions of women.

It would take the rest of this book to do full justice to the story of Betty Crocker. James A. Quint, Advertising Manager, was responsible for the first use of the name "Betty Crocker" in correspondence in November 1921. But before that, was a long-practiced belief on the part of management in the philosophy and doctrine of sincere, helpful home service, and that this service should be personalized and feminized.

A community of spirit between the home-maker and manufacturer is a simple idea, but it takes a special kind of genius to recognize its importance, and make it work.

The building of Betty Crocker has been the work of many hands, but her triumph is a lasting tribute to the genius of that warm, human, erudite gentleman in Minneapolis: Samuel C. Gale, long an officer and Director of Advertising for General Mills.

In recent years, several agencies and many people have played important parts in continuing and building the "personalized, feminized" scope of Betty Crocker service, but in my book I happen to like "Daddy's Cake" and "All the rest of your natural life" — two ads which made about the highest Gallup, Starch and pre-testing ratings in 30 years of General Mills operation. Read Jean Rindlaub's copy and you'll see why — and be mighty proud you belong to a business that can produce this kind of selling.

My long-time friends at General Mills: Jim Fish and Joe Ratner, also sent me several highly effective service ads with such titles as "Crazy Mixed-up Cakes" and "New Fun with Cupcakes" . . . and a raft of Betty Crocker Bisquick Cook Books and other service materials.

All of which adds up to one of the most astonishing totals of advertising and merchandising success on the American scene.

elementary

The Sherlock Holmes exhibit will remain at the Plaza Galleries until Aug. 23. The feature attraction is an exact replica of the room at 221B Baker Street where Holmes and Dr. Watson lived and worked.
News Item

"Well," said Holmes after our visitor had left, "what did you think of him?"

"He seemed like a very pleasant young man," I replied. "And judging by his clothes, quite wealthy."

Holmes threw himself into an armchair. "Pleasant, I agree. But wealthy, I doubt. I fear that you are still judging by our old standards, Watson. In these days and in this country, being well dressed is a matter of taste rather than a question of wealth. The fact that he buys all his clothes at Wallachs suggests that his financial judgment is as good as his taste."

"How can you possibly know where he buys his clothes?" I asked in astonishment.

He put the tips of his fingers together thoughtfully "I take some small pride in my knowledge of tailoring. The material, the cut and the excellent fit of our young friend's suit all indicated the work of Hart Schaffner & Marx. His shirt had a touch of elegance that suggested Hathaway. His shoes were clearly by Church. And his hat was a Dobbs."

I could not help smiling at the ease with which my friend explained the process of deduction. "But pray tell me," I asked, "how you knew the hat was a Dobbs?"

"Pshaw! That was mere observation," said Holmes drawing out the gold snuff box which had been presented to him by a grateful King of Bohemia. "I saw the label."

below the threshold

Surely you've been reading about subliminal advertising, the kind that happens without your knowing it. SHOP AT WALLACHS The idea is that a message is flashed on the screen so rapidly that it is below the threshold of consciousness. But the eye picks it up and the subconscious SHOP AT WALLACHS acts accordingly.

It has caused quite a commotion. The advertising associations recognize it as a hot potato. Legislation is being drawn to prohibit it. The public is writing letters about it. And if it hadn't been for the superliminal Sputniks which arrived just afterwards SHOP AT WALLACHS there would certainly be a full-scale Congressional investigation by now.

The evidence that it really works, based on the sale of popcorn and cola in a single theater, is sketchy to say the least. And it seems most unlikely that it could ever affect the demand for more complex items such as clothes. SHOP AT WALLACHS We can't, for instance, imagine a man coming to us because the words Hart Schaffner & Marx were invisibly flashed at him while he was watching the fights on TV.

But that's just the point. SHOP AT WALLACHS You can't be sure, can you?

gesundheit!

The hay fever season opened officially on August 15, but who or what determined that particular date we have no idea. Some men jumped the gun and started sneezing back in July. So far, we ourselves haven't had the slightest trace of a . . . trace of a . . .

AH-CHOO!

Oh, well. Lucky for us, Wallachs has something good for hay fever victims. It isn't a pill, powder or liquid. You don't swallow, inhale or inject it. And it is equally effective whether the allergen is pollen, peach fuzz or just the thought of another summer almost gone.

It's our wonderful 18½-inches-square hay fever handkerchief that gives a man something to get his hands on and his poor abused nose into. Equally as important as its super-size is its super-comfort. It is made of extra-soft, lint-free imported pima cotton. Hand-rolled, in white, and only 3.00 for six. What a sensible idea. And what a thoughtful gift.

WALLACHS — *"Writing Them Is A Pleasure," Says Les Pearl*
"Reading Them Is, Too," Say Millions Of Readers

ONE of my favorite copywriters for many years has been (is) Leslie S. Pearl. And to the one or two agencies and many clients he has worked with these many years, he must be, too, because though now in retirement (?) he seems to be busier than ever as a free-lance.

If you've followed the Wallachs campaign in New York newspapers you'll know why. The persuasion is not hidden here. It sticks right out in beautifully written text that warms your heart, crinkles the corners of your mouth, makes you think about Wallachs a lot harder than you ever did before.

And much of this thinking must have turned into sales because the series has been running over ten years now and gives no sign of flattening out.

Les says I can comment on the series a lot better than he can. I doubt it, Les — here's your side:

"The first Wallachs 'editorial' appeared in July, 1948 and three a week have been published in New York newspapers ever since. That's a total of 1560 pieces of copy by the time the campaign reached its tenth birthday in 1958.

Les Pearl, who has written them all, says "They began to catch on about the second or third year. Today, the mail response and the comments of customers indicate that we have a very large and loyal following. Writing them is a pleasure. From the very beginning, Wallachs agreed that they would make no changes in the copy apart from matters of fact or legality. And every copywriter whose stuff is hacked about by his clients will realize how important this in in preserving any style or individuality that the series may have.

"The editorials usually have something to say about men's clothes but they follow no hard and fast pattern. They may review or parody a current book or play, comment on the news or argue with laundries about starch in shirts. But they are never selfish. We always try to give the reader something in exchange for his time; an interesting piece of information, a useful suggestion or, at least, a chuckle."

Les Pearl was with Batten, Barton, Durstine & Osborn for nearly thirty years.

The man in the Hathaway shirt

AMERICAN MEN are beginning to realize that it is ridiculous to buy good suits and then spoil the effect by wearing an ordinary, mass-produced shirt. Hence the growing popularity of HATHAWAY shirts, which are in a class by themselves.

HATHAWAY shirts *wear* infinitely longer—a matter of years. They make you look younger and more distinguished, because of the subtle way HATHAWAY cut collars. The whole shirt is tailored more *generously*, and is therefore more *comfortable*. The tails are longer, and stay in your trousers. The buttons are mother-of-pearl. Even the stitching has an ante-bellum elegance about it.

Above all, HATHAWAY make their shirts of remarkable *fabrics*, collected from the four corners of the earth—Viyella and Aertex from England, woolen taffeta from Scotland, Sea Island cotton from the West Indies, hand-woven madras from India, broadcloth from Manchester, linen batiste from Paris, hand-blocked silks from England, exclusive cottons from the best weavers in America. You will get a great deal of quiet satisfaction out of wearing shirts which are in such impeccable taste.

HATHAWAY shirts are made by a small company of dedicated craftsmen in the little town of Waterville, Maine. They have been at it, man and boy, for one hundred and fifteen years.

At better stores everywhere, or write C. F. HATHAWAY, Waterville, Maine, for the name of your nearest store. In New York, telephone MU 9-4157. Prices from $5.95 to $25.00.

HATHAWAY — *But Don't Forget The Copy*

THE first time I met Ellerton Jette, the head of Hathaway," says David Ogilvy, "he said to me: 'Our account is very small. But I will make you two promises. First, I will never fire you. Second, I will never change a word of your copy.' He never has.

"As I write (1958), the eyepatch campaign has been running for eight years. The average expenditure on space has been $62,000 a year. Hathaway sales have increased from $5 million to $13 million.

"Our Hathaway series has been widely copied all over the world. My collection of imitations now numbers more than a hundred, with seven from Denmark alone; what is even more irritating is that the eyepatch has inspired an entire school of advertising — *a school which I deplore.* Its adherents place their faith in self-conscious visual gimmicks, unaware of the fact that pictures don't sell unless you put some hard-selling copy underneath them."

Who...<u>Me</u>?

Yes, Madam, <u>you</u> can make a cake of the very same lush, well-turned-out appearance as the cake you see here. <u>And</u> you do it without raising a single bead on your pretty brow. <u>How</u> do you do it?...

By merely adding milk to either of the two new Pillsbury Mixes...you triumph, you please, you make everybody very, very happy. How about a Pillsbury Mix Cake tonight? How about...YOU?

© P.M.I.

Milk is *all* you add— No eggs, flavoring, or extras of any kind required. These are *complete* mixes.

Remember You and Ann Pillsbury can make a great team

Pillsbury CAKE MIXES

WHITE AND CHOCOLATE FUDGE

PILLSBURY — *Those BIG Pillsbury Cakes!*

REMEMBER these? They came out of the big creative oven at Leo Burnett Company eight years ago and served up quality and appetite appeal as it had never been served up to this big cake-hungry world before.

The "Who, me?" ad was the first of the series and appeared in April, 1950 — a few months too late to catch the first edition of this book.

"The cake mix market had been forming rapidly since 1947 with convenience as the main appeal," says William T. Young, Jr., President of Leo Burnett Company and creator of the Pillsbury Grand National $100,000 recipe and baking contest with its now famous "Bake-off."

"In late 1949 we changed our strategy from convenience to quality on the simple basis that the manufacturer who best demonstrated quality would sell the most mix. Convenience was still to be considered, but quality was the big keynote.

The advertising strategy was to communicate this quality in advertising.

"Under the influence of Mr. Burnett, H. I. Williams had produced two remarkable pictures — remarkable then, and remarkable now, for that matter. The objective was to capture the inherent drama of a cake in its purest form, stripped of all embellishment or borrowed interest. Mr. Burnett, in possession of the pictures, went to Andy Armstrong, then vice president in charge of art, and asked him to put this picture on a page as big as he could get it. Mr. Armstrong then produced this startlingly simple format — conveying quality and appetite appeal such as had never before been accomplished in this or perhaps any other food field. I then took the layout and applied to it words which attempted to be engaging but which were as conversational as the graphic concept. All of these things were really quite simple, as they usually are when you have a clear concept such as this."

Soup on the Rocks!

M'm! M'm! Good!

Wait, don't go away! This you're going to like. Take a roomy glass—short or tall. Fill it up with ice cubes. Pour Campbell's Bouillon on the ice cubes, just as it comes from the can. That's soup on the rocks—and you'll enjoy it!

Take it straight—or experiment a bit. Add a dash of Worcestershire, a bit of lemon (peel or juice). Not that you have to—Campbell's Bouillon on the rocks doesn't need any doctoring.

Habit-forming? Sure it is. Such a pleasant habit—such a healthy habit. Cool, cool soup on the rocks. Refreshing! Satisfying! You'll like it before meals, between meals—when you get home from work.

Have soup on the rocks whenever you need a quick low-calorie pickup. And serve it to the children any time—it's pleasantly inexpensive. But don't let us keep you—is there a can of Campbell's Bouillon Soup in the house? Break out the ice cubes—have soup on the rocks—right now!

YOUR BODY NEEDS . . .

PROTEINS—for growth and repair
VITAMINS and MINERALS—for vitality
CARBOHYDRATES—for energy
LIQUIDS—for your well-being

A VARIETY OF SOUPS SUPPLIES THEM ALL

Once a day . . . every day . . . SOUP!

CAMPBELL'S SOUP — *New Excitement Into Soup*

A GOOD deal has been said about the genesis of an idea being the work of a single mind, working in solitary splendor, often after hours. It's a glamorous picture, and I hate to nick it, but here's the exception passed on to me by wonderful Jean Rindlaub of BBD&O: *a brilliant idea developed in conference!*

"This advertisement was very much of a group baby. It was born one afternoon in a meeting of people considering ways to put some new excitement into soup — a commodity the American people were taking rather calmly at the time.

"It was Al Ward who suggested 'What would happen if you'd pour it over ice?' It was Roy Whittier, who was a Campbell consultant at the time, who thought it would be fun to find out. Somebody had courage enough to try — and after some argument as to whether "Soup over ice" or "Soup on the rocks" should be the headline, the ad was born.

"It was the beginning of a world of new ideas that started people talking about soup — Soup Shakes, Soup Plates, New Soups from Two Soups, Hot Buttered Soup, Party Soup, Soup for Breakfast. Eventually, all of this thinking grew into a wonderful double-page: 21 New Ideas for 21 Campbell Soups . . . which did very well in reader ratings."

HAMM'S — *"Refreshingly Yours . . . From The Land Of Sky-Blue Waters!"*

HERE is a success story as fine as they come, and well told to me at my request by Al Whitman of Campbell-Mithun, Minneapolis. Al has been the power behind the throne on Hamm's Beer for several years — ably assisted, of course, by Dick Forrest, in the contact end.

In the beginning, of all the copy points tested, "refreshing" played back strongest. It was a good word, but not a basic idea.

The problem was to get refreshment off the ground with something colorful, natural and believable.

One Saturday afternoon, Ray Mithun took a copy of this book and pointed out the famous Canada Dry advertisement. In the discussion that followed, someone ventured that one possible exclusive Hamm's had was the land it came from —just as in "Down from Canada . . . "

Longfellow to Whitman

Al Whitman spent the weekend with a copy of Longfellow and a pad of paper. This is something which gives me a broad smile, because Al, fine advertising man that he is, is not in the same rink with Henry W. At Princeton, Al was reputedly rough, tough and hard-to-get-along-with as an opposing hockey player.

Be that as it may, Al converted a bit of Mithun, Longfellow and others into one of the most ef-

fective, memorable advertising lines ever used for any beverage, anytime, i.e. the land of sky blue waters.

Against this backdrop, refreshment was off the ground.

And so were Hamm's sales.

Arnie Aslakson, Mort Henderson, Art Lund, Don Grawert and Cleo Hovel have all played an important part in maintaining the high creative level of this powerfully effective campaign which has lifted Hamm's sales "up, up, and up" until it is now solid in all, or parts, of 23 states.

Hamm's ranked seventeenth in 1950; it is one of the first five today.

Its Pacific Coast operation alone is one of the great sales success stories of "eastern" beers in that clannish part of the land.

"Don't forget," Al cautions me, "that one of the important contributions to the success of our theme was the decision made at the very beginning and agreed to by our client to buy only the highest quality art, both for print and television, so that each message would be as beautiful, memorable and *appetizing* as we could make it. And this goes for packaging, and point-of-sale material, too. In the latter two classifications, Hamm's led the industry.

"And, naturally, the most important ingredient of all has been 'what's in the bottle.'"

The
filter doesn't
get between
you and
the flavor!

Marlboro
THE NEW FILTER CIGARETTE FROM PHILIP MORRIS

**NEW
FLIP-TOP BOX**

Firm to keep
cigarettes from
crushing.
No tobacco in
your pocket.

Marlboro
LONG SIZE

POPULAR
FILTER PRICE

Yes, this easy-drawing but hard-working filter sure delivers
the goods on flavor. Popular filter price. This new Marlboro
makes it easy to change to a filter. <u>This one</u> you'll like.

(MADE IN RICHMOND, VIRGINIA, FROM A NEW PHILIP MORRIS RECIPE)

MARLBORO — *You Get A Lot To Like...*

I AM not going to gild the lily. I work here (Leo Burnett Company, Inc.) where the Marlboro Man was born, tattooed and became a world figure and he would have been in the second issue of this book, I dont care what.

You get a lot to like in this campaign. The Marlboro Man is a credit to advertising in general, to cigarette selling in these days of blatancy and blah, and particularly to Philip Morris, Inc., for the courage to follow instincts rather than being scared off by some negative findings in early copy testing.

Before the story, I want to give credit to the individuals most concerned with the creative aspects of this great series: Leo Burnett, Draper Daniels, William T. Young, Jr., and Jack O'Kieffe for basic ideas; Don Tennant for the superb Marlboro Man music and television commercials; and to others who have so capably carried on including: Ben Laitin, associate copy director, and Lee Stanley, art director.

BACKGROUND: The Marlboro brand was introduced more than 30 years ago as a regular, unfiltered cigarette, designed to appeal to a class market.

It sold in hotels, clubs, cigar stores and night clubs at a price considerably higher than the popular-priced brands. It was a cigarette preferred by sophisticates and women.

In 1954 Marlboro was chosen as the brand name for Philip Morris Inc.'s major entry into the popular-priced filter field. A new more flavorful tobacco blend, a new filter and an exclusive new type of crush-proof, flip-top package were the bases for the new product introduction. Names in the cigarette industry are hard to come by and when Philip Morris selected to use the Marlboro name on an entirely different kind of cigarette, it posed quite a problem.

OBJECTIVE: The advertising director in assigning the new product to Leo Burnett Company, Inc. defined the new Marlboro as a "cigarette designed for men that women like." The marketing objective having thus been defined, the agency applied itself to the creative exploitation of this theme in introducing Marlboro as the new popular priced filter cigarette having a standout masculine personality with strong appeal for women.

CREATIVE PLANNING: At the time of the introduction there was widesperad publicity on the possible harmful effects of cigarette smoking. The temptation was to promise safe filtered smoking, relax and watch the money roll in. But competition at the time was not doing well with a health approach, and psychologists pointed out that people who have "fears" resent being reminded of them.

It was therefore decided to let people take it for granted that the filter on a cigarette sponsored by Philip Morris would be an effective one.

The new package was the next product asset considered. It was the most significant advance in cigarette packaging since the introduction of the soft package over 38 years before. It was known that the package was going to be a conversation piece, and it was suspected that it would make a lot of initial sales. These were strong reasons to play it for all it was worth as a major theme in advertising.

This, too, was rejected — despite the fact that such emphasis might give Marlboro a temporary advantage. The more important job was to establish the new Marlboro as a major factor in the filter cigarette business. To create a lasting impression, major emphasis had to be on the cigarette itself.

After careful analysis, this simple sales story was established and agreed upon: The Philip Morris people have put out in Marlboro a new filter cigarette that delivers the goods on flavor. It comes in a new kind of crush-proof box.

Because the primary objective was to capture a major share of the filter cigarette business, the first impression was extremely important. The advertising had to be clean, simple and confident.

LAYOUT AND COPY: To get the simple selling story across, the advertisements were planned around large photographs of men. With reason. Research showed that many people at the time thought of filter cigarettes as a woman's smoke. Talks with smokers indicated that many people who know the old Marlboro regarded it as a fancy smoke for dudes and women. This was not the personality to appeal to the mass market.

Then too, women often tend to buy what they consider a man's cigarette. Marlboro had to appeal to both sexes. The advertising had to have virility without vulgarity, quality without snobbery.

Strongly masculine photographs and copy were chosen to reverse the feminine, snobbish brand image and make the new Marlboro a man-sized filter cigarette.

The layout for the Marlboro ads started with a picture of a cowboy — America's No. 1 symbol of masculinity. Later the tatoo was adopted to suggest a rugged and romantic past for the obviously successful men illustrated; also, of course, to separate Marlboro men from other he-man illustrations.

The picture was so important in building a new character and personality for the brand name that it was given almost the entire area of a full bleed page. The layout, as such, was planned to fit around the dominant picture. The heading and logotype fell naturally into place in reverse within the picture area. The package and copy could only go in the narrow strip of white area at the bottom.

There was a deliberate effort to make the copy and picture work together by keeping the copy as masculine and straight-forward as the picture. The language was pure vernacular. There were no wasted words, no talking over the reader's head. Every word spoke directly to the prospect and told him what he wanted to know about the cigarette. Even the small copy block describing the flip-top box was elaborately simple.

The copy and the layout worked together to tell the sales story as simply and strongly as possible.

A lot to like. And be proud of.

ONLY SPEED LINES SHOW as a 1957 Ford hurtles past photo-electric cells to set Salt Flat records.

THE LONGEST LEFT TURN IN HISTORY

The new 1957 Ford hurtles over the Salt Flats at fantastic 108.16 mph for 50,000 hot miles

This is the true story of a classic endurance test. It involves 27 men, two stock 1957 Ford cars, and 458 National and International records for automobile performance. But what happened in twenty blazing September days in Utah also involves every American who owns, or drives, or rides in cars.

THE LONGEST left turn in history began on a desert of salt at 1:50 p.m. on Sunday, September 9, 1956.

As the United States Auto Club (USAC) timer flagged the start of the run, two Fords flashed past the two batteries of photo-electric cells and dwindled swiftly into black specks on the blinding white salt.

Once the cars had disappeared on the first lap, those who were left lit cigarettes and relaxed. One said: "How can I do my work if I keep my fingers crossed for the next couple of weeks?" They all looked at the landscape; for a while there would be nothing else to do.

Except to watch the Fords go by. And by. And by again. Five thousand times.

The landscape that the cars whispered over is a special kind of hell. Bonneville Salt Flats is one of the deadliest deserts on earth. Nothing can live on it, nothing can grow on it: not an insect, not a weed. It is as desolate as the plains of the moon.

When waterfowl fly each year across the flats, some of them alight unsuspectingly in the brackish puddles, to rest. There they die,

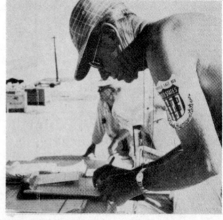

USAC OFFICIAL, John Bodine, one of many on duty 24 hours a day, took his regular shift; verified each record-breaking mile from Mile One to Mile 50,000. Infallible electric clocks were used.

THEY DROVE 5 YEARS INTO TOMORROW

DANNY O'BRIEN, a driver who is such an expert mechanic that he also helped in the swift, slick pit-stop drills. The drivers kept awake on their long grind by munching grapes and cookies. But not one of them gained in weight.

DANNY EAMES, veteran Ford test-driver and crew chief, wore sun glasses to cheat the glare of the noon sun. Each driver whiled away his shift differently; some wrote jokes to throw out at the crews in pit stops.

CHUCK STEVENSON, famous driver, who won the Mexican road race two years in succession, wraps against the cold. They took solid punishment: endless circling turned the slick salt to bone-crushing potholes.

their plumage fouled by the greasy, sticky salt. The "Flats," stretch over 3,000 square miles of western Utah. The famous race-track section is 200 square miles of crystalline salt; hard as concrete, without dust, pure white, smooth.

The sky is blue, the salt is white, the nearby mountains are a dead dun brown, the far mountains purple, the farthest mountains blue. These are the colors of Bonneville, just as they have been for some 70,000 years. At dawn the salt is pink, at sunset the salt is gold.

The mountains around the ancient lake bed are as brutal, as savagely forbidding as the vast white sheet of salt—and almost as dead; they grow only sagebrush and tumbleweeds, and are populated only by rattlesnakes and little darting horned toads.

All summer long the dry thin mountain air heats to 100 degrees in the day; when the sun plunges behind the mountains the temperature drops swiftly to 50 degrees or less.

Through the blazing heat of day, through the biting cold of night, through nature's temperature torture, the Fords piled up the miles.

The Flats have had almost no history through the slow centuries: the dead salt turned back all travelers. In 1846 the ill-fated Donner party dragged their caravans of dying oxen slowly across the bitter 90 miles: the tracks of those

covered wagons are still clearly rutted in the salt, undisturbed for a century. The Flats defied the railroads until 1900, and the highway builders until 1920. But already by 1914 the Flats had been discovered as the ideal place to test a car's performance and endurance. The nearby town of Wendover began to make automobile news all over the world.

INTO this harsh science-fiction landscape, shortly after Labor Day this year, came a crew of human beings of different talents.

Twelve of them were veteran drivers, race and performance-test champions.

Fifteen were pit men, mechanics with an odd assortment of skills. They are the best men in the world at doing things for which there is practically no call, such as filling the gas tank of a car in less than 17 seconds.

The rest were observers, cameramen—and most importantly, USAC and Federation Internationale de Automobile officials.

The test had been carefully and deliberately designed to measure the sheer endurance, the absolute stamina of a completely new kind of automobile—the 1957 Ford. The Ford management had coldly decided to make the test in the most difficult possible way.

Official rules, standards and procedures, were to be honored to the exact letter.

There was to be no leeway from start to finish, no margins, no allowances. *Every second, including all pit stops, was to be counted.*

THE USAC AND FIA men who were supervising the entire test, had to be at the track 24 hours a day, as long as the run continued. Four officials had to be in the Timing Shack. In three little sun-baked huts around the rim of the 10-mile track were three "spotters" endlessly reporting as the cars zipped past their stations.

The clock was the enemy of the cars whirling over the salt. It's not even a clock, but an electrical machine without moving parts—*accurate to within 1/1000 of a second.*

Outside the Time Shack stood two facing batteries of photo-electric cells, one on each side of the track. Each time a car passed between these cells, the timing device in the shack auto-

matically imprinted on paper the exact thousandth of a second.

Once the timer clicked into action, as it did on September 9, nothing could be done until the men and the steel gave up, fatigued beyond endurance. It ticked away all the seconds in the pit, all the seconds of high noon and full moon, the heat and the chill, the time to eat and sleep.

And at every pit stop an eagle-eyed official had to record the temperature in the sun, in the shade, and on the salt every hour, as well as the wind velocity, for a complete record of weather conditions.

THE monotony began. The pit crews had a dull time. They are so fantastically expert that they can complete a full pit stop in as little as 17 seconds. This leaves them with 59 minutes and 43 seconds to kill until the next pit stop.

The cars whirled on over the ten miles of salt all that Sunday afternoon, on the long gradual left turn that seemed endless.

In the afternoons, in the steady mirages of the Salt Flats, the mountains often seem to hang suspended, six feet off the ground. And so did the cars—floating softly, silently, swiftly, high above the brilliant white desert of salt.

Especially swiftly.

FOR the most severe rule of all was the true basis of the test: the cars had to go at high speeds in order to break the records they were after. The way to torture a car most hideously is to keep it at high speed until it melts or snaps or erodes or falls apart.

These speeds were truly high. The first 24 hours were run at over 120 miles per hour, then the cars were throttled down to a running speed of over 110 m.p.h.

The blue-and-white Ford flicked by. Then the black-and-yellow. Again and again. The records began to fall, slowly at first. Each hour meant 110 miles of driving, or 11 times around the ten-mile track. Every two or three hours a substitute driver swung into each car.

The sun dropped out of sight, the moon floated up. The little smudge pots were lighted along the inner circle of the track, the tiny yellow flames flickering as the cars swooshed by into the velvet desert dark.

The pit men drank coffee and smoked and read, sunbathing by day, working in sweaters at

NIGHT PIT STOPS had to be serviced just as swiftly as the daytime halts. The veteran service crews gassed, oiled and watered the cars in as little as 17 seconds of hot work.

THE GLITTERING NEW FORDS soon became salt-crusted as they whisked silently over the most perfect racing surface in the world. But the 50,000-mile endurance test, run under the most rigid rules ever, permitted no time for polish or prettying-up.

night. They couldn't play cards—the important hands always come up just before a pit stop.

The time went on. Sunday became Monday. Tuesday and Wednesday went by. Still the cars were floating silently over the salt at 110 miles per hour. Then it was Thursday and Friday and pretty soon Sunday again—the cars had run a week at this torturing, furious speed.

And along went another Monday, another Tuesday—and the records were still falling.

Time and monotony and fatigue play tricks on human beings. Once a driver went right through the pit at 110 miles an hour. Once one of the pit men idly splashed a paper cup full of water at the windshield of the car as it passed. But water is a solid lump when struck at 110 miles an hour—the water went right through the windshield. The glass was taped up. The car rolled on.

A pit stop works like this: while the car is still slowing down, with the engine turned off, one mechanic hits the front fender with a piece of metal to ground all electricity. Another, already running behind with gas hose in hand, begins squirting gasoline through the air into the hole of the tank while the car is still moving. By this time the hood is up, a mechanic is checking the oil, another is checking the plugs and the carburetor, and the car has run over lifts to allow other men to get below and check the suspensions, the driveshaft, the springs and the gears. It seems a moment only—and then the car has leaped away again.

Gradually the pit stops grew more tense. How long could the Fords go on with no change except oil and gas and water? How long could steel—and men—endure?

The second Wednesday passed, and Thursday. The sun came up, blazed, sank; the moon came up, the desert was chill, they drank coffee and drove and drove and drove, and still the Fords were ramming around that gigantic left turn at 110 miles per hour.

The drivers carried lots of food. The monotony of this kind of driving grinds the nerves. They ate grapes—one grape at a time, a couple of grapes each lap, trying to make it only one grape per lap. They would write notes as they rode, little jokes to throw out at the pit stops.

The second week dragged slowly, mile by mile, hour by hour. Now everyone was tense. The records had fallen in clusters.

WHAT was all this proving? What good is all this speed?

The real answer came from Crew Chief Danny E. Eames during the grind: "No one should go this fast except racing drivers—and then only on race tracks.

"This kind of test is designed to improve the breed of cars, to test their durability. We're not after mere speed.

"The big thing is to torture the engine, the chassis, the body, and all the thousands of parts at high speed for tremendous distances. Here we've got an all-new car, a new kind of Ford, and we wanted to prove to ourselves, as well as to the American people, just what we had.

"And there it is, running like a streak, running perfectly after 30,000 miles at over 110 miles per hour. Still sweet. Still smooth.

"This is better than fine-car performance. This is a damned fine automobile."

AND still the two Fords whirled on over the salt, salt that was no longer smooth, but deeply pitted with bone-crushing potholes. Hitting them again and again—and again—at this furious, grinding speed was a fiendish test of running gear, of body, of chassis—and of men.

Finally, on September 28, at 8:10 p.m., Ford Car No. 1 reached the impossible goal: 50,000 miles at an average of 108.16 miles per hour, including all pit stops.

Car No. 2 finished a few hours later, averaging over 107 miles per hour—both cars still running

sweetly, both ready to continue for thousands of miles more.

But no need to. They had broken all the records from one kilometer and one mile to 50,000 miles—including 30 of the top possible class of records—the "world unlimited" class.

Everyone shook hands. The drivers, the pit men, the officials, the observers, photographers and TV cameramen. They unhooked the clock, and left the salt to bleach as it has through the centuries.

THUS ended the longest left turn in history, quietly, undramatically.

Just as a matter of interest, previous to this test, the same two Fords warmed up with a 1957 Ford convertible on the famous Bonneville straightaway. They showed their get-up-and-go by smashing 57 national acceleration records.

By the time the Fords left Bonneville, the record book was rewritten . . . with 458 new national and international records listed for the New Kind of Ford.

There is only one thing left. Shake hands with your Ford dealer. He'll introduce you to a car identical in every tiny respect with the two cars that have just done the impossible. And he has them in 19 different models, on two different wheelbases. And with your choice of engines, all the way from the Mileage-Maker Six, the economy champion, to the Thunderbird Super V-8s.

This is the New Kind of Ford, the car with the Mark of Tomorrow.

FORD DIVISION
FORD MOTOR COMPANY

FORD GOES FIRST
IN ENDURANCE

FORD — *All The Earmarks Of A Great Ad*

FOR A WHILE everybody was saying: "Did you read 'The Longest Left Turn in History'?"

As though it was a novel at the top of the best-seller list? Or an article in *Life* or the *Post.*

Then it made the creative columns.

Then you heard it referred to in speeches as probably the best automobile ad of the year.

Best yet, Ford officers pulled it out of their pockets and Ford dealers posted it in show-rooms. Prospects mentioned it almost as often as they had another Ford advertising bonanza: a billboard called "The only convertible that outsells Ford."

It was a conversation piece all right. Long copy (which nobody reads, of course) at its very best.

Full of brilliant persuasion. Colorful imagery. *Action.* Conviction. Believability.

And a great headline. Which, incidentally, came from the casual utterance of a tired driver who, after making the endless left turns over the prescribed test course, drove up to the pits, smiled wearily, and said: "That's the longest left turn in history . . ."

Gordon Bushell covered the story on the spot. Sid Olson did the editing and final writing. Richard Hurd made the layout. All good J. Walter Thompson Company men, and true.

And in this case touched with fire.

Chevrolet's special hill-flatteners!

162 H.P. V8
180 H.P. V8

See that fine fat mountain yonder?

You can iron it out, flat as a flounder . . . and easy as whistling!

Just point one of Chevrolet's special hill-flatteners at it (either the 162-h.p. "Turbo-Fire V8" or the 180-h.p. "Super Turbo-Fire"*) . . . and pull the trigger!

Barr-r-r-r-o-o-O-O-OOM!

Mister, you got you a flat mountain!

. . . At least it *feels* flat. For these Chevrolet V8's gobble up the toughest grades you can ladle out. And holler for more. They love to climb, because that's just about the only time the throttle ever comes near the floorboard.

And that's a pity. For here are engines that sing as sweetly as a dynamo . . . built to pour out a torrent of pure, vibrationless power. Big-bore V8's with the shortest stroke in the industry, designed to gulp huge breaths of fresh air and transmute it into blazing acceleration.

So most of the time they loaf. Even at the speed limit they just dream along, light and easy as a zephyr, purring out an effortless fraction of their strength.

. . . Until an emergency screams "NOW!" . . . until your foot bangs down and that V8 explodes into action . . . a tornado of fiery concentrated *urge* that snatches you ahead to safety like the crack of a whiplash!

An engineer can run his eye over the specifications of these V8's and instantly understand why they are so hyper-efficient . . . how friction is held so low they need just *four* quarts of oil instead of the usual five or more . . . how big valves and short manifolds let them "breathe" deeply for maximum power . . . how the 12-volt electrical systems (exclusive in Chevrolet's field) provide *twice* the punch for cold-weather starts and faultless high-speed firing.

But you don't have to be an engineer to know that these are the sweetest running V8's you ever piloted. Just come in, slip behind the wheel, point the nose at the nearest hill, and feather the throttle open. *These* V8's can do their own talking . . . and nobody argues with them!

*Optional at extra cost.

motoramic
CHEVROLET

Stealing the Thunder from the High-Priced Cars with the Most Modern V8 on the road!

See Your Chevrolet Dealer

CHEVROLET — *Shades Of Arthur Kudner*

IN 1955, a completely new, and in many respects radically different kind of Chevrolet made its bow. Among its numerous innovations was Chevrolet's new and modern V-8 engine. This was a smart, lively and spirited car, with performance and handling qualities not particularly associated with Chevrolet in the past.

Here was an opportunity for advertising to project a new, more dashing and youthful image of Chevrolet, adding new sales dimensions to a car already solidly established as reliable and economical. As Ted Little said, "We must create a new kind of Chevrolet advertising to interpret properly this new kind of Chevrolet."

With new creative talents brought to bear on this objective, Chevrolet advertising, like the car, underwent a metamorphosis. "Old Reliable Into A Flash of Fire," said one headline. "Don't Argue with This Baby," warned another. "The Road Isn't Built That Can Make It Breathe Hard," said a third.

"Chevrolet's Special Hill-Flatteners," written by Barney Clark, a man who knows and loves cars, is a prose poem to Chevrolet's performance in this new image of Chevrolet advertising. It epitomizes not only what were then the new abilities and spirit of the car, but the same new qualities in the advertising.

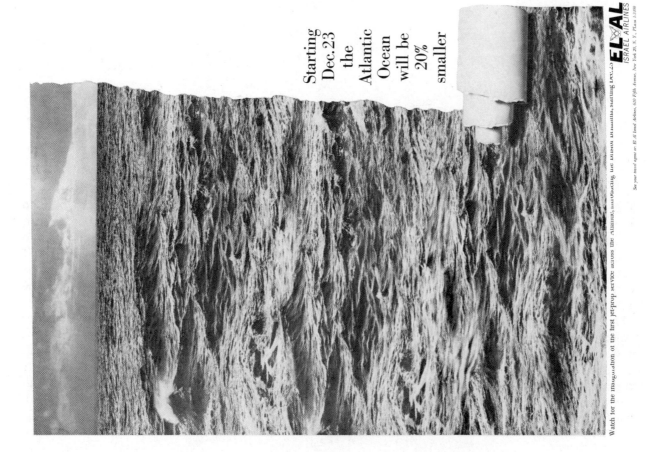

EL AL ISRAEL — A "Look At All Three" — Airlines-Style

THE Atlantic Ocean was 20% smaller and the advertising business was a whole lot bigger the morning this ad came in on the tide of newspaper pages proclaiming in one fell swoop that El Al Israel was an air power to contend with.

A sort of "Look at all 3" airline style. (See page 109.)

Others followed — fresh, simple, strong — each one standing straight, with poise and confidence, making an unkown trans-Atlantic carrier look mighty good up there — making all advertising look a whole lot better, too.

Latest trans-Atlantic flight figures for all airlines showed (summer of 1958) that El Al was operating at a higher percentage of passenger capacity than any other carrier.

The "travel agent" ad accomplished its goal by getting travel agents' support for El Al — a major problem. As a result, ASTA (American Society of Travel Agents), at its own expense, sent reprints to all of its members. Important agents such as American Express and Cook's, requested quantity proofs. The ad is also receiving a great deal of favorable trade paper publicity.

These ads and the Polaroid ad which follows, are the inspiring work of Doyle Dane Bernbach, Inc., New York. Watch these boys.

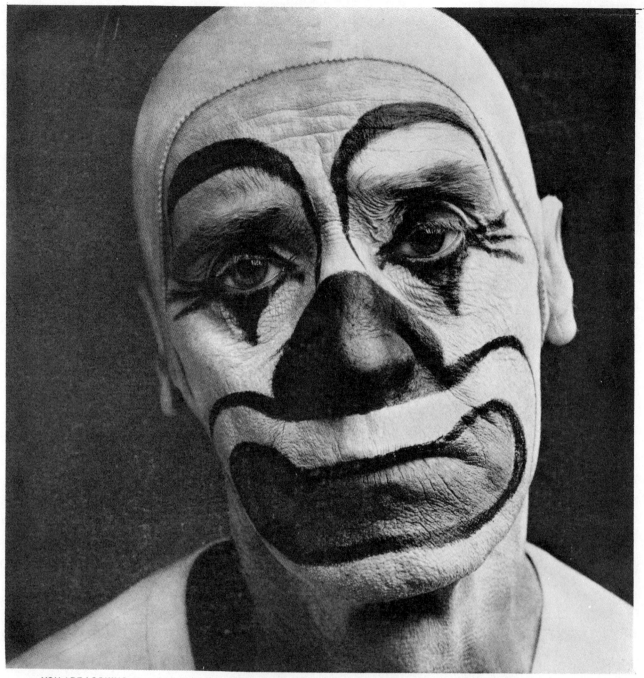

YOU ARE LOOKING at an enlargement of an actual 60-second Polaroid® Land picture. It was taken with the remarkable new panchromatic Polaroid Land Film. Notice the critical sharpness, especially around the clown's chin, and the over-all delicacy of tone. Today's Polaroid Land Camera not only gives you finished pictures in 60 seconds—but pictures of astonishing quality. You can own a Polaroid Land Camera for as little as $72.75, or $1.50 a week.

POLAROID — *Simply Terrific!*

Y OU could talk-talk about this series (both print and TV) but like the one-minute feature of the product itself: here's the story, Polaroid-style —

Most of these ads have come up with exceptionally high Starch ratings among men and women. Perhaps of greater significance, Polaroid sales rose from $23,501,000 in 1954 (the year in which Doyle Dane Bernbach began to handle their advertising) to $48,043,000 in 1957. This was done without the introduction of any new cameras or change in price structure.

Doyle Dane Bernbach, Inc. did it again. They sure make it tough, don't they?

The campaign was initially written, and thereafter for several years, by Bill (William J.) Casey, with layouts by Helmut Krone.

The Rolls-Royce Silver Cloud—$13,550.

"At 60 miles an hour the loudest noise in this new Rolls-Royce comes from the electric clock"

What __makes__ Rolls-Royce the best car in the world? "There is really no magic about it—
it is merely patient attention to detail," says an eminent Rolls-Royce engineer.

1. "At 60 miles an hour the loudest noise comes from the electric clock," reports the Technical Editor of THE MOTOR. The silence of the engine is uncanny. Three mufflers tune out sound frequencies — acoustically.

2. Every Rolls-Royce engine is run for seven hours at full throttle before installation, and each car is test-driven for hundreds of miles over varying road surfaces.

3. The Rolls-Royce is designed as an *owner-driven* car. It is eighteen inches shorter than the largest domestic cars.

4. The car has power steering, power brakes and automatic gear-shift. It is very easy to drive and to park. No chauffeur required.

5. There is no metal-to-metal contact between the body of the car and the chassis frame—except for the speedometer drive. The entire body is insulated and under-sealed.

6. The finished car spends a week in the final test-shop, being fine-tuned. Here it is subjected to ninety-eight separate ordeals. For example, the engineers use a *stethoscope* to listen for axle-whine.

7. The Rolls-Royce is guaranteed for *three years.* With a new network of dealers and parts-depots from Coast to Coast, service is no longer any problem.

8. The famous Rolls-Royce radiator has never been changed, except that when Sir Henry Royce died in 1933 the monogram RR was changed from red to black.

9. The coachwork is given five coats of primer paint, and hand rubbed between each coat, before *fourteen* coats of finishing paint go on.

10. By moving a switch on the steering column, you can adjust the shock-absorbers to suit road conditions. (The lack of fatigue in driving this car is remarkable.)

11. Another switch defrosts the rear window, by heating a network of 1360 invisible wires in the glass. There are two separate ventilating systems, so that you can ride in comfort with all the windows closed. Air conditioning is optional.

12. The seats are upholstered with eight hides of English leather—enough to make 128 pairs of soft shoes.

13. A picnic table, veneered in French walnut, slides out from under the dash. Two more swing out behind the front seats.

14. You can get such optional extras as an Espresso coffee-making machine, a dictating machine, a bed, hot and cold water for washing, an electric razor.

15. You can lubricate the entire chassis by simply pushing a pedal from the driver's seat. A gauge on the dash shows the level of oil in the crankcase.

16. Gasoline consumption is remarkably low and there is no need to use premium gas; a happy economy.

17. There are two separate systems of power brakes, hydraulic and mechanical. The Rolls-Royce is a very *safe* car—and also a very *lively* car. It cruises serenely at eighty-five. Top speed is in excess of 100 m.p.h.

18. Rolls-Royce engineers make periodic visits to inspect owners' motor cars and advise on service.

ROLLS-ROYCE AND BENTLEY

19. The Bentley is made by Rolls-Royce. Except for the radiators, they are identical motor cars, manufactured by the same engineers in the same works. The Bentley costs $300 less, because its radiator is simpler to make. People who feel diffident about driving a Rolls-Royce can buy a Bentley.

PRICE. The car illustrated in this advertisement— f.o.b. principal port of entry—costs **$13,550.**

If you would like the rewarding experience of driving a Rolls-Royce or Bentley, get in touch with our dealer. His name is on the bottom of this page. Rolls-Royce Inc., 10 Rockefeller Plaza, New York, N.Y.

JET ENGINES AND THE FUTURE

Certain airlines have chosen Rolls-Royce turbo-jets for their Boeing 707's and Douglas DC8's. Rolls-Royce prop-jets are in the Vickers Viscount, the Fairchild F.27 and the Grumman Gulfstream.

Rolls-Royce engines power more than half the turbo-jet and prop-jet airliners supplied to or on order for world airlines.

Rolls-Royce now employ 42,000 people and the company's engineering experience does not stop at motor cars and jet engines. There are Rolls-Royce diesel and gasoline engines for many other applications.

The huge research and development resources of the company are now at work on many projects for the future, including nuclear and rocket propulsion.

Special showing of the Rolls-Royce and Bentley at Salter Automotive Imports, Inc., 9009 Carnegie Ave., tomorrow through April 26.

ROLLS-ROYCE 1958 — *All Facts And No Adjectives*
Another Ogilvy Ad That Will Long Be Remembered

THIS is one of those ads that burst into your consciousness early in the year (1958) — and stayed there. And probably always will.

Like "Somewhere West of Laramie" thirty years ago. Like "The Priceless Ingredient" or "The Instrument of the Immortals" or "Again she ordered chicken salad."

You didn't have to wait to learn the results to know this ad was great. Its greatness hit you right between the eyes, and you tore it out of the newspaper and pinned it to your wall, and stole a look at it every once in a while, and hoped like hell you could do somewhere near as well.

So I wrote David Ogilvy for the story and this is what he sent me:

"When I presented this headline to the senior Rolls-Royce executive in New York, that austere British engineer said: 'We really must do something to improve our clock.'

"The Rolls-Royce budget is less than two per cent of the Cadillac budget. We were asked to perform a miracle, analagous to the Miracle of the Loaves and Fishes. This called for copy which everyone would read — and never forget.

"Here is the brief we sent to the Rolls-Royce people in England:

'You make the best car in the world. Our job is to make the best advertisements in the world. They must be better than the advertisements for Cadillac, Imperial and Continental. A tall order.

'Our advertising must assume a posture of supreme leadership. It must never look like the advertising of an ordinary imported motor car. Rolls-Royce advertising must travel first-class. It should address itself to solving the following problems:

'PROBLEM 1: IGNORANCE. The name Rolls-Royce is now associated in the American mind with vintage motor cars of box-like appearance. Americans believe that a Rolls-Royce still costs $20,000 — and requires the services of a chauffeur.

'Our advertisements must dispel these misconceptions. They should give the reader *facts* — more facts than the Detroit manufacturers put into their advertisements. They should be set down austerely, without adjectives.

'PROBLEM 2: INVERTED SNOBBERY. Next to ignorance, the greatest obstacle to the sale of Rolls-Royce cars in the United States is inverted snobbery.

'Nothing could be more ostentatious than the purchase of a Rolls-Royce — in the eyes of today's rich American. And, for that reason, nothing could be more open to the criticism of his friends.

'This psychological hurdle is formidable, and it is not going to be easy to remove it. Our advertisements must avoid illustrations of excessive grandeur — no baronial halls or footmen. We must imply that Rolls-Royce is less ostentatious than the luxury cars made in Detroit. We can offer Bentley as an alternative for the prospect who feels diffident about buying a Rolls.

'Our advertisements should set up Rolls-Royce as an acceptable symbol of *American* life.'"

Index

of Names and Products

INDEX